TEACHER'S ANNOTATED EDITION

Vocabulary Workshop

Level E

Jerome Shostak

Senior Series Consultant

Alex Cameron, Ph.D.
Department of English
University of Dayton
Dayton, Ohio

Series Consultants

Sylvia A. Rendón, Ph.D.
Coord., English Language Arts
Cypress-Fairbanks I.S.D.
Houston, Texas

Mel H. Farberman
Supervisor of Instruction
Brooklyn High Schools
New York City Board of Education
Brooklyn, New York

John Heath, Ph.D.
Department of Classics
Santa Clara University
Santa Clara, California

Sadlier-Oxford
A Division of William H. Sadlier, Inc.

Reviewers

The publisher wishes to thank for their comments and suggestions the following teachers and administrators, who read portions of the series prior to publication.

Anne S. Crane
Clinician, English Education
Georgia State University
Atlanta, GA

Arlene A. Oraby
Dept. Chair (Ret.), English 6–12
Briarcliff Public Schools
Briarcliff Manor, NY

Patricia M. Stack
English Teacher
South Park School District
South Park, PA

Susan W. Keogh
Curriculum Coordinator
Lake Highland Preparatory
Orlando, FL

Susan Cotter McDonough
English Department Chair
Wakefield High School
Wakefield, MA

Joy Vander Vliet
English Teacher
Council Rock High School
Newtown, PA

Mary Louise Ellena-Wygonik
English Teacher
Hampton High School
Allison Park, PA

Sr. M. Francis Regis Trojano
Sisters of St. Joseph (CSJ)
Educational Consultant
Boston, MA

Karen Christine Solheim
English Teacher
Jefferson High School
Jefferson, GA

Lisa Anne Pomi
Language Arts Chairperson
Woodside High School
Woodside, CA

Keith Yost
Director of Humanities
Tomball Ind. School District
Tomball, TX

Printed in the United States of America.
ISBN: 0-8215-7620-8
23456789/05 04 03 02

CONTENTS

INTRODUCTION

VOCABULARY WORKSHOP has for more than five decades been the leading program for systematic vocabulary development for grades 6–12. It has been proven a highly successful tool in helping students expand their vocabularies, improve their vocabulary skills, and prepare for the vocabulary strands of standardized tests.

This new edition of VOCABULARY WORKSHOP preserves and improves upon those key elements of the program that have made it so effective *and* introduces important new features that make the series more comprehensive in scope and current in approach to vocabulary instruction.

Key Elements

- At each Level, a **word list** of 300 main entries, plus hundreds of synonyms, antonyms, and other related words

- Proven and effective **five-step approach to instruction**, leading students to mastery of word meanings and usage

- Excellent **preparation for SAT I** and other standardized tests with strong correlations between word lists and words that frequently appear on the SAT, as well as practice in types and formats of exercises found on the SAT I

- Frequent **review and assessment** in both Student Text and in supplementary programs

New Features

- In each Unit and Review, **Vocabulary in Context**, a reading passage formatted to the SAT I reading comprehension sections that provides examples of how Unit words are used in context

- **Building with Classical Roots**, a Review exercise that acquaints students with Latin and Greek roots, and provides a strategy for finding the meaning of words derived from these roots

- In each Review, **Writer's Challenge**, an exercise that helps students improve their writing skills by applying what they have learned about the meaning and proper usage of selected Unit words

- **Enriching Your Vocabulary**, a Cumulative Review feature designed to broaden and enhance the students' knowledge and understanding of the relationships, history, and origins of the words that make up our rich and dynamic language

- Instruction in and examples of key vocabulary **strategies**—using context and using word structure—for decoding word meaning

- In the Units, expanded **Definitions** sections, which now include synonyms, antonyms, and complete, illustrative sentences for each part of speech of every taught word

- **Synonyms and Antonyms** sections that offer more examples of range of contexts and distinctions of usage

- Stress marks in **Pronunciation** sections that now reflect the system used in most leading dictionaries

- **Photographs** and color to engage student interest and illustrate reading and enrichment features

---

New Components

- For each Level, an **Annotated Teacher's Edition** that includes answers to all exercise items in the Student Text as well as valuable background information to help in lesson planning, instruction in vocabulary strategies, and assessment

- For each of Levels A–F, a **Test Generator CD-ROM** adds a new, secure assessment option to the program, eliminating the risk of "second-hand" tests that may distort assessment results

- For each of Levels A–F, an **Interactive Audio Pronunciation Program** now available in CD format as well as cassette—ideal for English Language Learners of all cultures and backgrounds, and for use in ESL classrooms

In the following pages of this Teacher's Edition, you will learn more about the VOCABULARY WORKSHOP program, including these new features and components, as well as how to get the most out of the program in your classroom.

OVERVIEW

"Pure Vocabulary" Approach: Systematic Vocabulary Instruction

The VOCABULARY WORKSHOP program focuses on words themselves, their meanings (both literal and figurative), their ranges of application (or usage), and their relationships with other words.

The approach is systematic in the sense that it begins with and builds upon a word list compiled to provide students with vocabulary they will encounter in their reading both in and out of the classroom. It is designed to prepare students with the vocabulary skills they will need in order to achieve higher-level reading proficiency and to succeed at standardized tests.

The VOCABULARY WORKSHOP systematic approach differs from a literature-based approach in that each Unit begins with a thorough consideration of the words themselves rather than with a reading selection featuring words to be studied. (This is not to say that VOCABULARY WORKSHOP cannot be profitably used as a complement to a literature-based approach. See pages T30–T31 for suggestions on how this might be done.)

Rather than in the circumstantial context of literature, VOCABULARY WORKSHOP introduces and exemplifies vocabulary usage in varied and controlled contexts. These range from short phrases to full sentences to the Vocabulary in Context reading passages that are new to this edition of the program.

For effective study, the "pure vocabulary" approach also offers these advantages:

- It provides unlimited flexibility in the choice and placement of grade-appropriate material.
- It avoids the problem of trying to deal with a literary passage both as literature and as a vehicle for vocabulary instruction.
- It focuses more directly and completely on the words themselves, their meanings, their usage, and their relationships with other words.
- By economizing space, it allows a greater range of practice, reinforcement, and enhancement.
- It allows maximum coverage to a maximum number of key words.

One of the cornerstones of the VOCABULARY WORKSHOP approach is intensive practice through varied and abundant "hands-on" exercises. This method ensures that students are provided with:

- maximum exposure to different meanings of the key words studied;
- maximum coverage of the range of each key word through its appearance in many different contexts;

• fullest understanding of the key words' relationships to other words.

The aim of the pattern of intensive practice is to include the words in the students' active, daily-use vocabulary. This implies the ability to use a given word not only in its literal, or narrow, sense but also in a figurative way as well. Furthermore, it means that students will be able to use the word with confidence both as speakers and as writers.

Grade-Level Placements

The chart below shows the suggested grade placement for each level of VOCABULARY WORKSHOP, depending on the overall ability of the student population involved.

In determining "proper" placement of a particular level of VOCABULARY WORKSHOP in a given situation, the following considerations should be taken into account:

• Grade placements are based on actual teacher experience and recommendations throughout the long course of VOCABULARY WORKSHOP's history.

• Differences in grade are reflected not only in the "difficulty" of the words presented but also in the "maturity" of the sentences and other contexts in which those words are used.

• Grade levels indicated in the chart should not be taken in too literal or rigorous a sense. A certain amount of experimentation, as well as the use of the diagnostic materials provided in the program, will establish the "correct" placement of a particular level in a given situation.

• The use of Level H with "above-average" students is designed to enhance preparation for the SAT I and other college-entrance examinations.

Grade Placements			
"Average" Students		"Above-Average" Students	
Level	Grade	Level	Grade
A	6	A	5
B	7	B	6
C	8	C	7
D	9	D	8
E	10	E	9
F	11	F	10
G	12	G	11
		H	12

Word Lists

Each Student Text in the VOCABULARY WORKSHOP program for Levels A–H contains 300 words organized in 15 Units.

Criteria for Selection

The selection of words for the VOCABULARY WORKSHOP program is based on four major criteria:

- currency in and usefulness for present-day American oral or written communication;
- frequency on recognized vocabulary lists;
- applicability to standardized tests, especially the SAT I;
- current grade-placement research.

General Sources

The lists of key words were developed from many sources:

- traditional, classic, and contemporary literature including novels, short stories, essays, newspaper and magazine articles, plays, films, videos, TV programs;
- spelling and vocabulary lists recognized as valid bases for teaching language skills at the middle and secondary levels;
- current subject-area textbooks, glossaries, and ancillary materials (especially for general, nontechnical terms).

Dictionary and Reference Sources

The following were the primary dictionary resources used for word (and definition) selection:

- *Webster's Third International Dictionary of the English Language* (unabridged)
- *Merriam-Webster's Collegiate Dictionary* (ninth and tenth editions)

Other supplementary dictionaries consulted included:

- *The American Heritage Dictionary of the English Language* (all three editions)
- *The Random House Dictionary of the English Language* (unabridged; both editions)
- *The Compact Edition of the Oxford English Dictionary*

Standard Word-Frequency Sources

Standard word-frequency studies were employed to evaluate and revise the words on the tentative lists. These included:

- *Primary*
  Dale-O'Rourke: *The Living Word Vocabulary*
  Carroll-Davies-Richman: *Word Frequency Book*

- *Supplementary*
  Harris-Jacobsen: *Basic Reading Vocabularies*
  Thorndike-Lorge: *The Teacher's Word Book of 30,000 Words*
  Zeno-Ivens-Millard-Duvvuri: *The Educator's Word Frequency Guide*

"Sliding-Scale" Placement

Each word list works on a sliding scale based on these principles:

- No word that Dale-O'Rourke indicates as known in a given grade is presented in that grade. Instead, where possible, it is presented 2 or 3 grades earlier.

- Each grade level contains a preponderance of words not known (according to Dale-O'Rourke) 2 or 3 grades later, with an admixture (in decreasing numbers) of words not known 4 or more grades later.

- The higher the grade, the larger the percentage of more difficult words contained on the word list. This was done to accommodate as many "SAT-type" words as possible in the key word lists for Grades 10–12.

PROGRAM COMPONENTS

This new edition of VOCABULARY WORKSHOP, Levels A–H, consists of the following components:

Components of the VOCABULARY WORKSHOP Program*
• **Student Texts,** 8 Levels (A–H)
• **Teacher's Annotated Editions,** 8 Levels (A–H)
• **Test Booklets** - Form A, 8 Levels (A–H) - Form B, 8 Levels (A–H) - Combined Answer Keys, 8 Levels (A–H)
• **Test Generator CD-ROM,** 6 Levels (A–F only)
• SAT-Type **TEST PREP Blackline Masters** (answers included), 8 Levels (A–H)
• **Interactive Audio Pronunciation Program,** 6 Levels (A–F only)

The components have been designed for use in an integrated year-long vocabulary program, as suggested in the chart on pages T23–T25.

*Note that, in its entirety, the VOCABULARY WORKSHOP program now includes Student Texts, Teacher's Editions, and Supplementary Testing Programs for Grades 3–5 (Levels Green, Orange, and Blue).

The Student Texts

All eight Student Texts (Levels A–H) present 300 key words and are organized in the same way: 15 Units of 20 words each; 5 Reviews (following Units 3, 6, 9, 12, and 15); and 4 Cumulative Reviews. Preceding the first Unit is a section titled The Vocabulary of Vocabulary and a Diagnostic Test. Concluding each Student Text is a Final Mastery Test.

Vocabulary of Vocabulary (Student Text pages 7–17)

The purpose of this section is to familiarize students with some of the terms, concepts, and strategies that will be introduced and applied in the program. The practice exercises that accompany the discussions are meant to clarify and consolidate the concepts involved.

Some of these terms (for example, *synonyms* and *antonyms*) will already be familiar to most students. However, teachers should not hesitate to review these terms if doing so seems advisable, even at the upper levels of the program. Other, more complex concepts (such as analogies and context), however, may require more instruction and practice, both as preparation for related exercises and as review or re-teaching for any students who have difficulty in successfully completing those exercises.

This is particularly true of analogies, which many students find especially challenging. Four pages of Vocabulary of Vocabulary are devoted to this important critical-thinking exercise so often found on standardized tests.

Diagnostic Test (Student Text pages 18–20)

A Diagnostic Test has been provided at the beginning of each Level as a means of assessing the students' overall vocabulary and test-taking skills. The Test covers a selection of key words introduced in the Level in question, and is presented in the form of 50 synonym and antonym items.

Although the Diagnostic Test may be presented as a timed speed test, with the specific aim of determining how many items students can answer in 10 or 15 minutes, it is better used as an informal assessment and/or motivational device. Speed will come when confidence and vocabulary fluency have developed.

The Units

At the heart of the Student Texts—and of the VOCABULARY WORKSHOP program—are the 15 Units in which the 300 key words are introduced.

The work of each Unit is divided into a unique 5-part structure designed to give maximum coverage to each of the key words given the space available.

Structure of the Unit
(20 words)
1. Definitions
2. Completing the Sentence
3. Synonyms and Antonyms
4. Choosing the Right Word
5. Vocabulary in Context

The following descriptions of the individual exercises in a typical Unit of Levels A–H are designed to aid the teacher in using the text to maximum effect in the classroom.

1. Definitions

The first section of each Unit provides definitions, parts of speech, pronunciation, synonyms, antonyms, and illustrative sentences.

Definitions

The definitions provided are not of the dictionary type. They are, for the most part, relatively brief and simple. The intent is to give students a reasonably good "core" idea of what each word means, without extensive detail or secondary connotations.

Generally, only a single meaning of maximum usefulness is given the student. However, several meanings may be indicated if they are distinct, if they appear to be more or less equally useful, or if they will enable students to prepare for the vocabulary-in-context strand of the Critical Reading section of the new SAT I.

Part of Speech

The part of speech of each word is indicated at the beginning of the definition, using a simple set of abbreviations. When a word functions as several parts of speech, the appropriate abbreviation appears before the corresponding definition. (An explanation of the abbreviations used can be found on page 6 of each Student Text).

Pronunciation

With each word listing, the pronunciation is indicated by means of a simple set of diacritical marks presented at the beginning of every Student Text (page 6).

The practice has been to indicate only 1 pronunciation, even where alternate pronunciations are sanctioned by the dictionary. There are only a few exceptions to this—for example, when a word changes its pronunciation in accordance with its use as different parts of speech (ob´ ject and ob ject´).

Note that once they have completed the first section of each Unit, students may utilize the **Interactive Audio Pronunciation Program** (Levels A–F only) for that Unit. This program provides about four hours of spoken material per Student Text, including pronunciations, part(s) of speech, definition(s), and illustrative usages. For further details about the use of the Audio Program in this and other ways, see page T21.

Synonyms and Antonyms

A list of synonyms and/or antonyms is given for each key word for which there is one or more of either. Some of these synonyms and antonyms will reappear in the Synonyms and Antonyms section (see page T13). By studying the given synonyms and antonyms, students will better understand the denotational family of words of which each key word is part, and by comparing specific usages of key words and their synonyms, students can better appreciate appropriate contexts for, and nuances in meaning and connotation represented by, these words.

Note that the lists of synonyms and antonyms are not meant to be exhaustive. Grade-level parameters have been taken into account; and obscure, archaic, and slang synonyms and antonyms have generally been avoided.

ILLUSTRATIVE SENTENCE

Concluding each key entry is an illustrative sentence including a blank space in which students must write the taught word. These sentences, although necessarily brief, provide a context that clarifies the meaning of each word and points up its idiomatic usage. By writing the word in such contextual settings, students begin to see how it can be used effectively in their own writing. Furthermore, the act of writing is in itself a form of reinforcement, and by writing the word the student must focus attention on its spelling as well.

2. COMPLETING THE SENTENCE

The next activity, Completing the Sentence, is a simple completion exercise in which students are asked to choose and write the word that logically and meaningfully fits into a blank in a given sentence.

When using this activity in the classroom, the teacher should bear in mind the following considerations:

- The sentences in this activity call for the literal or direct (as opposed to the metaphorical or extended) meaning of the words involved. This is an easier usage for students to grasp and provides a good foundation for the more sophisticated contexts that appear in Choosing the Right Word.

- The sentences are designed so that one and only one of the words fits in the given blank. Selection of the proper word has been facilitated by the introduction of context clues into each sentence.

- The words are to be used as the part of speech given in Definitions. The only exceptions are: Nouns given in the singular in Definitions may be plural in the sentences; verbs given in the base form in Definitions may be used in any tense or form (including participial) required by the sentence.

3. SYNONYMS AND ANTONYMS

In this section students are given phrases that include synonyms or antonyms as presented in the Definitions section, then must choose the appropriate key word for each phrase. Each of the 20 key Unit words is covered once either in the Synonyms or Antonyms part of the section. Besides reinforcing meanings, this exercise provides students with further examples of usage and context.

4. Choosing the Right Word

The fourth activity in each Unit is called Choosing the Right Word. In it students are asked to choose the member of a pair of words that more satisfactorily completes the sentence. At first appearance, this exercise may seem an easier activity than Completing the Sentence. In fact, however:

- sentences in this final activity are more mature linguistically and in subject matter;

- in many cases the words covered are used in a more figurative, extended, or abstract meaning;

- the part of speech or form of the key word has been changed (for example, from an adjective to an adverb) whenever convenient.

Accordingly, this activity is in reality more difficult than Completing the Sentence and requires real effort and a thorough understanding of the range of a word to complete successfully.

5. Vocabulary in Context

The fifth, and last, section of each Unit is an activity titled Vocabulary in Context. The activity is presented in the form of a reading passage, approximating a standardized-test format, into which five or six of the key Unit words have been woven. Its purpose is threefold:

- to give further examples of usage for the selected words;

- to offer an opportunity to derive meaning from context;

- to provide practice in the sort of vocabulary exercises found on standardized tests.

With this activity, it may prove helpful to refer students, if necessary, to the section of Vocabulary of Vocabulary (see Student Text pages 7–17) that serves as an introduction to the strategies involved in studying vocabulary in context.

Follow-Up Activities

Once the work of the Unit is completed, you may find it useful to give a writing exercise in which students may apply and illustrate what they have learned about the words introduced in the Unit.

Writing Essays or Stories

Students might be invited to create their own brief essays or short stories, and encouraged to use as many of the Unit's key words as is practical. (Students should, however, be discouraged from trying to "force" key words into their essays or stories indiscriminately, just for the sake of number alone. It is essential that students get in the habit of using these words correctly.) If they are to write essays, students might refer to the Vocabulary in Context passages as models.

WRITING SENTENCES

Depending on the ability level of individual students or of classes, you may prefer instead to administer a short writing exercise (5–10 items) such as the one shown below. This exercise is not so challenging as writing a story or essay but will give students an opportunity to "try out" some of the words they have learned, and provide the teacher with a means of assessing how well students have mastered the meaning and usage of these words.

Sample Writing Exercise (Level E)

Framing Sentences   On the lines provided, write an **original** sentence that illustrates the meaning and use of each of the following words. Do **not** merely copy one of the sentences given in the Student Text.

1. augment

_____

_____

_____

2. unkempt

_____

_____

_____

3. guise

_____

_____

_____

4. opulent

_____

_____

_____

5. intimation

_____

_____

_____

The Reviews

A Review follows every three Units. Every effort has been made to include all of the 60 key words at least once in the Review for the three corresponding Units.

Structure of the Review
1. Analogies
2. Word Associations
3. Vocabulary in Context
4. Choosing the Right Meaning
5. Antonyms
6. Word Families
7. Two-Word Completions
8. Building with Classical Roots
9. Writer's Challenge

SAT I SECTIONS

Four parts of each Review have been specially designed to meet the needs of students seriously preparing for the verbal part of the SAT I and similar standardized tests.

ANALOGIES (PART 1)

The first of these special SAT sections involves analogies.

- Analogies are valuable and revealing, not merely as a kind of mental gymnastics, but also as a means of pinning down the exact meanings of words and of remedying misconceptions or uncertainties about how those words are used.

- Analogies provide an excellent means for testing and refining the critical-thinking skills used on the college level.

- Words that receive the attention necessary to complete an analogy successfully are much more likely to become part of the student's active daily-use vocabulary.

It is impossible, of course, to catalog all the relationships that may be embodied in analogy questions. They are as open-ended as the mental capacity to manipulate ideas and terms. However, the analogies illustrated and discussed in Student Text pages 13–16 will be helpful in reviewing with the students a few of the general "types" that occur in the Reviews and Cumulative Reviews.

Note: In the Supplemental Answer Key on pages T38–T48, you will find explanations for the correct answers to all analogy exercises in the Student Text.

VOCABULARY IN CONTEXT (PART 3)

Like the Unit exercises that bear the same name, this activity is meant primarily as preparation for the vocabulary questions that appear in the SAT I and other standardized tests. Its format is changed in the Reviews, however, to more closely reflect the columnar format of standardized tests.

CHOOSING THE RIGHT MEANING (PART 4)

Focusing on usage-discrimination skills, this part of the Review challenges students to choose, from among two or more taught meanings of a word, the only one that the specific context will reasonably allow. This activity gives students useful practice in determining a word's meaning by careful attention to the context in which it appears, a skill assessed in the critical reading section of the SAT I.

Note: Explanations for the correct answers to the Choosing the Right Meanings can be found in the Supplemental Answer Key on pages T38–T48.

TWO-WORD COMPLETIONS (PART 7)

This part of the Reviews has been designed to familiarize students with the type of word-omission (cloze) exercise that appears on typical standardized tests, including the SAT I. Again the aim here is to refine students' critical-thinking skills. Context clues are embedded within the passages to guide students to the correct choice.

Note: Explanations for the correct answers to Two-Word Completions can be found in the Supplemental Answer Key on pages T38–T48.

OTHER SECTIONS OF THE REVIEW

WORD ASSOCIATIONS (PART 2)

The purpose of this activity is to reinforce and extend understanding of the meanings of key words with brief definitions or examples, situations, or allusions that in some way suggest key words.

ANTONYMS (PART 5)

As it requires of students that they recall the meaning of a key word in order to determine its opposite, this activity helps students "situate" a word within the cluster of words of related meanings.

WORD FAMILIES (PART 6)

This part extends the work of the Units by showing students that by learning one English word they often are acquiring a whole family of related words. It also provides practice in classifying words by part of speech.

BUILDING WITH CLASSICAL ROOTS (PART 8)

Building on the foundation laid down in the Vocabulary of Vocabulary section titled Vocabulary Strategy: Word Structure (Student Text pages 11–12), this part of the Reviews introduces students to English words derived from common Latin and Greek stems, and gives practice in the strategy of finding meaning by analyzing the parts of a word.

WRITER'S CHALLENGE (PART 9)

The concluding part of each Review provides an opportunity for students to apply to the writing and revising process what they have learned about word meanings and usage. Note that it is important that students understand that, apart from the conventions of Standard English (when applicable), there are no "rights" or "wrongs" in writing, and that this activity is meant to make them more aware of ways in which the choice of words affects the tone, clarity, and coherence of their written work.

The Cumulative Reviews

Once students have completed the Reviews (and any follow-up activities), they may turn to the Cumulative Reviews.

Of the four parts of the Cumulative Reviews, three mirror activities presented in the Reviews: Analogies, Choosing the Right Meaning, and Two-Word Completions. These are presented in the same format and serve the same purpose as their counterparts in the Reviews, primarily to give students practice in types of questions they will encounter on the SAT I and other standardized tests.

The fourth part of the Cumulative Review, Enriching Your Vocabulary, is designed to broaden and enhance student knowledge of the interesting origins, history, and relationships of the words that make up the English language.

The Final Mastery Test

The Final Mastery Test in the Student Text of Levels A–H is designed as a practice test of 100 items that gives students and teachers reasonably good insight into how much progress has been made during the year and what kind of additional work is in order.

The purpose of the Final Mastery Test is fourfold.

- It can serve as a dry run in preparation for the more formal (and "secure") tests available as optional components.

- It can serve as an informal evaluation of achievement to date.

- It can serve as a reinforcement activity.

- It can serve as a before-and-after comparison when used in conjunction with the Diagnostic Test.

For whichever purpose the test is used, it is both a testing and a teaching device, the culminating step in a process involving many class periods and, therefore, should be given careful attention.

Supplemental Assessment Components (Optional)

Test Generator CD-ROM (Levels A–F)

New to this edition, the Vocabulary Workshop Test Generator CD-ROM provides an array of secure student tests that support the Student Texts for Levels A–F. With the Test Generator, teachers may create countless unique vocabulary tests with a variety of question formats, all within seconds. With a database of more than 3,000 questions per Level, teachers never have to administer the same test twice.

The Test Generator CD-ROM provides:

* new and secure Unit Tests, Mastery Tests, Cumulative Tests, Diagnostic Tests, Mid-Year Tests, and Final Mastery Tests
* a wide assortment of question types to choose from: pronunciation, part of speech, spelling, definitions, synonyms and antonyms, sentence completions, sentence framing
* the ability to customize tests to include any number of questions and to assess any Unit in the Student Text
* a method of flagging questions so that they will not appear on other tests
* the option to save a test for future use
* an on-screen Help program
* a printed Teacher's Manual
* technical support

The Test Generator provides a convenient and secure source of assessment and/or extra practice. With the Test Generator CD-ROM, teachers may tailor tests to suit the specific needs of either individual students or an entire class.

The flexibility of the Test Generator makes it easy to use either as-needed or more systematically, as an integral part of the VOCABULARY WORKSHOP series. See pages T22–25 for recommendations on how it may be used in conjunction with the Student Text and other components of the program.

Test Booklets (Levels A–H)

Two Test Booklets (Form A and Form B) are available for each of Levels A–H. These Test Booklets have been designed to be used in alternating years, thereby reducing the risk of answers being passed on. Each Test Booklet contains a full set of testing materials and is designed to cover the work of one entire Level of the Student Text. Though the formats of the Test Booklets are the same, the items tested in any given section are completely different. The contents of the Test Booklets have been organized to reflect that of the Student Text, and include the following:

- preparatory test-taking tips for students

- a Warm-Up Test (corresponding to the Diagnostic Test in the Student Text)

- 15 Unit Tests each consisting of 25 items focusing on pronunciation, part of speech, spelling, definitions, synonyms, antonyms, and sentence completions

- 5 Cumulative Tests of 50 items each (plus 2 optional items)

The Warm-Up Test may serve either as an introduction to the Test Booklet as a whole or as an effective follow-up to the Diagnostic Test in the Student Text.

Each Unit Test has been designed for use as soon as the students have completed work on the Unit to which it corresponds or at any point thereafter.

Each Cumulative Test, including the Final Cumulative Test, covers all of the work of the Student Text to the point at which it occurs and is designed to be used after the corresponding Review in the Student Text.

Note that these tests may also serve as effective "lead-ins" to the SAT-oriented Cumulative Reviews in the Student Texts and to the SAT-oriented PREP Worksheets in the corresponding TEST PREP Blackline Masters.

For recommendations on how to employ the Test Booklets as part of the complete VOCABULARY WORKSHOP program, see pages T23–T29.

TEST PREP Blackline Masters (Levels A-H)

For further assessment options, a booklet of reproducible TEST PREP Blackline Masters is available for each Level A–H. The TEST PREP component is designed to provide both practice in working with SAT I type test questions and formats *and* review tests covering the entire content of the corresponding Student Text.

- Prep Tests approximate as closely as possible, given the vocabulary that is to be covered, the analogy and word-omission sections of the SAT I, and provide practice in the vocabulary-in-context strand with brief reading passages as well.

- Answer sheets provide an SAT I type test format to develop student ease and familiarity with standardized testing materials.

- Mastery Tests are meant to be used when students have completed the correspon-ding group of three Units in the Student Text. Each test covers basic Meanings, synonyms, antonyms, sentence completions, and analogies.

- Answer keys, including selected answer rationales, are provided for all tests.

For recommendations on the implementation of the TEST PREP Blackline Masters as part of the complete VOCABULARY WORKSHOP program, see pages T23–T25.

Interactive Audio Pronunciation Program (Levels A–F)

Now available in CD format as well as cassette, the Interactive Audio Pronunciation Program provides teachers and students with a convenient and effective means of teaching and learning the recommended pronunciations of all key words introduced in the Student Texts for Levels A–F. It is designed to be used either by the teacher in a classroom setting or by the student (either individually or in small groups) in a language laboratory or at home.

- Ideal for English Language Learners of all cultures and backgrounds, and for use in ESL classrooms.

- Students hear the recommended pronunciation of each word at least 6 times, both alone and in context.

- Full coverage is given to words with more than one recommended pronunciation.

- Students are provided with two opportunities to pronounce each word themselves.

- Pronunciations are followed by brief definitions based on those given in the Student Text.

- Usage examples in complete-sentence form extend student knowledge of how to use a word correctly in their speech and writing.

- Teacher's notes for the program are provided in Spanish as well as English.

For recommendations on when to use the program, see the chart on pages T22–25.

Implementing the Program

The format of the VOCABULARY WORKSHOP program allows for great flexibility. The teacher can easily adjust the activity assignments to conform to the special needs of an entire class, of groups within the class, or of individual students.

Schedule for the Year (28 Weeks)

The chart on pages T23–T25 shows how the various components of the VOCABULARY WORKSHOP program for Levels A–H can be scheduled effectively over an academic year lasting 28 weeks.

The following notes should prove helpful when adapting the chart to individual needs:

- Though the chart shows a disposition of material over 28 weeks, the time period can be extended to as many as 34 weeks simply by increasing to two weeks the time allotment for the items under weeks 6, 11, 16, 21, 26, and 28.

- It is not to be supposed that every item listed under Follow-Up Activities is meant to be covered during the week specified. The listings here are designed to offer teacher options from which to choose in order to tailor the VOCABULARY WORKSHOP program to the specific needs of a particular class. This is also true of the sections or subsections into which some of the Follow-Up components are divided.

KEY

IAPP = Interactive Audio Pronunciation Program, Levels A–F only

BLM = *TEST PREP Blackline Masters*

TB A/B = Test Booklet Form A/Form B

TG = Test Generator CD-ROM

Using the Program Over the Year (28 Weeks)

Note: "Framing Sentences" and "Story/Essay Writing" are to be supplied by the teacher.

Week	Student Text	Follow-Up Activities
1	Vocabulary of Vocabulary	
2	Diagnostic Test	Warm-Up Test (TB A/B) Warm-Up Prep Test (BLM)
3	Unit 1 IAPP	Framing Sentences Story/Essay Writing Unit Test 1 (TB A/B) Unit Test 1 (TG)
4	Unit 2 IAPP	Framing Sentences Story/Essay Writing Unit Test 2 (TB A/B) Unit Test 2 (TG)
5	Unit 3 IAPP	Framing Sentences Story/Essay Writing Unit Test 3 (TB A/B) Unit Test 3 (TG)
6	Review 1-3	Mastery Test 1–3 (BLM) Mastery Test (TG)
7	—	Cumulative Test 1–3 (TB A/B) Prep Worksheet 1–3 (BLM)
8	Unit 4 IAPP	Framing Sentences Story/Essay Writing Unit Test 4 (TB A/B) Unit Test 4 (TG)
9	Unit 5 IAPP	Framing Sentences Story/Essay Writing Unit Test 5 (TB A/B) Unit Test 5 (TG)
10	Unit 6 IAPP	Framing Sentences Story/Essay Writing Unit Test 6 (TB A/B) Unit Test 6 (TG)

(Continued on pg. T24)

(Continued from pg. T23)

Week	Student Text	Follow-Up Activities
11	Review 4–6	Mastery Test 4–6 (BLM) Mastery Test (TG)
12	Cumulative Review 1–6	Cumulative Test 1–6 (TB A/B) Prep Worksheet 4–6 (BLM)
13	Unit 7 IAPP	Framing Sentences Story/Essay Writing Unit Test 7 (TB A/B) Unit Test 7 (TG)
14	Unit 8 IAPP	Framing Sentences Story/Essay Writing Unit Test 8 (TB A/B) Unit Test 8 (TG)
15	Unit 9 IAPP	Framing Sentences Story/Essay Writing Unit Test 9 (TB A/B) Unit Test 9 (TG)
16	Review 7–9	Mastery Test 7–9 (BLM) Mastery Test (TG) Mid-Year Test (TG)
17	Cumulative Review 1–9	Cumulative Test 1–9 (TB A/B) Prep Worksheet 7–9 (BLM) Cumulative Test (TG)
18	Unit 10 IAPP	Framing Sentences Story/Essay Writing Unit Test 10 (TB A/B) Unit Test 10 (TG)
19	Unit 11 IAPP	Framing Sentences Story/Essay Writing Unit Test 11 (TB A/B) Unit Test 11 (TG)
20	Unit 12 IAPP	Framing Sentences Story/Essay Writing Unit Test 12 (TB A/B) Unit Test 12 (TG)

Week	Student Text	Follow-Up Activities
21	Review 10–12	Mastery Test 10–12 (BLM) Mastery Test (TG)
22	Cumulative Review 1–12	Cumulative Test 1–12 (TB A/B) Prep Worksheet 1–12 (BLM) Cumulative Test (TG)
23	Unit 13 IAPP	Framing Sentences Story/Essay Writing Unit Test 13 (TB A/B) Unit Test 13 (TG)
24	Unit Test 14 IAPP	Framing Sentences Story/Essay Writing Unit Test 14 (TB A/B) Unit Test 14 (TG)
25	Unit 15 IAPP	Framing Sentences Story/Essay Writing Unit Test 15 (TB A/B) Unit Test 15 (TG)
26	Review 13–15	Mastery Test 13–15 (BLM) Mastery Test (TG)
27	Cumulative Review 1–15	Cumulative Test 1–15 (TB A/B) Prep Worksheet 13–15 (BLM) Cumulative Test (TG)
28	Final Mastery Test	Cumulative Mastery Test (BLM) Cumulative Prep Test (BLM) Final Test (TG)

Using the Units

On the top of these 2 pages the teacher will find 2 models for using the Units effectively on a weekly basis. Though there is no single formula or plan that will be sure to yield optimum results all the time, the models presented here and on the next 2 pages are designed to get the teacher thinking about how best to adapt the program to the needs of individual classes.

KEY: IAPP = Interactive Audio Pronunciation Program

TB = Test Booklet Form A or B

TG = Test Generator CD-ROM

** Item to be supplied by teacher/student

Assignment	
Classwork	
Homework	

MODEL B: 5 Sessions/Periods (20 Minutes)		
Assignment	**Day 1**	**Day 2**
Classwork	**1.** Collect Framing Sentences **2.** Review Unit Test **3.** Present Definitions	Review Completing the Sentences
Homework	**1.** Completing the Sentence **2.** IAPP	Synonyms and Antonyms

Using the Reviews

On the bottom of these 2 pages the teacher will find 2 models for using the Reviews effectively on a weekly basis.

Assignment	
Classwork	
Homework	

MODEL B: 5 Sessions/Periods (20 Minutes)		
Assignment	**Day 1**	**Day 2**
Classwork	Present Analogies	**1.** Review homework **2.** Present Choosing the Right Meaning
Homework	**1.** Word Associations **2.** Antonyms	Vocabulary in Context

Weekly Lesson Plans

Day 1	Day 2	Day 3
1. Collect Framing Sentences** 2. Present Definitions	1. Review Completing the Sentence, Synonyms and Antonyms 2. Present Choosing the Right Word and Vocabulary in Context	1. Unit Test (TB or TG) 2. Review last week's Framing Sentences**
1. Completing the Sentence, Synonyms and Antonyms 2. IAPP	Test Study	Framing Sentences**

Day 3	Day 4	Day 5
Review Synonyms and Antonyms	1. Review Choosing the Right Word 2. Review Vocabulary in Context	1. Unit Test (TB or TG) 2. Review last week's Framing Sentences
Choosing the Right Word	Test Study	Framing Sentences**

Day 1	Day 2	Day 3
Present: Word Associations Vocabulary in Context Word Families	Review homework Present: Antonyms Building with Classical Roots Choosing the Right Meaning	1. Mastery Test (TB or TG) 2. Review homework
1. Analogies 2. Two-Word Completions	1. Test Study 2. Writer's Challenge	Remedial work as required

Day 3	Day 4	Day 5
Review homework Present Two-Word Completions	Mastery Test (TB or TG)	1. Review Mastery Test 2. Review homework
Test Study Word Families	1. Building with Classical Roots 2. Writer's Challenge	Remedial work as required

Using the Cumulative Reviews

On the top of these 2 pages the teacher will find 2 models for using the Cumulative Reviews effectively on a weekly basis.

Assignment
Classwork
Homework

MODEL B: 5 Sessions/Periods (20 Minutes)		
Assignment	**Day 1**	**Day 2**
Classwork	Present Cumulative Review	Cumulative Test Parts 1–4 (TB)
Homework	Test Study	Test Study

Implementing the Weekly Schedules

The following may prove helpful when adapting the foregoing schedules to specific situations.

- The models shown are, as their designation suggests, purely models—that is, starting points. Accordingly, the teacher is expected to adapt them to the particular situation at hand.

- The models make only minimal use of the Follow-Up Activities suggested earlier and no use whatsoever of the Alternative Approaches to Using the Program suggested on the following pages. The teacher should in all cases feel free to introduce such alternative approaches as convenient.

- Place assignments and timings are to some extent hypothetical. Teachers should switch items around and adjust timings as needed. Similarly, items may be modified or deleted and new items inserted as the teacher sees fit.

- Multiple listings in a Day's entry for either Classwork or Homework are to be seen as options from which the teacher should select appropriate material. It is unlikely that the teacher could cover all the suggested material in the indicated time allotment.

- With some adjustment, the allotments for each Day can accommodate a 2- or 4-day arrangement. There is usually too much material to cover in 1 day, and a 1-day approach is, therefore, not suggested.

MODEL A: 3 Sessions/Periods (35–40 Minutes)		
Day 1	**Day 2**	**Day 3**
Present Cumulative Review	Cumulative Test (TB or TG)	**1.** Review Cumulative Test **2.** Review Prep Worksheet
Test Study	Prep Worksheet	Remedial Work as Required

Day 3	**Day 4**	**Day 5**
Cumulative Test Parts 5–6 (TB)	Review Cumulative Test	Review Prep Worksheet
—	Prep Worksheet	Remedial Work as Required

Alternative Approaches to Using the Program

Writing Approach

Research has shown that vocabulary acquisition is maximized when learning is authentically contextualized—when learners have a "real-life" purpose for acquiring and using a new word. Activities such as the following can provide these authentic contexts.

- Students can create journals or logs in which they use the key words to express experiences, thoughts, or feelings that are personally meaningful. They are free to keep these entries for their eyes only or to share them with others.

- Students can use the key words in personal letters to friends and relatives or in letters to the editor of the school or local newspaper. Students should write about subjects of real interest and concern to them.

- Students can use the key words to write descriptions of people they know or characters they are interested in. These character sketches or personality profiles may be written for a class yearbook, for a book report, or as a reference for a friend.

Literature-Based Approach

The VOCABULARY WORKSHOP program can be combined with some of the items listed below to form a *literature-based* approach to vocabulary study. Each of the items listed has been surveyed for use of some of the key words presented in the specified level of VOCABULARY WORKSHOP. Seeing the words they are studying in classic world literature will reinforce student appreciation of the value of possessing a good active-use vocabulary.

Classic Literature To Use With The Program

Levels D and E

Louisa May Alcott *Little Women*

Maya Angelou *I know Why the Caged Bird Sings*

Ray Bradbury *Fahrenheit 451*

Charlotte Brontë *Jane Eyre*

Emily Brontë *Wuthering Heights*

Pearl S. Buck *The Good Earth*

Lewis Carroll *Alice's Adventures in Wonderland*

Willa Cather *My Antonia*

Sandra Cisneros *The House on Mango Street*

Daniel Defoe *Robinson Crusoe*

Charles Dickens *A Tale of Two Cities*

Arthur Conan Doyle *The Hound of the Baskervilles*

George Eliot *Silas Marner*

William Golding *Lord of the Flies*

Frank Herbert *Dune*

Harper Lee *To Kill a Mockingbird*

Carson McCullers *Member of the Wedding*

Nicholasa Mohr *El Bronx Remembered*

Walter Dean Myers *Fallen Angels*

George Orwell *Animal Farm*

Alan Paton *Cry, the Beloved Country*

John Steinbeck *The Pearl*

Level F

Sherwood Anderson *Winesburg, Ohio*

James Baldwin *Go Tell It on the Mountain*

Stephen Crane *The Red Badge of Courage*

Kate Chopin *The Awakening*

Ralph Ellison *Invisible Man*

Louise Erdrich *Love Medicine*

Jack Finney *Time and Again*

F. Scott Fitzgerald *The Great Gatsby*

Joseph Heller *Catch-22*

Ernest Hemingway *A Farewell to Arms*

Zora Neale Hurston *Their Eyes Were Watching God*

Nathaniel Hawthorne *The Scarlet Letter*

Henry James *Washington Square*

Maxine Hong Kingston *Woman Warrior*

N. Scott Momaday *The Way to Rainy Mountain*

Toni Morrison *Beloved*

John Steinbeck *The Grapes of Wrath*

Amy Tan *The Joy Luck Club*

Mark Twain *The Adventures of Huckleberry Finn*

Kurt Vonnegut, Jr. *Slaughterhouse Five*

Alice Walker *The Color Purple*

Edith Wharton *The House of Mirth* and *The Age of Innocence*

Richard Wright *Black Boy*

Levels G and H

Margaret Atwood *The Handmaid's Tale*

Chinua Achebe *Things Fall Apart*

Jane Austen *Pride and Prejudice*

Joseph Conrad *Lord Jim* and *Heart of Darkness*

Charles Dickens *David Copperfield*

Isak Dinesen *Out of Africa*

George Eliot *The Mill on the Floss*

Thomas Hardy *The Return of the Native*

Aldous Huxley *Brave New World*

James Joyce *A Portrait of the Artist as a Young Man*

Gabriel Garcia Marquez *One Hundred Years of Solitude*

Mark Mathabane *Kaffir Boy*

V.S. Naipaul *A House for Mr. Biswas*

Mary Shelley *Frankenstein*

Muriel Spark *The Prime of Miss Jean Brodie*

Jonathan Swift *Gulliver's Travels*

Virginia Woolf *A Room of One's Own* and *To the Lighthouse*

To coordinate reading and vocabulary study, the following may prove helpful:

- Instruct students to devote a special notebook to vocabulary. As they come across key words in their reading, they should head a page of the notebook with the word; copy the title of the work; and then indicate (a) the definition of the word used in that sentence, (b) its part of speech, and (c) whether it is used in a literal or figurative sense.

- Students may then be instructed to check *Bartlett's Familiar Quotations* for other famous examples of the use of the key word in question. These may be copied into the notebook and shared with others in the class.

Content-Area Approach

VOCABULARY WORKSHOP can be used to enhance student understanding and use of vocabulary in subjects such as social studies and history, science and health, and other curriculum areas.

In the following list of nonfiction print and video titles you will find works that relate in content to Vocabulary in Context exercises appearing in specific Units and Reviews of the VOCABULARY WORKSHOP Student Texts for Levels D–H. Students may wish to read or view some of these works and report on the topics and issues that they treat. In their reports, whether oral or written, students should be encouraged to use words they have come to know through their Student Texts.

Author & Title	Level & Unit
Lisa Aldred, *Thurgood Marshall*	Level G, U6; H, U6
Catherine Allgor, *Parlor Politics*	Level G, Unit 7
Isaac Asimov, "The Eureka Phenomenon" from *Left Hand of the Election*	Level E, Review 13–15
Russell Baker, *Growing Up*	Level E, U15; H, U4
Rachel Carson, *Silent Spring*	Level G, Unit 2
Agnes DeMille, "The Kosloff School" from *Dance to the Piper*	Level E, Unit 10
Benjamin Franklin, *The Autobiography*	Level E, Unit 3
James Herriot, *All Creatures Great and Small*	Level D, Unit 12
J. S. Holliday, *The World Rushed In*	Level E, Review 7–9
Washington Irving, *Dietrich Knickerbocker's A History of New York*	Level H, Review 10–12
Charles Kuralt, "Noah Webster's Dictionary" from *Dateline America*	Level H, Unit 2
Brian Lanker, "Daisy Bates," in *I Dream a World: Portraits of Black Women Who Changed America*	Level H, Unit 6
Patricia Lauber, *Volcano: The Eruption and Healing of Mt. St. Helens*	Level D, Unit 15
Bill Littlefield, *Champions*	F, Rev 4–6; H, U5, 12
John McPhee, "The Loch Ness Monster" from *Pieces of the Frame*	Level F, Unit 8
Tsuneo Nakamura, *Gentle Giant*	Level D, Unit 13
Ann Petry, *Harriet Tubman: Conductor on the Underground Railroad*	Level E, Unit 6
Franklin D. Roosevelt, *War Message to Congress, December 8, 1941*	Level F, Unit 11
Amy Tan, *The Joy Luck Club*	Level D, Unit 3
Ellen Harkins Wheat, Jacob Lawrence, *American Painter*	Level H, Unit 8

Title & Distributor Videos	Level & Unit
American Cinema (Discovery Channel Video)	Level F, Unit 1
American Photography (PBS Home Video)	Level F, Unit 7
American Visions (PBS Home Video)	E, U9; F, U3; G, U5; H, Rev. 1–3
Baseball: A Film by Ken Burns (PBS Home Video)	Level F, U5; Level H, U5
Cold War (PBS Home Video)	Level D, Unit 5
Flyers (PBS Home Video)	Level F, Review 1–3
Frank Lloyd Wright (PBS Home Video)	Level F, Unit 3
Gold Fever (PBS Home Video)	Level E, Review 7–9
The Great Depression (History Channel Video)	Level E, Unit 15
The Great Ships: Sailing Collection (History Channel Video)	Level E, Unit 7
John Ringling: Master of the Big Top (PBS Home Video)	Level E, Unit 1
Ken Burns' America: Statue of Liberty (PBS Home Video)	Level D, Unit 7
Liberty! The American Revolution (PBS Home Video)	D, U1, E, U3; F, U13; G, U4; H, U9
Not for Ourselves Alone (PBS Home Video)	Level H, Unit 7
Reflections on Elephants (National Geographic Video)	Level F, Review 7–9
Surviving the Dust Bowl (PBS Home Video)	Level H., Unit 14
Trains Unlimited (History Channel Video)	Level F, Unit 14
The Ultimate Guide: Birds of Prey (Discovery Channel Video)	Level E, Unit 12

Other content-related activities to which students might apply vocabulary study are:

- Working in pairs or small groups, they can choose sentences from Completing the Sentence or Choosing the Right Word and discuss a larger context in which these sentences could have appeared, such as a history or mathematics textbook, a daily newspaper, a book review, a personal letter, or a scientific article.

- Students can work together to link individual vocabulary words to a particular content area. Then working in pairs, they can find "real-world" examples of the words used in context in that content area.

- Students can work cooperatively to create sentence and paragraph contexts that illustrate the meaning of the content-area words that they have identified.

Useful Classroom Techniques

Classroom experience and research have shown that some students learn more readily when they can exercise a great deal of personal choice and can interact with others. VOCABULARY WORKSHOP can be adapted in the following ways to accommodate such students.

Cooperative Activities

Working cooperatively does not just mean working in proximity to other students or dividing an assignment or project into discrete tasks. Rather it means that students take individual and collective responsibility for the learning of all members of the group and for the successful completion of the group goal. Students who cooperate to develop their vocabulary should maintain an ongoing dialog to monitor the comprehension of all group members.

Oral and Kinesthetic

One student can write the key words in a given unit on the chalkboard while the rest of the class is divided into pairs or small groups. A member of each group will read a numbered item from the Unit aloud. The rest of the group will confer and then supply the required vocabulary word. The student reader will evaluate each answer and give reasons why it is correct or incorrect based on the word's definition and any context clues.

Students in groups can discuss the shades of meaning or connotations among selected synonyms and antonyms for a given Unit and among the alternative answers in Choosing the Right Meaning.

Students can work together to create puns, riddles, Tom Swifties, and limericks to illustrate the multiple meanings of appropriate vocabulary words. They may want to collect and publish their creations in illustrated books or an audio-anthology.

Members of a group can work together to improvise stories, skits, or pantomimes that illustrate the meaning of the key word in a given Unit, while other group members guess the word being illustrated.

Written

- Students can work cooperatively to brainstorm their own vocabulary word lists, based on their current reading and writing in all areas of the curriculum and on their personal reading and writing experiences.

- The class can collaborate to create their own Unit, covering vocabulary words they have chosen. Different groups can be assigned to develop each of the unit activities.

- Students may want to create their own mini-dictionaries, based on the word lists in VOCABULARY WORKSHOP or on categories of words that are especially meaningful or useful to them, such as sports, fashion, music, and career terms.

- Students can make use of semantic mapping and other graphic devices, such as flow charts, to generate new vocabulary or to demonstrate understanding of word relationships. Semantic mapping, or webbing, can be used to illustrate word families, synonyms, and antonyms. Flow charts can illustrate etymological and grammatical relationships.

Alternative Types of Assessment

The following types of assessment may be used in addition to or in lieu of the objective-scoring materials provided in the VOCABULARY WORKSHOP, Levels A–H. The emphasis here is on monitoring understanding rather than on ranking students.

Self-Evaluation

Students can use their journals to reflect on their own process of learning and use of new words. They may consider, for example, which words from VOCABULARY WORKSHOP they understood quickly and used frequently and why. They may want to use these insights to design their own vocabulary-acquisition strategies.

Teacher-Student Conferencing

Meetings take place at every stage of the vocabulary-acquisition process. Meeting over time allows teachers to assess students' developing understanding of words as used in specific contexts.

Observation

Using a checklist of 2 or 3 important criteria, the teacher can observe and evaluate students while they are interacting in groups or engaging in other oral activities. Teachers can also probe for deeper levels of comprehension by asking students to clarify or give reasons for their choice of word or context.

Peer Evaluation

Students meet in pairs or small groups to develop standards or criteria to evaluate their vocabulary acquisition. They then apply their standards to their peers' oral or written expression, giving positive feedback and concrete suggestions for improvement.

Portfolio Assessment

By having students collect and save self-selected samples of their writing over a period of time, teachers have an ongoing record of students' vocabulary development and of their facility in using words in context.

Multimodal Assessment

Students with strong nonverbal competencies can be given the opportunity to demonstrate in nonverbal media their understanding of new vocabulary. For example, they can draw, paint, model, dance, compose music, or construct objects to communicate their comprehension of a word and its definition.

TEACHER RESOURCES

The following lists have been compiled to assist the teacher in the effective presentation of the VOCABULARY WORKSHOP program, Levels A–H.

I. DICTIONARIES

Recommended

Merriam-Webster's Collegiate Dictionary [Tenth Edition] (Springfield, MA: Merriam-Webster, 2000)

Webster's Third New International Dictionary (Springfield, MA: G. & C. Merriam, 1993)

American Heritage Dictionary (Boston: Houghton Mifflin, 2000)

Oxford English Dictionary [Compact Edition] (Oxford: Oxford University Press, 1971)

Skeat, W.W. *A Concise Etymological Dictionary of the English Language* (NY: G.P. Putnam, 1980)

Supplemental

12,000 Words [A Supplement to Webster's *Third International Dictionary*] (Springfield, MA: Merriam-Webster, 1993)

The Random House Dictionary of the English Language [Unabridged Edition] (NY: Random House, 1987)

II. THESAURI

Recommended

Roget's II The New Thesaurus (Boston: Houghton Mifflin, 1995)

Random House Roget's Thesaurus (NY: Random House, 2001)

Rodale, J. [Revised by Urdang, L. and La Roche, N.] *The Synonym Finder* (Emmaus, PA: Rodale Press, 1979)

Supplemental

Chapman, R.L. (Ed.). *Roget A to Z* (NY: Harper Perennial, 1994)

Laird, C. *Webster's New World Thesaurus* (NY: Warner Books, 1990)

Roget's International Thesaurus [Fifth Edition] (NY: HarperCollins, 1992)

Abate, F. *The Oxford Dictionary and Thesaurus: The Ultimate Language Reference for American Readers* (NY: Oxford University Press, 1996)

III. OTHER REFERENCE WORKS

Recommended

Carroll, J., Davies, P., and Richman, B. *Word Frequency Book* (Boston: Houghton Mifflin, 1971)

Dale, E. and O'Rourke, J. *The Living Word Vocabulary* (Chicago: Scott & Fetzer, 1981)

Supplemental

Harris, A. and Jackson, M. *Basic Reading Vocabularies* (NY: Macmillan, 1982)

Thorndike, E. and Lorge, I. *The Teacher's Book of 30,000 Words* (NY: Teachers College Press, Columbia University, 1968)

IV. HISTORY

General

Baugh, A.C. and Cable, T. *A History of the English Language* [Third Edition] (Englewood Cliffs, NJ: Prentice-Hall, 1992)

Carver, C. *A History of English in Its Own Words* (NY: HarperCollins, 1991)

Jespersen, O. *Growth and Structure of the English Language* (Chicago: University of Chicago Press, 1982)

McCrum, R., Cran, W., and MacNeil, R. *The Story of English* (NY: Penguin, 1993)

Myers, L.M. *The Roots of Modern English* (Boston: Little, Brown, 1961)

Pyles, T. *The Origins and Development of the English Language* [Fourth Edition] (NY: Harcourt, Brace, Jovanovich, 1993)

Robinson, O. *Old English and Its Closest Relatives* (Stanford, CA: Stanford University Press, 1993)

American English

Dillard, J.L. *All-American English* (NY: Random House, 1975)

Dillard, J.L. *American Talk* (NY: Random House, 1976)

Flexner, S.B. *I Hear America Talking* (NY: Simon & Schuster, 1976)

Mencken, H.L. *The American Language* (NY: Alfred A. Knopf, 1979)

V. OTHER USEFUL RESOURCES

A Dictionary of American Idioms (Woodbury, NY: Barron's Educational Series, Inc., 1995)

Bryson, B. *A Dictionary of Troublesome Words* (NY: Viking Penguin, 1988)

Carroll, D. *Dictionary of Foreign Terms in the English Language* (NY: Hawthorn Books, 1973)

Dixson, R. *Essential Idioms in English* (Englewood Cliffs, NJ: Pearson ESL, 1993)

Evans, I.H. (Ed.) *Brewer's Dictionary of Phrase & Fable* (NY: Harper & Row, 2000)

Harrison, G. *Vocabulary Dynamics* (NY: Warner Books, 1992)

Hendrickson, R. *The Dictionary of Eponyms* (NY: Stein and Day, 1985)

Morris, W. and M. *Morris Dictionary of Word & Phrase Origins* (NY: Harper & Row, 1988)

Orgel, J.R. *Building an Enriched Vocabulary* (NY: William H. Sadlier, Inc., 1999)

Paxson, W. *New American Dictionary of Confusing Words* (NY: NAL-Dutton, 1990)

Room, A. *Dictionary of Contrasting Pairs* (NY: Routledge Educational Series Inc., 1988)

Room, A. *The Penguin Dictionary of Confusibles* (NY: Penguin Books, 1989)

Shipley, J. *Dictionary of Word Origins* (Glenville, IL: Greenwood Press, 1988)

Smith, R. *Dictionary of English Word-Roots* (Totowa, NJ: Littlefield, Adams & Co., 1980)

Spears, R. *Slang and Euphemisms* (NY: NAL-Dutton, 1991)

Webster's Word Histories (Springfield, MA: Merriam-Webster, 1989)

ANSWERS TO EXERCISES IN REVIEWS AND CUMULATIVE REVIEWS

REVIEW UNITS 1–3

Analogies (page 42)

1. (a) A means the opposite of B.
2. (b) Living in an A suggests B.
3. (c) A indicates that the mouth is B, just as C indicates that the eyes are D.
4. (d) A is something that a person would B.
5. (b) An A is caused by a great deal of B.
6. (a) A means the same as B.
7. (a) An A would not be likely to be B.
8. (d) A means the same as B.
9. (c) A means the opposite of B.
10. (c) An A is something that is not supposed to be B.
11. (c) An A is something that comes B something else in time.
12. (b) A means the opposite of B.
13. (d) An A is concerned with B matters.
14. (c) A means the opposite of B.
15. (c) A indicates a B feeling.
16. (b) A refers to (is a quality of) B.
17. (a) The tone of A is B.
18. (a) The tone of A is B.

Choosing the Right Meaning (page 45)

1. (a) (Clue: How easy would it be to attack steep mountain fastnesses?) (c): wrong sense of word for context (ws); (b), (d): irrelevant to meaning of word (ir).

2. (b) (Clue: What kind of self-image would a megalomaniac ["person with delusions of grandeur"] have?) (a), (d): ws; (c): ir.

3. (c) (Contrast clue: "a . . . triumphs" implies activity.) (a), (d): ws; (b): ir.

4. (d) (Clue: *kaustos* = "burnt.") (a), (b): not close enough because neither conveys a sense of burning; (c): ir.

5. (b) (Clue: "in prose and verse.") (c): ws; (a): ir; (d): too weak.

Two-Word Completions (page 47)

1. (a) intimation (Restatement clue: "inkling") . . . duplicity (Restatement clue: "double-dealing")

2. (c) averse (Restatement clue: "always . . . at") . . . wary (Restatement clue: "look . . . leap")

3. (d) insidious (Inference clue: How might you describe a disease whose effects aren't noticeable?) . . . retrogress (Contrast clue: "no longer improving but")

4. (c) belligerent (Restatement clue: "walk . . . shoulder") . . . alienated (Contrast clue: "have . . . friends")

5. (d) verbatim (Inference clue: How wouldn't you be able to reproduce something if it were too long for your needs?) . . . delete (Inference clue: What must you do to a passage to get it down to the size you need?)

6. (b) cursory (Inference clues: What is the nature of a glance? If one doesn't have the time to do something properly, what kind of job does one do?) . . . scrutinize (Inference clues: What would one call a careful reading of a report? How would one prepare oneself to discuss a report in detail?)

REVIEW UNITS 4–6 _____

Analogies (page 72)

1. (a) The tone of A is B.
2. (c) A means the same as B.
3. (c) A is the cure for B.
4. (d) A means the same as B.
5. (d) A means the same as B.
6. (a) The tone of A is B.
7. (c) To A is to move in a way that is not B.
8. (d) An A is someone who would by definition be B.
9. (b) A means the opposite of B.
10. (d) An A is by definition something that is B.
11. (b) Someone who is A another person cannot B.
12. (c) If A is thought up ahead of time (preplanned), it is considered B.
13. (b) A is the verb associated with flourishing a B.
14. (b) The direction of movement indicated by A is B.
15. (c) A means the opposite of B.
16. (d) A describes a B that is strong.
17. (a) A means the opposite of B.
18. (c) A indicates that there is B of something.

Choosing the Right Meaning (page 75)

1. (a) (Clue: To do what the sentence says, what must a foreign policy be?) (d): ws; (b), (c): ir.

2. (d) (Clue: What would happen to many lives during a holocaust [= "vast slaughter"]?) (b), (c): ws; (a): ir.

3. (b) (Clue: What kind of person would not be party to sharp practice [= unethical behavior]?) (c): ws; (a), (d): ir.

4. (c) (Clue: Is Tolkien's a literal or a figurative/abstract voyage?) (a): ws (too literal); (b), (d): ir.

5. (c) (Clue: In a moment of crisis what would a nation do with its hopes of safety?) (d): ws; (a), (b): ir.

Two-Word Completions (page 77)

1. (a). attain (Restatement clue: "achieved") . . . esteem (Restatement clue: "fame")

2. (d) assent (Inference clue: When you sign a contract, what do you do in regard to the agreement it contains?) . . . explicitly (Contrast clue: "so vaguely")

3. (b) solace (Inference clue: What would comforting knowledge be likely to provide?) . . . repose (Contrast clue: "strife")

4. (b). omniscient (Inference clue: If you had to use what you knew to learn something else, what wouldn't you be?) . . . infallible (Inference clue: If you had to be careful to avoid making mistakes, what wouldn't you be?)

5. (d) irony (Inference clue: How would you characterize a situation in which a reformer is him- or herself guilty of the very fault he/she is campaigning to correct?) . . . venal (Inference clue: What would a corrupt politician be likely to be?)

6. (c) ascertain (Inference clue: What might school trustees do in regard to the identity of a mysterious donor of a gift?) . . . benefactor (Restatement clue: "donor")

7. (c) panaceas (Inference clue: What are elixirs supposed to be?) . . . virulent (Inference clue: What would a bogus elixir be likely to be?)

CUMULATIVE REVIEW I

Analogies (page 81)

1. (d) Someone who lacks A can justly be described as B.
2. (a) An A is a facial expression that shows B, or you would A to show B.
3. (b) Something that is A cannot be B.
4. (b) You use your A to B.
5. (d) That which is A has B to it.
6. (c) If something is A, you can B it.
7. (b) An A that suddenly appears can justly be said to B.
8. (c) If you remove something from your A, you B it.
9. (c) A means the same as B.
10. (b) To be A means that a person exercises great B in regard to something.

Choosing the Right Meaning (pages 81–82)

1. (b) (Clue: "speak . . . hand.") (a): ws; (c), (d): ir.

2. (a) (Clue: Context indicates grief as the result of loss.) (b), (d): ws; (c): ir.

3. (b). (Clue: What kind of a smile would make a person feel foolish and uncomfortable?) (d): ws; (a), (c): ir.

4. (d) (Clue: "enterprise" indicates a literal, not an abstract, usage.) (a), (b), (c): ws (too abstract).

5. (c) (Clue: The context suggests the preliminary moves in or before a battle.) (a), (b): not specific enough because neither suggests movement into battle formation; (d): ir.

Two-Word Completions (page 82)

1. (d) coercion (Restatement clue: "open violence and") . . . extirpate (Restatement clue: "root out . . . of")

2. (c) infallible (Inference clues: What is the nature of the cure a panacea professes to offer? How would you describe a remedy that worked all the time?) . . . unkempt (Inference clue: What kind of person would need the services of a barber?)

3. (b) chivalrous (Inference clue: How would you describe an action that was reminiscent of the knights of old? Restatement clue: "magnanimous") . . . punitive (Restatement clue: "or retaliatory")

4. (a) culinary (Inference clue: What kind of knowledge does a chef have?) . . . bequeath (Inference clue: What does one do with a precious heirloom?)

5. (d) reiterated (Inference clue: What verb would aptly describe saying something for the umpteenth time?) . . . affiliated with (Contrast clue: "independent"; Inference clue: Does an independent candidate have any connection with any organized political party?)

REVIEW UNITS 7–9

Analogies (page 105)

1. (d) A means the same as B.
2. (d) An A is overly concerned with matters of B.
3. (d) A means the opposite of B.
4. (c) Something that is A has a great deal of B.
5. (a) An A that is clear may properly be called B.
6. (c) The tone of A is B.
7. (a) A means the opposite of B.
8. (d) B is the extreme of A.
9. (c) Someone who is A could not be accused of B.
10. (a) Someone who is A lacks B.
11. (b) An A is something that would by nature B a person.
12. (b) An A is a way of getting redress for a B.
13. (b) Someone who is A would be likely to take/make B for something.
14. (a) A properly refers to B.
15. (b) A person would be likely to A if he or she was B.
16. (c) Someone who is A possesses all B.
17. (c) A means the same as B.
18. (a) A means the opposite of B.

Choosing the Right Meaning (page 108)

1. (a) (Clue: Context dictates a technical use of the word.) (b), (c), (d): ws (i.e., non-technical).

2. (b) (Contrast clue: "usual.") (d): ws; (a), (c): ir.

3. (d) (Clue: "overblown"; think of some characteristics of soapbox oratory.) (a), (b): ws; (c): ir (= "without order").

4. (c) (Clue: "until . . . in.") (a): ws; (b), (d): ir.

5. (b) (Clue: In a burial at sea what would you do with a dead body vis-à-vis the sea and God?) (a), (c): ws; (d): ir.

Two-Word Completions (page 110)

1. (d) omnivorous (Contrast clue: "turning . . . nose") . . . unpalatable (Inference from "turning . . . dish" and "unpleasant")

2. (a) turbulent (Contrast clue: "normally calm"; Inference clue: What happens to lake waters during a storm?) . . . buffeted (Restatement clue: "slapped"; Inference from "like . . . blender")

3. (a) chastised (Inference clue: What would an enraged party leader do to someone who had bolted to the opposition during a crucial vote?) . . . renegades (Inference clue: What would you call people who had unexpectedly bolted to the opposition party?)

4. (b) commend (Restatement clue: "give praise") . . . reprehensible (Inference from "where . . . due")

5. (c) interred (Restatement clue: "laid to rest") . . . consecrated (Restatement clue: "hallowed")

6. (c) vociferous (Restatement clue: "deafening") . . . apathy (Contrast clue: "enthusiasm")

CUMULATIVE REVIEW II

Analogies (page 114)

1. (c) Something that is A has by definition B to it.
2. (c) One would use A to B someone.
3. (b) An A is a building that would by definition be B.
4. (b) A means the opposite of B.
5. (c) Someone who was A would B everything.
6. (d) Something that is A has the ability to B something else.
7. (d) A describes a B that is heavy, dark, and forbidding.
8. (a) An animal that is proverbially A is a B.
9. (a) An A would by definition be B.
10. (d) Someone who was A would have a great deal of B.

Choosing the Right Meaning (pages 114–115)

1. (d) (Clue: What kind of prose would a fanatic write?) (a): ws; (c): too restrictive; (b): ir.

2. (a) (Clue: What kind of solutions might people intent on attaining their own ends propose?) (d): ws; (b), (c): ir.

3. (b) (Clue: "animosities" suggests a figurative sense of the word.) (a): ws (too literal); (c), (d): ir.

4. (d) (Clue: How would a ship make its way in storm-tossed seas?) (a), (b): too weak; (c): ir.

5. (c) (Clue: "views" suggests an abstract sense; Contrast clue: "orthodox.") (a): ws (too literal); (b), (d): ir.

Two-Word Completions (page 115)

1. (b) ironies (Inference clue: How would you describe the death by hanging of a judge who had hanged so many others?) . . . assiduously (Inference clue: How would a person who was implacable be likely to act?)

2. (a) allocated (Inference clue: What does one do with one's fortune in one's will?) . . . altruistic (Inference clues: What type of endeavors are sheltering the homeless and feeding the hungry? With what type of endeavor would a philanthropist be concerned?)

3. (d) uncanny (Restatement clue: "eerie") . . . apprehension (Restatement clue: "fear and")

4. (c) decrepit (Inference clue: How would you describe a hoary relic?) . . . musty (Inference clue: How would a house that had been closed up for many years smell?)

5. (a) revel (Restatement clue: "take delight") . . . adversary (Contrast clue: "Though . . . friend's")

Review Units 10–12 _____

Analogies (page 138)

1. (a) The tone of A is B.
2. (a) Someone who is A has a great deal of B.
3. (c) An A is used to measure B.
4. (a) The tone of A is B.
5. (c) An A is by definition B something.
6. (d) An A is by definition a person who would be likely to make use of B.
7. (c) Someone who is A could also be described as feeling B.
8. (d) Something that is A can be discerned by the sense of B.
9. (c) An A is by definition B.
10. (c) A means the same as B.
11. (d) A is a great deal more severe than B.
12. (b) A properly refers to B, or A describes a B that is pleasing and full.

(Continued on pg. T44)

(Continued from pg. T43)

13. (b) A means the opposite of B.
14. (b) A means the opposite of B.
15. (b) A means the opposite of B.
16. (c) An A is someone who would by definition B money.
17. (b) An A is an animal that Bs.
18. (a) If something is A, a person cannot B it.

Choosing the Right Meaning (page 141)

1. (d) (Clue: Since no middle ground exists, how definite would the division between rich and poor be?) (a), (b), (c): ws.

2. (b) (Clue: Sentence suggests a literal meaning of the word.) (d): ws; (a), (c): ir.

3. (b) (Clue: What quality might prove irresistible?) (a), (c), (d): ir.

4. (a) (Clue: Context indicates the mathematical sense of the word.) (b), (c), (d): ws.

5. (c) (Clue: Sentence suggests a document listing daily activities and the time allotted for them.) (a), (b): ws; (d): ir.

Two-Word Completions (page 143)

1. (a) sinuous (Inference clue: How would you describe a trail that is full of curves?) . . . respite (Inference clue: Why would experienced skiers stop on a dangerous trail?)

2. (b) alluded (Inference clue: What would a name-dropper be likely to do?) . . . misnomer (Inference clue: What wouldn't "name-dropper" be when applied to a person who constantly alludes to the celebrities he knows?)

3. (c) compunction (Inference clue: What wouldn't a revolutionary court feel when trying a dictator who had committed many crimes?) . . . retribution (Inference clue: What would a revolutionary court seek to obtain when trying that dictator?)

4. (b) crestfallen (Inference clue: How would you feel if you had lost a championship game in an upset defeat?) . . . coveted (Inference clue: How would you describe your attitude toward a trophy that you were trying hard to win?)

5. (d) conflagration (Restatement clue: "flames") . . . acrid (Inference clue: How would a person describe the stench of burning rubber?)

6. (c) trenchant (Contrast clue: "tired old . . . decades") . . . platitudes (Restatement clue: "observations" that are "tired . . . decades")

7. (a) disheveled (Inference clue: How would a person look if his trousers were rumpled and his shirttails were hanging out after romping around all afternoon with a child?) . . . askew (Inference clue: How would a person's tie be likely to look if his trousers were rumpled and his shirttails were hanging out?)

Analogies (page 147)

1. (b) If something is A, a person would not B it.
2. (b) Someone with a lot of A may properly be described as having B.
3. (a) A means the opposite of B.
4. (c) If something is A, a person cannot B it.
5. (d) Something that is A has a lot of B.
6. (a) A means the same as B.
7. (d) A means the opposite of B.
8. (d) Something that is A has B.
9. (a) To A something is to express a B for it.
10. (c) If something is A, a person can B it.

Choosing the Right Meaning (page 147–148)

1. (c) (Clue: "lambs, kids.") (a): ws; (b), (d): ir.

2. (a) Clue: "normal.") (c): ws; (b), (d): ir.

3. (c) (Clue: What might a car's engine be on a very cold day?) (b): ws; (a), (d): ir.

4. (d) (Clue: What kind of royal lands would the king be trying to recover?) (b): too strong; (a), (c): ir.

5. (b) (Clue: "a cold heart.") (d): ws; (a), (c): ir.

Two-Word Completions (page 148)

1. (b) facility (Restatement clue: "ease and") . . . plagiarized (Inference clue: What would someone be likely to have done if his or her claims about original work had been called into question?)

2. (d) revelry (Restatement clue: "carousing") . . . nocturnal (Inference clue: When would something be taking place if it interrupted the quiet of the night?)

3. (c) superficial (Inference clue: How would you describe a resemblance that was perceived at first glance only?) . . . discern (Inference clue: What would be likely to happen if you gave something closer inspection?)

4. (c) allure (Inference clue: What would something that is irresistibly attractive possess?) . . . destitute (Restatement clue: "poor")

5. (a) professes (Contrast clue: "but . . . show") . . . sophomoric (Restatement clue: "and uncouth"; Contrast clue: "learned and refined")

Analogies (page 171)

1. (a) A means the opposite of B.
2. (b) Parallel actions: To A a B is to awaken it.
3. (c) An A is the B as/of something else.
4. (c) A indicates that a person talks too B.
5. (b) To A something is to make it B.
6. (c) A means the opposite of B.
7. (a) Someone who is A lacks B.
8. (c) B is the extreme of A.
9. (b) A means the opposite of B.
10. (d) One is said to A if one gives up a B, or to A a B is to give it up.
11. (d) Someone who is A could properly be said to B.
12. (b) Someone who is A would be likely to B a person.
13. (b) A properly applies to B.
14. (c) One applies for and obtains an A to protect a B.
15. (a) The tone of A is B.
16. (d) A means the opposite of B.
17. (d) Someone who is A has the ability to B other things.
18. (a) Someone who exhibits A could properly be called B.

Choosing the Right Meaning (page 174)

1. (d) (Clue: What is an anesthetic used for?) (a), (c): ws; (b): ir.

2. (a) (Clue: How are mountains usually located with regard to a valley?) (b), (c), (d): ws.

3. (b) (Clue: With what would laws about patents be concerned?) (c): ws; (a), (d): ir.

4. (c) (Clue: "principled.") (a), (d): ws; (b): ir.

5. (a) (Clue: "tranquil.") (b), (d): ws (these refer to people, rather than to things like a brook); (c): ir.

Two-Word Completions (page 176)

1. (d). droll (Inference clue: How would you describe an offbeat sense of humor?) . . . asset (Inference clue: What would a droll sense of humor be likely to be in a competition for class wit?)

2. (b) facsimiles (Contrast clue: "real thing") . . . infinitesimal (Contrast clue: "what . . . cost")

3. (b) alleviate (Inference clue: What would a supply of winter uniforms do in regard to the hardships faced by troops?) . . . militated (Inference clue: How might an ammunition shortage and an ominous weather forecast affect plans for an attack?)

4. (c) reticent (Restatement clue: "I keep . . . myself") . . . receptive (Contrast clue: "he . . . it")

5. (a) edict (Inference clue: How did the Roman emperors of old rule?) . . . mandatory (Contrast clue: "optional")

6. (d) implacable (Inference clue: How would one describe a foe of people who posed a threat to his or her security?) . . . magnanimous (Restatement clue: "evenhanded")

7. (a) stipulated (Contrast clue: "Though . . . rule out"; Inference clue: What does a warranty usually contain?) . . . abrasive (Inference clue: What kind of cleansers would damage a tile floor? Contrast clue: "Though . . . mild")

CUMULATIVE REVIEW IV

Analogies (pages 180–181)

1. (b) Something that is A has the ability to B a person.
2. (d) If you give up an A, you may properly be said to B it.
3. (b) A is by definition B.
4. (b) Someone who was A would lack B.
5. (a) Someone who is A is by definition full of B.
6. (d) A means the same as B.
7. (c) A means the same as B.
8. (c) Something that is A can be discerned by the sense of B.
9. (c) An A is used for B.
10. (b) Something that is A has a great deal of B to it.
11. (b) If you have an A for something, you B it.
12. (c) A means the opposite of B.
13. (b) A means the same as B.
14. (a) If you retract an A, you B it.
15. (d) An A is someone who by definition would not show or possess B.
16. (c) Inordinate A could properly be characterized as B.
17. (d) Something that is A has the capacity to B something else.
18. (a) If you were A, you would most certainly feel B.
19. (d) If something is A, you can B it.
20. (d) A person would use A to B someone else.
21. (a) A means the opposite of B.
22. (b) Someone who is A would not possess B.

Choosing the Right Meaning (page 181)

1. (c) (Clue: How might one describe Vivien Leigh's famous interpretation of Scarlett O'Hara?) (a): ws; (b), (d): ir.

2. (d) (Clue: "will feed us.") (a), (b): too mild, no sense of starvation implied; (c): ir.

3. (c) (Contrast clue: "dull.") (a), (b): ws; (d): too general, no sense of sharpening implicit in word.

4. (d) (Clue "jewel-encrusted.") (a), (b), (c): ws.

5. (a) (Clue: Reference is to lilacs.) (c), (d): ws (these refer more to people than to things); (b): ir.

6. (b) (Clue: What would happen to one's head as sleep set in?) (a), (c), (d): ws.

Two-Word Completions (pages 182–183)

1. (d) exponents (Inference clue: How did Copernicus and Galileo feel about the sun-centered theory of the universe?) . . . vanguard (Inference clue: As a result of their views, what place do Copernicus and Galileo hold in the "scientific revolution" that has led to men walking on the moon?)

2. (a) skulking (Inference clue: What verb would suggest furtive movement in an alleyway?) . . . premeditated (Contrast clue: "rather than . . . chance")

3. (b) jeopardy (Inference clue: What would an attack on an exposed flank do to a battle formation?) . . . deployed (Inference clue: What do you do with reserve troops in order to reinforce a battle formation?)

4. (b) grotesque (Restatement clue: "bizarre") . . . protrude (Inference clue: What is the position of a hunting trophy hung over a fireplace in reference to the wall it's hanging on?)

5. (c) chagrin (Inference clue: What feeling would an upset defeat produce in you?) . . . complacent (Inference clue: How might a string of easy victories affect your attitude toward your abilities?)

6. (c) somnolent (Inference clue: What kind of effect would a droning voice and tired platitudes have on you?) . . . stultifying (Inference clue: same question)

7. (d) lolling (Inference clue: What does one do on a beach on a sunny day? Restatement clue: "bask") . . . inclement (Contrast clue: "fine," "but")

8. (c) extant (Inference clue: If you can still see a particular way of life, what must it necessarily be?) . . . obsolete (Inference clue: If you cannot see this particular way of life elsewhere, what must it necessarily be in other parts?)

9. (a) discrepancies (Restatement clue: "and inconsistencies") . . . feasible (Inference clue: Would it be possible for a story that was full of discrepancies and inconsistencies to convince a jury?)

10. (a) adversaries (Inference clue: What were the Capulets and the Montagues?) . . . quell (Inference clue: Why would the authorities be called when a riot breaks out?)

11. (a) extolled (Inference clue: What would critics who offered lavish praise have thought of a novel?) . . . tepid (Inference clue: What kind of welcome must the novel have received if the author was perplexed and disappointed by the reaction?)

12. (c) wastrel (Inference clue: What would you call someone who squandered something?) . . . assets (Restatement clue: "nest egg")

13. (d) amicable (Contrast clue: "ugly") . . . fracas (Restatement clue: "dispute"; Inference clue: What do you call a dispute that suddenly turns violent?)

14. (b) apprehensive (Inference clue: How would a military governor feel if his measures had failed to achieve their goal?) . . . reprisals (Inference clue: What measures do the authorities of an occupying force usually take against acts of sabotage?)

Vocabulary Workshop

Level E

Jerome Shostak

Senior Series Consultant

Alex Cameron, Ph.D.
Department of English
University of Dayton
Dayton, Ohio

Series Consultants

Sylvia A. Rendón, Ph.D.
Coord., English Language Arts
Cypress-Fairbanks I.S.D.
Houston, Texas

Mel H. Farberman
Supervisor of Instruction
Brooklyn High Schools
New York City Board of Education
Brooklyn, New York

John Heath, Ph.D.
Department of Classics
Santa Clara University
Santa Clara, California

Sadlier-Oxford
A Division of William H. Sadlier, Inc.

Reviewers

The publisher wishes to thank for their comments and suggestions the following teachers and administrators, who read portions of the series prior to publication.

Anne S. Crane
Clinician, English Education
Georgia State University
Atlanta, GA

Susan W. Keogh
Curriculum Coordinator
Lake Highland Preparatory
Orlando, FL

Mary Louise Ellena-Wygonik
English Teacher
Hampton High School
Allison Park, PA

Lisa Anne Pomi
Language Arts Chairperson
Woodside High School
Woodside, CA

Arlene A. Oraby
Dept. Chair (Ret.), English 6–12
Briarcliff Public Schools
Briarcliff Manor, NY

Susan Cotter McDonough
English Department Chair
Wakefield High School
Wakefield, MA

Sr. M. Francis Regis Trojano
Sisters of St. Joseph (CSJ)
Educational Consultant
Boston, MA

Keith Yost
Director of Humanities
Tomball Ind. School District
Tomball, TX

Patricia M. Stack
English Teacher
South Park School District
South Park, PA

Joy Vander Vliet
English Teacher
Council Rock High School
Newtown, PA

Karen Christine Solheim
English Teacher
Jefferson High School
Jefferson, GA

Photo Credits

Allsport Photography/Simon Bruty: 149; *Archive*: 163; *Corbis*/Bettman: 27, 41, 123; Francis G. Mayer: 64; Jacob and Gwendolyn Lawrence/North Carolina Museum of Art: 71; Owen Franken: 83; Joe McDonald: 97; Corcoran Gallery: 104; Ron Austing: 137; *FPG*: Gary Buss: 57; *National Gallery of Art*/Antonio Frascon: 130; *New York Historical Society*: 170; *Photodisc*: 184; *Stone*/Wayne R. Bilenduke: 34, 156; Austin Brown: 90; Andy Sachs: 116.

PREFACE

For over five decades, VOCABULARY WORKSHOP has proven a highly successful tool for guiding systematic vocabulary growth. It has also been a valuable help to students preparing for the vocabulary-related parts of standardized tests. In this, the latest edition of the series, many new features have been added to make VOCABULARY WORKSHOP even more effective in increasing vocabulary and improving vocabulary skills.

The **Definitions** sections in the fifteen Units, for example, have been expanded to include synonyms and antonyms and for each taught word an illustrative sentence for each part of speech.

In the **Synonyms** and **Antonyms** sections, exercise items are now presented in the form of phrases, the better to familiarize you with the range of contexts and distinctions of usage for the Unit words.

New to this edition is **Vocabulary in Context**, an exercise that appears at the end of each Unit and in the Reviews. In this exercise, you will read an expository passage containing a selection of Unit words. In addition to furnishing you with further examples of how and in what contexts Unit words are used, this exercise will also provide you with practice with vocabulary questions in standardized-test formats.

In the five Reviews, you will find two important new features, in addition to Analogies, Two-Word Completions, and other exercises designed to help you prepare for standardized tests. One of these new features, **Building with Classical Roots**, will acquaint you with Latin and Greek roots from which many English words stem and will provide you with a strategy that may help you find the meaning of an unknown or unfamiliar word.

Another new feature, **Writer's Challenge**, is designed to do just that—challenge you to improve your writing skills by applying what you have learned about meanings and proper usage of selected Unit words.

Finally, another new feature has been introduced in the four Cumulative Reviews. **Enriching Your Vocabulary** is meant to broaden and enhance your knowledge and understanding of the relationships, history, and origins of the words that make up our rich and dynamic language.

In this Level of VOCABULARY WORKSHOP, you will study three hundred key words, and you will be introduced to hundreds of other words in the form of synonyms, antonyms, and other relatives. Mastery of these words will make you a better reader, a better writer and speaker, and better prepared for the vocabulary parts of standardized tests.

CONTENTS

PRONUNCIATION KEY

The pronunciation is indicated for every basic word introduced in this book. The symbols used for this purpose, as listed below, are similar to those appearing in most standard dictionaries of recent vintage. The author has consulted a large number of dictionaries for this purpose but has relied primarily on *Webster's Third New International Dictionary* and *The Random House Dictionary of the English Language (Unabridged)*.

There are, of course, many English words for which two (or more) pronunciations are commonly accepted. In virtually all cases where such words occur in this book, the author has sought to make things easier for the student by giving just one pronunciation. The only significant exception occurs when the pronunciation changes in accordance with a shift in the part of speech. Thus we would indicate that *project* in the verb form is pronounced prə jekt', and in the noun form, präj' ekt.

It is believed that these relatively simple pronunciation guides will be readily usable by the student. It should be emphasized, however, that the *best* way to learn the pronunciation of a word is to listen to and imitate an educated speaker.

Vowels	ā	lake	e	str*e*ss	ü	l*oo*t, n*ew*
	a	m*a*t	ī	kn*i*fe	ù	f*oo*t, p*u*ll
	â	c*a*re	i	s*i*t	ə	r*u*g, brok*e*n
	ä	b*a*rk, b*o*ttle	ō	fl*o*w	ər	b*ir*d, bett*er*
	aù	d*ou*bt	ô	*a*ll, c*o*rd		
	ē	b*ea*t, word*y*	oi	*oi*l		

Consonants	ch	*ch*ild, lec*t*ure	s	*c*ellar	wh	*wh*at
	g	*g*ive	sh	*sh*un	y	*y*earn
	j	*g*entle, bri*dg*e	th	*th*ank	z	i*s*
	ŋ	si*ng*	t̶h̶	*th*ose	zh	mea*s*ure

All other consonants are sounded as in the alphabet.

Stress	The accent mark *follows* the syllable receiving the major stress: en rich'

Abbreviations	*adj.* adjective	*n.* noun	*prep.* preposition
	adv. adverb	*part.* participle	*v.* verb
	int. interjection	*pl.* plural	

See page T21 for information about the Interactive Audio Pronunciation Program.

THE VOCABULARY OF VOCABULARY

There are some interesting and useful words that are employed to describe and identify words. The exercises that follow will help you to check and strengthen your knowledge of this "vocabulary of vocabulary."

Denotation and Connotation

The **denotation** of a word is its specific dictionary meaning. Here are a few examples:

Word	Denotation
eminent	distinguished or noteworthy
cumbersome	hard to handle or manage
remember	call to mind

The **connotation** of a word is its **tone**—that is, the emotions or associations it normally arouses in people using, hearing, or reading it. Depending on what these feelings are, the connotation of a word may be *favorable* (*positive*) or *unfavorable* (*negative, pejorative*). A word that does not normally arouse strong feelings of any kind has a *neutral* connotation. Here are some examples of words with different connotations:

Word	Connotation
eminent	favorable
cumbersome	unfavorable
remember	neutral

Exercises In the space provided, label the connotation of each of the following words **F** for "favorable," **U** for "unfavorable," or **N** for "neutral."

_U_ **1.** mediocre		_U_ **3.** reek		_N_ **5.** plan	
_N_ **2.** article		_F_ **4.** intrepid		_F_ **6.** illustrious	

Literal and Figurative Usage

When a word is used in a **literal** sense, it is being employed in its strict (or primary) dictionary meaning in a situation (or context) that "makes sense" from a purely logical or realistic point of view. For example:

Yesterday I read an old tale about a knight who slew a *fire-breathing* dragon.

In this sentence, *fire-breathing* is employed literally. The dragon is pictured as breathing real fire.

Sometimes words are used in a symbolic or nonliteral way in situations that do not "make sense" from a purely logical or realistic point of view. We call this nonliteral application of a word a **figurative** or **metaphorical** usage. For example:

Suddenly my boss rushed into my office *breathing fire*.

In this sentence *breathing fire* is not being used in a literal sense. That is, the boss was not actually breathing fire out of his nostrils. Rather, the expression is intended to convey graphically that the boss was very angry.

Exercises   *In the space provided, write* **L** *for "literal" or* **F** *for "figurative" next to each of the following sentences to show how the italicized expression is being used.*

___L___ **1.** Tom *danced* with Sally at the prom.

___F___ **2.** All kinds of delightful images *dance* across the pages of that novel.

___F___ **3.** As long as we don't have the funds to produce this project, it will have to stay *on the back burner.*

Synonyms

A **synonym** is a word that has *the same* or *almost the same* meaning as another word. Here are some examples:

eat—consume   clash—conflict
hurt—injure   fire—discharge
big—large   slim—slender

Exercises   *In each of the following groups, circle the word that is most nearly the* **synonym** *of the word in* **boldface** *type.*

1. amuse	**2. hidden**	**3. melody**	**4. neat**
(a. delight)	a. conquered	a. bar	a. dull
b. fancy	b. hated	b. staff	(b. tidy)
c. clear	c. admired	c. violin	c. overworked
d. deport	(d. concealed)	(d. tune)	d. sloppy

Antonyms

An **antonym** is a word that means *the opposite* of or *almost the opposite* of another word. Here are some examples:

enter—leave   happy—sad
wild—tame   leader—follower
buy—sell   war—peace

Exercises   *In each of the following groups, circle the word that is most nearly the* **antonym** *of the word in* **boldface** *type.*

1. fix	**2. fiction**	**3. honest**	**4. difficult**
a. trouble	a. ideal	a. profitable	(a. easy)
b. please	(b. truth)	(b. deceitful)	b. forceful
c. change	c. novel	c. gentle	c. stubborn
(d. break)	d. notion	d. loud	d. boring

VOCABULARY STRATEGY: USING CONTEXT

How do you go about finding the meaning of an unknown or unfamiliar word that you come across in your reading? You might look the word up in a dictionary, of course, provided one is at hand. But there are two other useful strategies that you might employ to find the meaning of a word that you do not know at all or that is used in a way that you do not recognize. One strategy is to analyze the **structure** or parts of the word. (See pages 15 and 16 for more on this strategy.) The other strategy is to try to figure out the meaning of the word by reference to context.

When we speak of the **context** of a word, we mean the printed text of which that word is part. By studying the context, we may find **clues** that lead us to its meaning. We might find a clue in the immediate sentence or phrase in which the word appears (and sometimes in adjoining sentences or phrases, too); or we might find a clue in the topic or subject matter of the passage in which the word appears; or we might even find a clue in the physical features of a page itself. (Photographs, illustrations, charts, graphs, captions, and headings are some examples of such features.)

One way to use context as a strategy is to ask yourself what you know already about the topic or subject matter in question. By applying what you have learned before about deserts, for example, you would probably be able to figure out that the word *arid* in the phrase "the arid climate of the desert" means "dry."

The **Vocabulary in Context** exercises that appear in the Units and the **Choosing the Right Meaning** exercises that appear in the Reviews and Cumulative Reviews both provide practice in using subject matter or topic to determine the meaning of given words.

When you do the various word-omission exercises in this book, look for **context clues** built into the sentence or passage to guide you to the correct answer. Three types of context clues appear in the exercises in this book.

A **restatement clue** consists of a *synonym* for, or a *definition* of, the missing word. For example:

> "I'm willing to <u>tell</u> what I know about the matter," the reporter said, "but I can't _____ my sources."
> a. conceal   b. defend   c. find   (d. reveal)

In this sentence, *tell* is a synonym of the missing word, *reveal*, and acts as a restatement clue for it.

A **contrast clue** consists of an *antonym* for, or a phrase that means the *opposite* of, the missing word. For example:

> "I'm trying to <u>help</u> you, <u>not</u> (**assist,**(**hinder**))you!" she exclaimed in annoyance.

In this sentence, *help* is an antonym of the missing word, *hinder*. This is confirmed by the presence of the word *not*. *Help* thus functions as a contrast clue for *hinder*.

An **inference clue** implies but does not directly state the meaning of the missing word or words. For example:

> A utility infielder has to be a very _____
> player because he is a veritable jack-of-all-trades on the
> _____ diamond.
>
> a. veteran . . . football
> b. versatile . . . baseball
> c. experienced . . . hockey
> d. energetic . . . golf

In this sentence, there are several inference clues: (a) the term *jack-of-all-trades* suggests the word *versatile* because a jack-of-all-trades is by definition versatile; the word *utility* in the term *utility infielder* suggests the same thing; (b) the words *infielder* and *diamond* suggest *baseball* because they are terms employed regularly in that sport. Accordingly, all these words are inference clues because they suggest or imply, but do not directly state, the missing word or words.

Exercises   *Use context clues to choose the word or words that complete each of the following sentences or sets of sentences.*

1. Jonathan Swift once said that he didn't like people as a group but that he could put up with them _____.
   a. collectively
   b. regularly
   c. individually
   d. occasionally

2. "Don't take the _____ off the line yet," Mom told me as I searched around for the clothespin bag. "It is still _____ to the touch."
   a. laundry . . . damp
   b. telephone . . . dull
   c. wash . . . dry
   d. clothes . . . dirty

3. If you will supply the dishes for the picnic, I will (**furnish,** eat) the food.

VOCABULARY STRATEGY: WORD STRUCTURE

One important way to build your vocabulary is to learn the meaning of word parts that make up many English words. These word parts consist of prefixes, suffixes, and **roots**, or **bases**. A useful strategy for determining the meaning of an unknown word is to "take apart" the word and think about the parts. For example, when you look at the word parts in the word *invisible,* you find the prefix *in-* ("not") + the root *-vis-* ("see") + the suffix *-ible* ("capable of"). From knowing the meanings of the parts of this word, you can figure out that *invisible* means "not capable of being seen."

Following is a list of common prefixes. Knowing the meaning of a prefix can help you determine the meaning of a word in which the prefix appears.

Prefix	Meaning	Sample Words
bi-	two	bicycle
com-, con-	together, with	compatriot, contact
de-, dis-	lower, opposite	devalue, disloyal
fore-, pre-	before, ahead of time	forewarn, preplan
il-, im-, in-, ir-, non-, un-	not	illegal, impossible, inactive, irregular, nonsense, unable
in-, im-	in, into	inhale, import
mid-	middle	midway
mis-	wrongly, badly	mistake, misbehave
re-	again, back	redo, repay
sub-	under, less than	submarine, subzero
super-	above, greater than	superimpose, superstar
tri-	three	triangle

Following is a list of common suffixes. Knowing the meaning and grammatical function of a suffix can help you determine the meaning of a word.

Noun Suffix	Meaning	Sample Nouns
-acy, -ance, -ence, -hood, -ity, -ment, -ness, -ship	state, quality, or condition of, act or process of	adequacy, attendance, persistence, neighborhood, activity, judgment, brightness, friendship
-ant, -eer, -ent, -er, -ian, -ier, -ist, -or	one who does or makes something	contestant, auctioneer, resident, banker, comedian, financier, dentist, doctor
-ation, -ition, -ion	act or result of	organization, imposition, election

Verb Suffix	Meaning	Sample Verbs
-ate	to become, produce, or treat	validate, salivate, chlorinate
-en	to make, cause to be	weaken
-fy, -ify, -ize	to cause, make	liquefy, glorify, legalize

Adjective Suffix	Meaning	Sample Adjectives
-able, -ible	able, capable of	believable, incredible
-al, -ic	relating to, characteristic of	natural, romantic
-ful, -ive, -ous	full of, given to, marked by	beautiful, protective, poisonous
-ish, -like	like, resembling	foolish, childlike
-less	lacking, without	careless

A **base** or **root** is the main part of a word to which prefixes and suffixes may be added. Many roots come to English from Latin, such as *-socio-,* meaning "society," or from Greek, such as *-logy-,* meaning "the study of." Knowing Greek and Latin roots can help you determine the meaning of a word such as *sociology,* which means "the study of society."

In the **Building with Classical Roots** sections of this book you will learn more about some of these Latin and Greek roots and about English words that derive from them. The lists that follow may help you figure out the meaning of new or unfamiliar words that you encounter in your reading.

Greek Root	Meaning	Sample Word
-astr-, -aster-, -astro-	star	astral, asteroid, astronaut
-auto-	self	autograph
-bio-	life	biography
-chron-, chrono-	time	chronic, chronological
-cosm-, -cosmo-	universe, order	microcosm, cosmopolitan
-cryph-, -crypt-	hidden, secret	apocryphal, cryptographer
-dem-, -demo-	people	epidemic, democracy
-dia-	through, across, between	diameter
-dog-, -dox-	opinion, teaching	dogmatic, orthodox
-gen-	race, kind, origin, birth	generation
-gnos-	know	diagnostic
-graph-, -graphy-, -gram-	write	graphite, autobiography, telegram
-log-, -logue-	speech, word, reasoning	logic, dialogue
-lys-	break down	analysis
-metr-, -meter-	measure	metric, kilometer
-micro-	small	microchip
-morph-	form, shape	amorphous
-naut-	sailor	cosmonaut
-phon-, -phone-, -phono-	sound, voice	phonics, telephone, phonograph
-pol-, -polis-	city, state	police, metropolis
-scop-, -scope-	watch, look at	microscope, telescope
-tele-	far off, distant	television
-the-	put or place	parentheses

Latin Root	Meaning	Sample Word
-cap-, -capt-, -cept-, -cip-	take	capitulate, captive, concept, recipient
-cede-, -ceed-, -ceas-, -cess-	happen, yield, go	precede, proceed, decease, cessation
-cred-	believe	incredible
-dic-, -dict-	speak, say, tell	indicate, diction
-duc-, -duct-, -duit-	lead, conduct, draw	educate, conduct, conduit
-fac-, -fact-, -fect-, -fic-, -fy-	make	faculty, artifact, defect, beneficial, clarify
-ject-	throw	eject
-mis-, -miss-, -mit-, -mitt-	send	promise, missile, transmit, intermittent
-note-, -not-	know, recognize	denote, notion
-pel-, -puls-	drive	expel, compulsive
-pend-, -pens-	hang, weight, set aside	pendulum, pension
-pon-, -pos-	put, place	component, position
-port-	carry	portable
-rupt-	break	bankrupt
-scrib-, -scribe-, -script-	write	scribble, describe, inscription
-spec-, -spic-	look, see	spectator, conspicuous
-tac-, -tag-, -tang-, -teg-	touch	contact, contagious, tangible, integral
-tain-, -ten-, -tin-	hold, keep	contain, tenure, retinue
-temp-	time	tempo
-ven-, -vent-	come	intervene, convention
-vers-, -vert-	turn	reverse, invert
-voc-, -vok-	call	vocal, invoke

WORKING WITH ANALOGIES

Today practically every standardized examination involving vocabulary, especially the SAT-I, employs the **analogy** as a testing device. For that reason, it is an excellent idea to learn how to read, understand, and solve such verbal puzzles.

What Is an Analogy?

An analogy is a kind of equation using words rather than numbers or mathematical symbols and quantities. Normally, an analogy contains two pairs of words linked by a word or symbol that stands for an equal sign (=). A complete analogy compares the two pairs of words and makes a statement about them. It asserts that the logical relationship between the members of the first pair of words is *the same as* the logical relationship between the members of the second pair of words. This is the only statement a valid analogy ever makes.

Here is an example of a complete analogy. It is presented in two different formats.

Format 1
maple is to tree as rose is to flower

Format 2
maple : tree :: rose : flower

Reading and Interpreting Analogies

As our sample indicates, analogies are customarily presented in formats that need some deciphering in order to be read and understood correctly. There are a number of these formats, but you need concern yourself with only the two shown.

Format 1: Let's begin with the format that uses all words:

maple is to tree as rose is to flower

Because this is the simplest format to read and understand, it is the one used in the student texts of VOCABULARY WORKSHOP. It is to be read exactly as printed. Allowing for the fact that the word pairs change from analogy to analogy, this is how to read every analogy, no matter what the format is.

Now you know how to read an analogy. Still, it is not clear exactly what the somewhat cryptic statement "maple is to tree as rose is to flower" means. To discover this, you must understand what the two linking expressions *as* and *is to* signify.

- The word *as* links the two word pairs in the complete analogy. It stands for an equal sign (=) and means "is the same as."

- The expression *is to* links the two members of each word pair, so it appears twice in a complete analogy. In our sample, *is to* links *maple* and *tree* (the two words in the first pair) and also *rose* and *flower* (the two words in the second word pair). Accordingly, the expression *is to* means "the logical relationship between" the two words it links.

Putting all this information together, we can say that our sample analogy means:

The logical relationship between a *maple* and a *tree* is *the same as* (=) the logical relationship between a *rose* and a *flower*.

Now you know what our sample analogy means. This is what every analogy means, allowing for the fact that the word pairs will vary from one analogy to another.

Format 2: Our second format uses symbols, rather than words, to link its four members.

maple : tree :: rose : flower

This is the format used on the SAT-I and in the *TEST PREP Blackline Masters* that accompany each Level of VOCABULARY WORKSHOP. In this format, a single colon (:) replaces the expression *is to*, and a double colon (::) replaces the word *as*. Otherwise, format 2 is the same as format 1; that is, it is read in exactly the same way ("maple is to tree as rose is to flower"), and it means exactly the same thing ("the logical relationship between a *maple* and a *tree* is the same as the logical relationship between a *rose* and a *flower*").

Completing Analogies

So far we've looked at complete analogies. However, standardized examinations do not provide the test taker with a complete analogy. Instead, the test taker is given the first, or key, pair of words and then asked to *complete* the analogy by selecting the second pair from a given group of four or five choices, usually lettered *a* through *d* or *e*.

Here's how our sample analogy would look on such a test:

1. maple is to tree as
a. acorn is to oak
b. hen is to rooster
c. rose is to flower
d. shrub is to lilac

or

1. maple : tree ::
a. acorn : oak
b. hen : rooster
c. rose : flower
d. shrub : lilac

It is up to the test taker to complete the analogy correctly.

Here's how to do that in just four easy steps!

Step 1: *Look at the two words in the key (given) pair, and determine the logical relationship between them.*

In our sample analogy, *maple* and *tree* form the key (given) pair of words. They indicate the key (given) relationship. Think about these two words for a moment. What is the relationship of a maple to a tree? Well, a maple is a particular kind, or type, of tree.

Step 2: *Make up a short sentence stating the relationship that you have discovered for the first pair of words.*

For our model analogy, we can use this sentence: "A maple is a particular kind (type) of tree."

Step 3: *Extend the sentence you have written to cover the rest of the analogy, even though you haven't completed it yet.*

The easiest way to do this is to repeat the key relationship after the words *just as*, leaving blanks for the two words you don't yet have. The sentence will now read something like this:

A maple is a kind (type) of tree, just as a ? is a kind of ? .

Step 4: *Look at each of the lettered pairs of words from which you are to choose your answer. Determine which lettered pair illustrates the same relationship as the key pair.*

The easiest and most effective way to carry out step 4 is to substitute each pair of words into the blanks in the sentence you made up to see which sentence makes sense. Only one will.

Doing this for our sample analogy, we get:

    a. A maple is a kind of tree, just as an acorn is a kind of oak.
    b. A maple is a kind of tree, just as a hen is a kind of rooster.
    c. A maple is a kind of tree, just as a rose is a kind of flower.
    d. A maple is a kind of tree, just as a shrub is a kind of lilac.

Look at these sentences. Only *one* of them makes any sense. Choice *a* is clearly wrong because an acorn is *not* a kind of oak. Choice *b* is also wrong because a hen is *not* a kind of rooster. Similarly, choice *d* is incorrect because a shrub is *not* a kind of lilac, though a *lilac* is a kind of shrub. In other words, the two words are in the wrong order. That leaves us with choice *c*, which says that a rose is a kind of flower. Well, that makes sense; a rose is indeed a kind of flower. So, choice *c* must be the pair of words that completes the analogy correctly.

Determining the Key Relationship

Clearly, determining the nature of the key relationship is the most important and the most difficult part of completing an analogy. Since there are literally thousands of key relationships possible, you cannot simply memorize a list of them. The table on page 14, however, outlines some of the most common key relationships. Study the table carefully.

Table of Key Relationships

Complete Analogy	Key Relationship
big is to **large** as **little** is to **small**	**Big** means the same thing as **large**, just as **little** means the same thing as **small**.
tall is to **short** as **thin** is to **fat**	**Tall** means the opposite of **short**, just as **thin** means the opposite of **fat**.
brave is to **favorable** as **cowardly** is to **unfavorable**	The tone of **brave** is **favorable**, just as the tone of **cowardly** is **unfavorable**.
busybody is to **nosy** as **klutz** is to **clumsy**	A **busybody** is by definition someone who is **nosy**, just as a **klutz** is by definition someone who is **clumsy**.
cowardly is to **courage** as **awkward** is to **grace**	Someone who is **cowardly** lacks **courage**, just as someone who is **awkward** lacks **grace**.
visible is to **see** as **audible** is to **hear**	If something is **visible**, you can by definition **see** it, just as if something is **audible**, you can by definition **hear** it.
invisible is to **see** as **inaudible** is to **hear**	If something is **invisible**, you cannot **see** it, just as if something is **inaudible**, you cannot **hear** it.
frigid is to **cold** as **blistering** is to **hot**	**Frigid** is the extreme of **cold**, just as **blistering** is the extreme of **hot**.
chef is to **cooking** as **tailor** is to **clothing**	A **chef** is concerned with **cooking**, just as a **tailor** is concerned with **clothing**.
liar is to **truthful** as **bigot** is to **fair-minded**	A **liar** is by definition not likely to be **truthful**, just as a **bigot** is by definition not likely to be **fair-minded**.
starvation is to **emaciation** as **overindulgence** is to **corpulence**	**Starvation** will cause **emaciation**, just as **overindulgence** will cause **corpulence**.
practice is to **proficient** as **study** is to **knowledgeable**	**Practice** will make a person **proficient**, just as **study** will make a person **knowledgeable**.
eyes are to **see** as **ears** are to **hear**	You use your **eyes** to **see** with, just as you use your **ears** to **hear** with.
sloppy is to **appearance** as **rude** is to **manner**	The word **sloppy** can refer to one's **appearance**, just as the word **rude** can refer to one's **manner**.
learned is to **knowledge** as **wealthy** is to **money**	Someone who is **learned** has a great deal of **knowledge**, just as someone who is **wealthy** has a great deal of **money**.

Exercises   In each of the following, circle the item that best completes the analogy. Then explain the key relationship involved.

1. doctor is to **medical** as
a. general is to naval
b. plumber is to social
c. detective is to financial
d. lawyer is to legal

2. clear is to **cloudy** as
a. timid is to fearful
b. bright is to dark
c. costly is to expensive
d. swift is to famous

3. meet is to **encounter** as
a. recall is to remember
b. wink is to nod
c. walk is to run
d. raise is to lower

4. deafening is to **loud** as
a. sweltering is to cold
b. freezing is to rainy
c. sizzling is to windy
d. blinding is to bright

VOCABULARY AND WRITING

When you study vocabulary, you make yourself not only a better reader but also a better writer. The greater the number of words at your disposal, the better you will be able to express your thoughts. Good writers are always adding new words to their personal vocabularies, the pool of words that they understand *and* know how to use properly. They use these words both when they write and when they revise.

There are several factors to consider when choosing words and setting the tone of your writing. First, your choice of words should suit your purpose and your audience. If you are writing an essay for your history teacher, you will probably want to choose words that are formal in tone and precise in meaning. If you are writing a letter to a friend, however, you will probably choose words that are more informal in tone and freer in meaning. Your **audience** is the person or people who will be reading what you write, and your **purpose** is the reason why you are writing. Your purpose, for example, might be to explain; or it might be to describe, inform, or entertain.

Almost any kind of writing—whether a school essay, a story, or a letter to a friend—can be improved by careful attention to vocabulary. Sometimes you will find, for example, that one word can be used to replace a phrase of five or six words. This is not to say that a shorter sentence is always better. However, readers usually prefer and appreciate **economy** of expression. They grow impatient with sentences that plod along with vague, unnecessary words rather than race along with fewer, carefully chosen ones. Writing can also be improved by attention to **diction** (word choice). Many writers use words that might make sense in terms of *general* meaning but that are not precise enough to convey *nuances* of meaning. In the **Writer's Challenge** sections of this book, you will have an opportunity to make word choices that will more clearly and precisely convey the meaning you intend.

Exercises   *Read the following sentences, paying special attention to the words and phrases underlined. From the words in the box, find better choices for the underlined words and phrases.*

1. The Berlin Wall was <u>erased</u> in 1989 by almost 1000 soldiers from East and West Germany.

disputed	scuffled	(razed)	canceled

2. Natural resources such as oil and coal are not evenly <u>spread far and wide</u> across the globe.

(distributed)	assaulted	abandoned	acquired

3. I left my money in the care of a(n) <u>clever and businesslike</u> accountant.

impressive	fertile	thrifty	(shrewd)

4. After Ernest Hemingway lost the notebooks that contained much of his writing, he was never able to <u>imitate</u> them.

abandon	provoke	(reproduce)	transport

5. Twelfth-century alchemists tried to <u>modify</u> copper and lead into gold.

swindle	transport	expand	(convert)

DIAGNOSTIC TEST

This test contains a sampling of the words that are to be found in the exercises in this Level of VOCABULARY WORKSHOP. It will give you an idea of the types of words to be studied and their level of difficulty. When you have completed all the units, the Final Mastery Test at the end of this book will assess what you have learned. By comparing your results on the Final Mastery Test with your results on the Diagnostic Test below, you will be able to judge your progress.

Synonyms

*In each of the following groups, circle the word or phrase that **most nearly** expresses the meaning of the word in **boldface** type in the given phrase.*

1. a **stentorian** voice
   (a. loud)   b. grating   c. high   d. hushed

2. a **musty** closet
   a. large   b. concealed   (c. smelly)   d. locked

3. **delete** a portion of the selection
   a. read   (b. cross out)   c. emphasize   d. misunderstand

4. unable to **acquiesce**
   (a. go along with)   b. leave   c. obtain   d. understand

5. **cogent** reasoning
   a. false   b. organized   c. dulled   (d. forceful)

6. chemicals that **adulterate** the food
   a. consume   (b. pollute)   c. purify   d. color

7. no longer **extant**
   (a. in existence)   b. happy   c. in prison   d. visible

8. an **adroit** driver
   a. careful   b. experienced   (c. skillful)   d. careless

9. **copious** notes
   a. scribbled   b. clever   c. imitative   (d. plentiful)

10. an **unkempt** appearance
   a. sudden   (b. untidy)   c. necessary   d. voluntary

11. **accede** to their requests
   a. listen   (b. consent)   c. object   d. refer

12. a **poignant** scene
   a. humorous   (b. moving)   c. tiresome   d. noisy

13. the **belligerent** nations
   a. neighborly   b. wealthy   (c. hostile)   d. poor

14. seek **redress**
   a. health   (b. remedy)   c. shelter   d. advantage

15. **turbulent** days
   (a. violent)   b. boring   c. rainy   d. sunny

16. gnarled tree trunks
a. damaged   b. cut   c. knotty   d. tall

17. scrupulous attention to details
a. expert   b. careful   c. slight   d. childish

18. part of an **insidious** plan
a. treacherous   b. recent   c. awkward   d. logical

19. compatible couples
a. married   b. divorced   c. like-minded   d. elderly

20. plead for **clemency**
a. justice   b. mercy   c. understanding   d. release

21. lost in the **holocaust**
a. confusion   b. struggle   c. results   d. great fire

22. embark at once
a. cut   b. notice   c. cover   d. board

23. endemic plants and animals
a. interesting   b. native   c. peculiar   d. valuable

24. a **cursory** examination
a. hasty   b. thorough   c. very painful   d. rewarding

25. offer as a **panacea**
a. cure-all   b. substitute   c. moneymaker   d. token

26. reprehensible behavior
a. worthy   b. blameworthy   c. criminal   d. remarkable

27. an **officious** guard
a. efficient   b. hired   c. powerful   d. meddlesome

28. altruistic motives
a. unselfish   b. complex   c. obvious   d. inner

29. deride our efforts
a. compliment   b. mock   c. defend   d. extend

30. a clever **artifice**
a. worker   b. reaction   c. statement   d. trick

Antonyms

*In each of the following groups, circle the word or expression that is most nearly **opposite** in meaning to the word in **boldface** type in the given phrase.*

31. a **voluminous** report
a. valuable   b. brief   c. learned   d. written

32. with **negligible** results
a. substantial   b. curious   c. negative   d. unexpected

33. retrogress in ability
a. fall behind   b. advance   c. fail   d. bask

34. a worthy **adversary**
a. undertaking   b. opponent   c. ally   d. cause

35. since the plan appears to be **feasible**
  a. uncomplicated b. innocuous (c. unworkable) d. inexpensive

36. an overly **indulgent** parent
  a. energetic b. unconcerned (c. strict) d. confident

37. made some very **trenchant** comments
  a. revealing b. strange c. amusing (d. inane)

38. a truly **virulent** strain of the virus
  a. unusual (b. mild) c. recent d. deadly

39. a **dearth** of ideas
  a. lack b. choice c. source (d. abundance)

40. a **loquacious** person
  (a. tight-lipped) b. openhanded c. farsighted d. narrow-minded

41. a **suave** young man
  a. clever (b. boorish) c. haughty d. kindly

42. **perpetuate** a family tradition
  a. defend b. observe (c. discontinue) d. question

43. a **meticulous** worker
  a. diligent b. contented c. retired (d. careless)

44. a **callous** attitude
  (a. sensitive) b. hostile c. surprising d. distant

45. **quell** an armed uprising
  a. report (b. instigate) c. join d. crush

46. the **placid** waters of the lake
  a. peaceful (b. agitated) c. polluted d. sparkling

47. **venal** arrangements
  a. workable (b. honorable) c. corrupt d. helpful

48. **disparaged** their achievements
  a. criticized b. studied c. reported (d. praised)

49. **quiescent** volcanoes
  a. dormant b. imposing (c. active) d. small

50. **misconstrue** its meaning
  a. question (b. understand) c. dislike d. enjoy

 **Definitions**

Note carefully the spelling, pronunciation, part(s) of speech, and definition(s) of each of the following words. Then write the word in the blank space(s) in the illustrative sentence(s) following. Finally, study the lists of synonyms and antonyms given at the end of each entry.

1. adulterate
(ə dəl′ tə rāt)

(*v.*) to corrupt, make worse by the addition of something of lesser value

Hospitals take strict precautions to assure that nothing _____**adulterates**_____ the blood supply.

SYNONYMS: contaminate, pollute, sully
ANTONYMS: purify, purge, expurgate

2. ambidextrous
(am bi dek′ strəs)

(*adj.*) able to use both hands equally well; very skillful; deceitful, hypocritical

Occasionally a teacher will come across a child who displays _____**ambidextrous**_____ abilities when taught to write.

SYNONYMS: versatile, facile
ANTONYMS: clumsy, all thumbs, maladroit

3. augment
(ôg ment′)

(*v.*) to make larger, increase

Many couples have to _____**augment**_____ their income in order to pay the mortgage on a new home.

SYNONYMS: enlarge, supplement, amplify
ANTONYMS: decrease, diminish

4. bereft
(bi reft′)

(*adj., part.*) deprived of; made unhappy through a loss

Individuals who live to be very old may eventually find themselves completely _____**bereft**_____ of friends and family.

SYNONYM: bereaved
ANTONYMS: replete, well provided

5. deploy
(di ploi′)

(*v.*) to position or arrange; to utilize; to form up

A bugle call is a signal used to _____**deploy**_____ troops for inspection, parade, or battle.

SYNONYMS: station, organize

6. dour
(daůr)

(*adj.*) stern, unyielding, gloomy, ill-humored

Dickens's Mr. Gradgrind in the novel *Hard Times* is an example of a character with a _____**dour**_____ and sullen disposition.

SYNONYMS: harsh, bleak, forbidding, saturnine
ANTONYMS: cheery, inviting, genial

7. fortitude
(fôr' ti tüd)

(*n.*) courage in facing difficulties

The residents of the Mississippi delta showed remarkable
_____**fortitude**_____ during and after the flood
that destroyed their homes and businesses.

SYNONYMS: resolve, steadfastness, mettle
ANTONYMS: fearfulness, timidity, faintheartedness

8. gape
(gāp)

(*v.*) to stare with open mouth; to open the mouth wide; to open wide

First-time visitors to Niagara Falls can be expected to
_____**gape**_____ at the spectacular sights
nature has provided for them.

SYNONYMS: gawk, ogle

9. gibe
(jīb)

(*v.*) to utter taunting words; (*n.*) an expression of scorn

The recruits rushed into battle so that no one could
_____**gibe**_____ at them for cowardice.

Voters may reject a candidate who resorts to personal
_____**gibes**_____ instead of discussing the issues.

SYNONYMS: (*v.*) ridicule, mock, deride, jeer
ANTONYMS: (*n.*) compliment, praise

10. guise
(gīz)

(*n.*) an external appearance, cover, mask

The thieves gained entry to the home by presenting
themselves in the _____**guise**_____
of police officers.

SYNONYMS: costume, semblance, pretense

11. insidious
(in sid' ē əs)

(*adj.*) intended to deceive or entrap; sly, treacherous

The investigators uncovered an _____**insidious**_____
scheme to rob people of their life savings.

SYNONYMS: cunning, underhanded, perfidious
ANTONYMS: frank, ingenuous, aboveboard

12. intimation
(in tə mā' shən)

(*n.*) a hint, indirect suggestion

They were too proud to give any _____**intimation(s)**_____ of
their financial difficulties.

SYNONYMS: clue, indication, inkling

13. opulent
(äp' yə lənt)

(*adj.*) wealthy, luxurious; ample; grandiose

The tour guide showed us the _____**opulent**_____
living quarters of the royal family.

SYNONYMS: rich, lavish, plentiful, abundant
ANTONYMS: poverty-stricken, wretched, destitute

14. pliable
(plī′ ə bəl)

(*adj.*) easily bent, flexible; easily influenced

Spools of _____**pliable**_____ copper wire are standard equipment for many kinds of maintenance workers, including electricians.

SYNONYMS: supple, adaptable, resilient
ANTONYMS: rigid, inflexible, recalcitrant

15. reiterate
(rē it′ ə rāt)

(*v.*) to say again, repeat

Effective speakers often _____**reiterate**_____ an important statement for emphasis.

SYNONYMS: restate, rehash, recapitulate

16. stolid
(stäl′ id)

(*adj.*) not easily moved mentally or emotionally; dull, unresponsive

_____**Stolid**_____ people can generally be expected to take most things in stride.

SYNONYMS: impassive, phlegmatic
ANTONYMS: emotional, oversensitive, high-strung

17. tentative
(ten′ tə tiv)

(*adj.*) experimental in nature; uncertain, hesitant

Negotiators have come up with a _____**tentative**_____ agreement that will keep both sides at the bargaining table past the strike deadline.

SYNONYMS: provisional, inconclusive
ANTONYMS: definite, conclusive, confirmed

18. unkempt
(ən kempt′)

(*adj.*) not combed; untidy; not properly maintained; unpolished, rude

According to my parents, the latest fashions make me and my friends look _____**unkempt**_____.

SYNONYMS: sloppy, disheveled, disordered, rough
ANTONYMS: well-groomed, tidy, neat, natty

19. verbatim
(vər bā′ təm)

(*adj., adv.*) word for word; exactly as written or spoken

Newspapers often publish the _____**verbatim**_____ text of an important political speech.

At the swearing-in ceremony, the Chief Justice reads each line of the Oath of Office, and the new President repeats it _____**verbatim**_____.

SYNONYM: (*adj.*) exact; (*adv.*) precisely
ANTONYM: (*adj.*) paraphrased

20. warily
(wâr′ ə lē)

(*adv.*) cautiously, with great care

The hikers made their way _____**warily**_____ up the steep and rocky trail.

SYNONYMS: carefully, prudently, gingerly
ANTONYMS: recklessly, heedlessly, incautiously

Completing the Sentence

From the words for this unit, choose the one that best completes each of the following sentences. Write the word in the space provided.

1. What a tragedy that in the twilight of her life the unfortunate woman should be _____**bereft**_____ of all her loved ones!

2. We learned that beneath his _____**stolid**_____ exterior there was a sensitive, highly subtle, and perceptive mind.

3. Having learned to respect the power in his opponent's fists, the boxer moved _____**warily**_____ around the center of the ring.

4. Her unchanging facial features and controlled voice as she received the news gave no _____**intimation**_____ of her true feelings.

5. An experienced baseball manager _____**deploys**_____ his outfielders according to the strengths and weaknesses of the opposing batters.

6. At the risk of being boring, let me _____**reiterate**_____ my warning against careless driving.

7. To this day, historians are still debating whether or not Aaron Burr was guilty of a(n) _____**insidious**_____ plot to break up the United States.

8. Since I need the speaker's exact words for my report, I have asked the stenographer to take down the speech _____**verbatim**_____.

9. The _____**dour**_____ expressions on the jurors' faces as they grimly filed back into the courtroom did not bode well for the defendant.

10. Many ballplayers can bat from either side of the plate, but they cannot throw well with each hand unless they are _____**ambidextrous**_____.

11. Why would someone who is usually so neat and tidy appear in public in such a(n) _____**unkempt**_____ state?

12. As the magician's assistant seemed to vanish into thin air, the entire audience _____**gaped**_____ in amazement.

13. Perhaps I would be bored with the _____**opulent**_____ lifestyle of a millionaire, but I'm willing to try it.

14. How can you tell whether the chopped-meat patty you ate for lunch had been _____**adulterated**_____ with artificial coloring and other foreign substances?

15. America's earliest settlers faced the hardships of life on the frontier with faith and _____**fortitude**_____.

16. The company commander called his troops together and asked for more volunteers to _____**augment**_____ the strength of the raiding party.

17. The twigs that were to be woven into the basket were soaked in water to make them more _____**pliable**_____.

18. In Shakespeare's famous tragedy *Othello*, Iago comes to Othello in the ___guise___ of a friend but proves to be a deadly enemy.

19. Why should I be the object of all those ___gibes___ just because I'm wearing a three-piece suit on campus?

20. Since his acceptance of the invitation was only ___tentative___, the hostess may be one man short at the dinner party.

Synonyms

*Choose the word from this unit that is **the same** or **most nearly the same** in meaning as the **boldface** word or expression in the given phrase. Write the word on the line provided.*

1. deprived of the companionship of a beloved pet   bereft

2. the **stern** faces of the ancestral portraits   dour

3. stared at the huge jaws of the crocodile   gaped

4. gave no **indication** of being nervous   intimation

5. rehash the same old theories   reiterate

6. station the remaining guards at the exits   deploy

7. appeared in the **costume** of a cowboy   guise

8. polluted the water with toxic chemicals   adulterated

9. need to **increase** the computer's memory   augment

10. an **underhanded** attack on my good name   insidious

11. the **supple** limbs of a dancer   pliable

12. jeer at the mistakes of the rookies   gibe

13. proceeded **carefully** in unknown waters   warily

14. a group of tired and **untidy** travelers   unkempt

15. attended a **lavish** holiday banquet   opulent

Antonyms

*Choose the word from this unit that is **most nearly opposite** in meaning to the **boldface** word or expression in the given phrase. Write the word on the line provided.*

16. a person with a **high-strung** temperament   stolid

17. displayed **timidity** under fire   fortitude

18. a **paraphrased** version of the announcement   verbatim

19. surprisingly **maladroit** handling of the ball   ambidextrous

20. a **definite** date for the party   tentative

Choosing the Right Word

Circle the **boldface** word that more satisfactorily completes each of the following sentences.

1. Do you believe that the curriculum has been (**deployed, adulterated**) by the inclusion of courses on aspects of popular culture?

2. Because the situation is changing so rapidly, any plans we make to deal with the emergency can be no more than (**verbatim, tentative**).

3. What they call their "(**insidious, pliable**) outlook on life" seems to be simply a lack of any firm moral standards.

4. Recruits who complain of the cold should try to show a little more intestinal (**fortitude, intimation**) in facing the elements.

5. Let us not forget that the early fighters for women's rights were greeted with the (**gibes, guises**) of the unthinking mob.

6. In this scene of wild jubilation, my (**stolid, tentative**) roommate continued to eat his peanut butter sandwich as though nothing had happened.

7. Have you heard the joke about the (**ambidextrous, opulent**) loafer who was equally adept at not working with either hand?

8. Though all hope of victory had faded, the remaining troops continued to resist the enemy with a (**bereft, dour**) tenacity.

9. How annoying to hear the same silly advertising slogans (**gaped, reiterated**) endlessly on television!

10. Because of my inexperience, I did not recognize at first his (**insidious, ambidextrous**) attempts to undermine our employer's confidence in me.

11. The young prince, who much preferred blue jeans, had to dress in the (**stolid, opulent**) robes designed for the coronation.

12. The ticking grew louder as the bomb squad (**warily, pliably**) opened the package found on the grounds of the governor's residence.

13. The speaker (**deployed, adulterated**) all the facts and figures at her command to buttress her argument.

14. I must have been (**bereft, pliable**) of my senses when I bought that old car!

15. There we were at the very edge of the cliff, with our front wheels about to plunge into a (**gaping, intimating**) ravine!

16. I soon found out that my supposed friend had taken it upon himself to repeat (**unkempt, verbatim**) every word I said about Frieda's party.

17. A sort of heaviness in the air and an eerie silence were the first real (**reiterations, intimations**) of the approaching cyclone.

18. By studying the reactions of simpler life forms, researchers have greatly (**adulterated, augmented**) our knowledge of human behavior.

19. One of the chief reasons for your dateless weekends is undoubtedly your (**opulent, unkempt**) appearance.

20. Do you expect me to listen to a lot of tired old ideas dressed up in the (**fortitude, guise**) of brilliant new insights?

Vocabulary in Context

Read the following passage, in which some of the words you have studied in this unit appear in **boldface** type. Then complete each statement given below the passage by circling the letter of the item that is **the same** or **almost the same** in meaning as the highlighted word.

Circuses

(Line)

Circuses have been entertaining people for thousands of years. At the public games in ancient Rome, for example, riders stood on the bare backs of horses and raced around circular tracks while the assembled crowds **gaped** in wonder and astonishment. In fact, the word *circus* comes from the Latin word for "circle" or "oval."

(5)　　Jugglers, those **ambidextrous** performers who throw many objects into the air and keep them in constant motion, have an even more ancient history. Egyptian wall paintings and early Greek sculptures show jugglers, many of them women, balancing

(10)　balls and clubs in the air. In the Americas, pictures of jugglers tossing torches have been found in ancient ruins.

In the Middle Ages, performers called *jesters* entertained royalty and commoners

(15)　alike with jokes and physical comedy. Shakespeare features court jesters in some of his plays, where they often function as more than mere clowns. In *King Lear*, for example, the Fool speaks a great

(20)　deal of sense but cloaks it in the **guise** of foolishness.

Circus poster, 1944

The modern circus began in England in 1768, when a man named Philip Astley presented fancy horseback riding,

(25)　acrobatic acts, and clowns, accompanied by live music. Astley's circus was quickly imitated in America. A century later, showmen such as P. T. Barnum **augmented** these spectacles with a great variety of acts, including trapeze artists, tightrope walkers, trained animals, and dancers.

The clowns, however, are at the heart of any circus. Awkward and **unkempt**, the

(30)　clowns strut and stumble in outlandish clothes and makeup, delighting one and all with their antics. Who can keep from laughing when a dozen clowns climb out of a tiny car?

---

1. The meaning of **gaped** (line 3) is
a. gasped
b. gawked
c. cheered
d. protested

2. Ambidextrous (line 5) most nearly means
a. skillful
b. ungainly
c. amazing
d. ancient

3. Guise (line 20) is best defined as
a. business
b. name
c. tradition
d. semblance

4. The meaning of **augmented** (line 27) is
a. beautified
b. spoiled
c. enlarged
d. tamed

5. Unkempt (line 29) most nearly means
a. disheveled
b. silly
c. lovable
d. ugly

Definitions

Note carefully the spelling, pronunciation, part(s) of speech, and definition(s) of each of the following words. Then write the word in the blank space(s) in the illustrative sentence(s) following. Finally, study the lists of synonyms and antonyms given at the end of each entry.

1. adroit
(ə droit′)

(*adj.*) skillful, expert in the use of the hands or mind

Many rodeo performers are ____**adroit**____ at twirling a rope while on horseback.

SYNONYMS: clever, deft, dexterous, slick
ANTONYMS: clumsy, inept, all thumbs

2. amicable
(am′ ə kə bəl)

(*adj.*) peaceable, friendly

Sometimes mediation by a neutral individual can lead to an ____**amicable**____ settlement of a dispute.

SYNONYMS: congenial, neighborly, cordial
ANTONYMS: hostile, antagonistic

3. averse
(ə vərs′)

(*adj.*) having a deep-seated distaste; opposed, unwilling

You are not likely to become a marathon runner if you are ____**averse**____ to strenuous exercise.

SYNONYMS: disinclined, loath
ANTONYMS: favorably disposed, eager, keen

4. belligerent
(bə lij′ ə rənt)

(*adj.*) given to fighting, warlike; combative, aggressive; (*n.*) one at war, one engaged in war

I did not expect such a ____**belligerent**____ answer to my request for directions.

After each ____**belligerent**____ signed the peace treaty, the war was declared officially over.

SYNONYMS: (*adj.*) assertive, truculent, pugnacious
ANTONYMS: (*adj.*) peaceful, conciliatory, placid

5. benevolent
(bə nev′ ə lənt)

(*adj.*) kindly, charitable

The newcomers had nothing but ____**benevolent**____ feelings toward all their neighbors.

SYNONYMS: benign, well-meaning
ANTONYMS: malicious, spiteful, malevolent

6. cursory
(ker′ sə rē)

(*adj.*) hasty, not thorough

The mayor gave a final ____**cursory**____ glance at the text of her speech before mounting the podium.

SYNONYMS: quick, superficial, perfunctory
ANTONYMS: thorough, painstaking, careful

7. duplicity
(dü plis′ ə tē)

(*n.*) treachery, deceitfulness

We found it difficult to believe that our good friend could be capable of such _____ duplicity _____ .

SYNONYMS: fraud, double-dealing, chicanery

8. extol
(ek stōl′)

(*v.*) to praise extravagantly

Many inspiring stories and plays have been written that _____ extol _____ the heroic deeds of Joan of Arc.

SYNONYMS: glorify, applaud, acclaim, hail
ANTONYMS: criticize, belittle, disparage

9. feasible
(fē′ zə bəl)

(*adj.*) possible, able to be done

Our city needs to develop a _____ feasible _____ plan of action for dealing with storms and other emergencies.

SYNONYMS: workable, practicable, viable
ANTONYMS: unworkable, impractical

10. grimace
(grim′ əs)

(*n.*) a wry face, facial distortion; (*v.*) to make a wry face

The _____ grimace _____ of the refugee in the photograph reveals the pain of homelessness.
Most people _____ grimace _____ at the mere sound of the dentist's drill.

SYNONYMS: (*n.*) pained expression, facial contortion
ANTONYMS: (*n.*) smile, grin; (*v.*) beam

11. holocaust
(häl′ ə kôst)

(*n.*) a large-scale destruction, especially by fire; a vast slaughter; a burnt offering

Journalists at the time were eager to interview survivors of the Chicago _____ holocaust _____ .

SYNONYMS: conflagration, devastation, annihilation
ANTONYMS: deluge, inundation

12. impervious
(im pər′ vē əs)

(*adj.*) not affected or hurt by; admitting of no passage or entrance

It is best to store flour in a container with a plastic cover that is _____ impervious _____ to moisture.

SYNONYMS: impenetrable, resistant, proof against
ANTONYMS: porous, permeable, vulnerable

13. impetus
(im′ pə təs)

(*n.*) a moving force, impulse, stimulus

The coming of winter gave a new _____ impetus _____ to the appeals for food and clothing for needy families.

SYNONYMS: impulse, incentive, spur
ANTONYMS: curb, hindrance, impediment, constraint

14. jeopardy
(jep′ ər dē)

(*n.*) danger
Experienced mountaineers know that a single mistake can put an entire expedition in serious _____**jeopardy**_____ .
SYNONYMS: risk, hazard, peril
ANTONYMS: safety, security

15. meticulous
(mə tik′ yə ləs)

(*adj.*) extremely careful; particular about details
If you have a full-time job outside the home, you may find it exceedingly difficult to be a _____**meticulous**_____ housekeeper.
SYNONYMS: fastidious, painstaking, fussy
ANTONYMS: careless, negligent, sloppy

16. nostalgia
(nä stal′ jə)

(*n.*) a longing for something past; homesickness
Looking at old scrapbooks and reading old letters can bring on a vague sense of _____**nostalgia**_____ for days gone by and friends no longer near.

17. quintessence
(kwin tes′ əns)

(*n.*) the purest essence or form of something; the most typical example
Risking one's own life to save the lives of others is considered the _____**quintessence**_____ of selfless valor.
SYNONYMS: paragon, exemplar

18. retrogress
(re trə gres′)

(*v.*) to move backward; to return to an earlier condition
In the novel, the survivors of a nuclear explosion _____**retrogress**_____ into a state of barbarism and anarchy.
SYNONYMS: revert, degenerate, decline
ANTONYMS: advance, evolve, progress

19. scrutinize
(skrüt′ ə nīz)

(*v.*) to examine closely
Lawyers are paid to _____**scrutinize**_____ legal papers and explain the fine print to their clients.
SYNONYMS: inspect, pore over
ANTONYMS: skim, scan, glance at

20. tepid
(tep′ id)

(*adj.*) lukewarm; unenthusiastic, marked by an absence of interest
A cup of _____**tepid**_____ tea will not warm you up on a chilly morning.
SYNONYMS: insipid, halfhearted, wishy-washy
ANTONYMS: heated, excited, enthusiastic

Completing the Sentence

From the words for this unit, choose the one that best completes each of the following sentences. Write the word in the space provided.

1. Our physical education instructor _____**extols**_____ the virtues of regular exercise.

2. For centuries, Switzerland has avoided becoming a(n) _____**belligerent**_____ in the conflicts that have scarred the rest of Europe.

3. When I realized how bad the brakes of the old car were, I feared that our lives were in _____**jeopardy**_____.

4. What good is a plastic raincoat that is _____**impervious**_____ to water if it also prevents any body heat from escaping?

5. As the old soldier watched the parade, he was suddenly overcome with _____**nostalgia**_____ for the youthful years he spent in the army.

6. King Arthur's Knights of the Round Table were the _____**quintessence**_____ of chivalry.

7. A triple reverse looks mighty impressive on the chalkboard, but I doubt that the play will prove _____**feasible**_____ on the football field.

8. A(n) _____**cursory**_____ examination of my luggage was enough to show me that someone had been tampering with it.

9. An expert from the museum _____**scrutinized**_____ the painting, looking for telltale signs that would prove it to be genuine or expose it as a forgery.

10. If you are _____**averse**_____ to hard study and intensive reading, how do you expect to get through law school?

11. If, as you claim, you really like raw oysters, why do you make such an eloquent _____**grimace**_____ every time you swallow one?

12. My teacher counseled me to keep up my studies, or my performance in class might once again _____**retrogress**_____ into mediocrity.

13. When I heard you speaking French so fluently, my determination to master that language received a fresh _____**impetus**_____.

14. Because I was looking forward to a hot bath, I was disappointed at the feeble stream of _____**tepid**_____ water that flowed into the tub.

15. The accountant's records—neat, accurate, and complete in every respect—show that she is a most _____**meticulous**_____ worker.

16. Although he shows no particular talent as a worker, he is exceptionally _____**adroit**_____ at finding excuses for not doing his job.

17. Regarding Native Americans as "bloodthirsty savages," Europeans were rarely able to maintain _____**amicable**_____ relations with them.

18. No one doubted the _____ benevolent _____ intentions of the program for community improvement, but it was ruined by mismanagement.

19. We must not forget the millions of people who were ruthlessly slaughtered by the Nazis in the _____ holocaust _____ of World War II.

20. Only when we learned that the embezzler had tried to cast suspicion on his innocent partner did we realize the extent of his _____ duplicity _____ .

Synonyms

*Choose the word from this unit that is **the same** or **most nearly the same** in meaning as the **boldface** word or expression in the given phrase. Write the word on the line provided.*

1. another **incentive** to do a good job — impetus
2. a shocking case of **fraud** — duplicity
3. rescued dozens of people from the **large fire** — holocaust
4. described as the **paragon** of graciousness — quintessence
5. a brief spell of **homesickness** — nostalgia
6. staged a **painstaking** re-creation of a famous battle — meticulous
7. respond with a **pugnacious** gesture — belligerent
8. not **practicable** during the winter months — feasible
9. **revert** to a pattern of self-destructive behavior — retrogress
10. in **danger** of losing your reputation for honesty — jeopardy
11. made a **quick** estimate of the crowd's size — cursory
12. **resistant** to the usual methods of treatment — impervious
13. a **halfhearted** response to the appeal for donations — tepid
14. a tendency to **glorify** the talents of our friends — extol
15. a remarkably **congenial** group of people — amicable

Antonyms

*Choose the word from this unit that is **most nearly opposite** in meaning to the **boldface** word or expression in the given phrase. Write the word on the line provided.*

16. **skimmed** the article for the main ideas — scrutinized
17. a **smile** in the face of danger — grimace
18. was **favorably disposed** to borrowing money — averse
19. a single **clumsy** stroke of the painter's brush — adroit
20. had a **malevolent** influence on the society — benevolent

Choosing the Right Word

*Circle the **boldface** word that more satisfactorily completes each of the following sentences.*

1. News of famine in various parts of the world has given added (**nostalgia, impetus**) to the drive to increase food production.

2. On the morning of the picnic, the sky was gray and overcast, but suddenly the sun came out and smiled on us (**benevolently, adroitly**).

3. Because I was not even born when the Beatles were at the height of their popularity, their albums do not fill me with (**duplicity, nostalgia**).

4. The lawyer's (**adroit, belligerent**) questioning slowly but surely revealed the weaknesses in his opponent's case.

5. Anyone who is (**averse, cursory**) to having a girls' hockey team in our school doesn't know what's been happening in recent years.

6. When I saw my sister land in a tree on her first parachute jump, my interest in learning to skydive became decidedly (**tepid, adroit**).

7. In the Sherlock Holmes stories, we read of the evil Professor Moriarty, whose (**duplicity, quintessence**) was almost a match for Holmes's genius.

8. Do you think you are being fair in passing judgment on my poem after such a (**cursory, benevolent**) reading?

9. The nightmare that continues to haunt all thoughtful people is a nuclear (**holocaust, jeopardy**) in which our civilization might be destroyed.

10. Though it may appear rather ordinary to the casual reader, Lincoln's Gettysburg Address is to me the (**impetus, quintessence**) of eloquence.

11. I knew you would be (**impervious, meticulous**) in caring for my plants, but I did not expect you to water them with a medicine dropper!

12. Carelessness in even minor details may (**extol, jeopardize**) the success of a major theatrical production.

13. His parents tried to encourage an interest in literature, music, and art, but he seemed (**amicable, impervious**) to such influences.

14. Some civil engineers believe that someday it may be (**feasible, averse**) to derive a large part of our energy directly from the sun.

15. It was rude of you to (**retrogress, grimace**) so obviously when the speaker mispronounced words and made grammatical errors.

16. (**Extolling, Scrutinizing**) other people's achievements is fine, but it is no substitute for doing something remarkable of your own.

17. Though the peace talks began with an exchange of lofty sentiments, they soon (**retrogressed, grimaced**) into petty squabbling and backbiting.

18. It made me very uncomfortable to see the suspicion with which the wary customs officer (**scrutinized, extolled**) my passport.

19. Providing a powerful defense force for our nation does not mean that we are taking a (**belligerent, meticulous**) attitude toward any other nation.

20. After shouting at each other rather angrily, the participants in the roundtable discussion calmed down and parted (**feasibly, amicably**).

Read the following passage, in which some of the words you have studied in this unit appear in **boldface** type. Then complete each statement given below the passage by circling the letter of the item that is *the same* or *almost the same* in meaning as the highlighted word.

Fire Fight

(Line

There was literally a **holocaust** in the western United States in the summer of 1988. Major fires destroyed all plant life in eight areas in and around Yellowstone National Park. In the park itself, one million acres were consumed by wildfire. What caused this disaster? Can such a calamity be prevented from happening again?

A spark of lightning or human carelessness might have provided the original (5) **impetus** for the fires. But the combination of drought conditions and a long-standing buildup of leaf litter and decaying wood on the floor of the forest fed and sustained the flames. Even the very latest and most sophisticated fire-fighting techniques were (10) ineffective against the blaze.

Periodic droughts cannot be prevented, and debris accumulates on the forest floor naturally. Occasional small fires are part of the natural cycle and help clear the forest floor and reduce the risk of (15) larger fires. However, the fire-management policies of the U.S. Forest Service and the National Parks Service emphasized aggressive fire-fighting efforts, which included quenching these small, naturally occurring fires. This seemingly (20) **benevolent** policy of fire fighting was responsible for saving many acres of private property and parkland.

In the wake of the 1988 fires, however, many scientists challenged this policy of fire (25) prevention. They asked Congress to **scrutinize** its impact. Did it put millions of acres of forest in **jeopardy** in the long run? The scientists ignited a political firestorm. Not surprisingly, many politicians and members of the public were **averse** to (30)

Pine trees ablaze in Yellowstone

changing a policy that had saved so much valuable land. It will no doubt take years for this dispute to be settled.

---

1. The meaning of **holocaust** (line 1) is
a. heat wave
b. accident
c. debate
d. conflagration

2. Impetus (line 6) most nearly means
a. spur
b. calamity
c. action
d. story

3. Benevolent (line 21) is best defined as
a. spiteful
b. benign
c. effective
d. outdated

4. The meaning of **scrutinize** (line 26) is
a. condemn
b. avoid
c. welcome
d. examine

5. Jeopardy (line 28) most nearly means
a. reserve
b. darkness
c. peril
d. limbo

6. Averse (line 30) is best defined as
a. loath
b. open
c. resigned
d. committed

Definitions

Note carefully the spelling, pronunciation, part(s) of speech, and definition(s) of each of the following words. Then write the word in the blank space(s) in the illustrative sentence(s) following. Finally, study the lists of synonyms and antonyms given at the end of each entry.

1. adversary
(ad′ vər ser ē)

(*n.*) an enemy, opponent

A best friend off the tennis court can also be a fierce _____**adversary**_____ on it.

SYNONYMS: antagonist, rival, foe
ANTONYMS: friend, ally, supporter, confederate

2. alienate
(ā′ lē ə nāt)

(*v.*) to turn away; to make indifferent or hostile; to transfer, convey

Gossiping and backbiting are bad habits that are bound to _____**alienate**_____ friends.

SYNONYMS: separate, drive apart, estrange
ANTONYMS: befriend, attract, captivate, reconcile

3. artifice
(är′ tə fis)

(*n.*) a skillful or ingenious device; a clever trick; a clever skill; trickery

Even the most renowned art experts were completely taken in by the forger's _____**artifice**_____ .

SYNONYMS: ruse, stratagem, contrivance

4. coerce
(kō ərs′)

(*v.*) to compel, force

Dictators try to _____**coerce**_____ their subjects into obedience by threatening them or their families with punishment.

SYNONYMS: pressure, bully, intimidate, constrain
ANTONYMS: persuade, cajole

5. craven
(krā′ vən)

(*adj.*) cowardly; (*n.*) a coward

Those who urged Great Britain to make peace with Hitler were criticized for their _____**craven**_____ attitude.

It is a mistake to assume that everyone who refuses to go to war is a _____**craven**_____ who lacks patriotism.

SYNONYMS: (*adj.*) fearful, fainthearted, pusillanimous
ANTONYMS: (*adj.*) brave, courageous, valiant

6. culinary
(kyü′ lə ner ē)

(*adj.*) of or related to cooking or the kitchen

Cooking shows on television have helped many people to master the secrets of the _____**culinary**_____ arts.

7. delete
(di lēt')

(v.) to erase, wipe out, cut out

Crime labs can determine whether an attempt has been made to _____delete_____ material from audiotapes.

SYNONYMS: remove, cancel, expunge
ANTONYMS: insert, add, retain, include

8. demise
(di mīz')

(n.) a death, especially of a person in a lofty position

Traditionally, the tolling of church bells has announced the _____demise_____ of a monarch.

SYNONYMS: decease, passing away; downfall
ANTONYMS: birth, beginning, commencement

9. exhilarate
(eg zil' ə rāt)

(v.) to enliven, cheer, give spirit or liveliness to

The first landing on the moon, in the summer of 1969, _____exhilarated_____ the nation.

SYNONYMS: stimulate, excite, gladden
ANTONYMS: discourage, dispirit, dishearten, inhibit

10. fallow
(fal' ō)

(adj.) plowed but not seeded; inactive; reddish-yellow; (n.) land left unseeded; (v.) to plow but not seed

After a month without a date, I decided that my social life was definitely in a _____fallow_____ period.

In the drought-stricken region, there were millions of acres of _____fallow_____.

Farmers often _____fallow_____ a third of their fields each year to restore the chemical balance of the soil.

SYNONYMS: (adj.) unproductive, inert, dormant
ANTONYMS: (adj.) productive, fertile, prolific

11. harass
(hə ras')

(v.) to disturb, worry; to trouble by repeated attacks

The judge repeatedly cautioned the prosecuting attorney not to _____harass_____ the witness.

SYNONYMS: annoy, pester, bedevil, beleaguer

12. inclement
(in klem' ənt)

(adj.) stormy, harsh; severe in attitude or action

During an _____inclement_____ New England winter, heavy snowfalls may bring highway traffic to a standstill.

SYNONYMS: blustery, tempestuous, implacable
ANTONYMS: mild, gentle, balmy, tranquil

13. muse
(myüz)

(v.) to think about in a dreamy way, ponder

Philosophers have always _____mused_____ on the meaning of life.

SYNONYMS: meditate, contemplate, daydream

14. negligible
(neg' lə jə bəl)

(*adj.*) so unimportant that it can be disregarded

After taxes are deducted, a small raise in salary may result in a _____negligible_____ increase in take-home pay.

SYNONYMS: trivial, inconsequential, insignificant
ANTONYMS: significant, crucial, momentous

15. perpetuate
(pər pech' ü āt)

(*v.*) to make permanent or long lasting

In most cultures, people try to _____perpetuate_____ the customs of their ancestors.

SYNONYMS: continue, preserve, prolong indefinitely
ANTONYMS: discontinue, abolish, abandon

16. precedent
(pres' ə dənt)

(*n.*) an example that may serve as a basis for imitation or later action

We hope that students at other schools in our city will follow our _____precedent(s)_____ in volunteer work and charitable contributions.

SYNONYMS: guide, tradition, model

17. punitive
(pyü' nə tiv)

(*adj.*) inflicting or aiming at punishment

The general led a _____punitive_____ expedition against the rebel forces.

SYNONYMS: penalizing, retaliatory

18. redress
(rē dres')

(*v.*) to set right, remedy; (*n.*) relief from wrong or injury

An apology can go a long way to _____redress_____ the hurt feelings caused by an insensitive comment or a thoughtless act.

The accident victims will seek _____redress_____ for the injuries they suffered in the train crash.

SYNONYMS: (*v.*) rectify, correct, mitigate

19. sojourn
(sō' jərn)

(*n.*) a temporary stay; (*v.*) to stay for a time

No matter how short your _____sojourn_____ in Paris, you must take time to go to the Louvre.

Many American graduates _____sojourn_____ abroad before they begin working full-time at home.

SYNONYMS: (*n.*) visit, stopover, brief stay

20. urbane
(ər bān')

(*adj.*) refined in manner or style, suave

An _____urbane_____ host puts guests at ease by appearing totally confident and unruffled no matter what happens.

SYNONYM: elegant
ANTONYMS: crude, uncouth, boorish

Completing the Sentence

From the words for this unit, choose the one that best completes each of the following sentences. Write the word in the space provided.

1. The deserted buildings and the land lying _____ **fallow** _____ hinted at the troubles the farmers in the area were experiencing.

2. His charmingly _____ **urbane** _____ manner and keen wit made him a much sought-after guest at social gatherings.

3. The full extent of my _____ **culinary** _____ skill is preparing scrambled eggs on toast.

4. Since both cars had virtually come to a halt by the time their bumpers met, the damage was _____ **negligible** _____.

5. Magicians rely on sleight of hand and other forms of _____ **artifice** _____ to deceive their unsuspecting audiences.

6. As I lay under the old apple tree, I began to _____ **muse** _____ on the strange twists of fate that had led to the present situation.

7. Their bad manners and insufferable conceit _____ **alienated** _____ even those who were most inclined to judge them favorably.

8. The coach emphasized that the way to stop our opponents' passing game was to _____ **harass** _____ their receivers and blitz their quarterback.

9. I advise you to _____ **delete** _____ from your statement all the words that people are likely to find personally offensive.

10. The coach took me off the starting team as a(n) _____ **punitive** _____ measure for missing two days of practice.

11. When planning our trip to the Southwest, we made sure to set aside two days for a(n) _____ **sojourn** _____ at the Grand Canyon.

12. At first we watched the game with relatively little emotion, but we became so _____ **exhilarated** _____ by our team's strong comeback that we began to cheer loudly.

13. If we continue to elect unworthy people to public office, we will simply _____ **perpetuate** _____ the evils that we have tried so hard to correct.

14. Their _____ **craven** _____ behavior at the first sign of danger was a disgrace to the uniform they wore.

15. When the snowstorm lasted into a second day, we listened attentively to the radio to find out if our school was among those closed because of the _____ **inclement** _____ weather.

16. The _____ **demise** _____ of an administration in the United States is never a crisis because a newly elected administration is waiting to take over.

17. When citizens feel that something is wrong, they have a right under the First Amendment to ask their government for a(n) _____ **redress** _____ of grievances.

18. In 1858, Abraham Lincoln held a series of debates with Stephen Douglas, his

_____ adversary _____ in the contest for U.S. Senator from Illinois.

19. When Grandfather stubbornly refused to eat his vegetables, he set a(n) __ precedent __ that was immediately followed by the children.

20. There are far more subtle ways of _____ coercing _____ a person into doing what you want than twisting his or her arm.

Synonyms

*Choose the word from this unit that is **the same** or **most nearly the same** in meaning as the **boldface** word or expression in the given phrase. Write the word on the line provided.*

1. pestered by flies and mosquitoes   harassed

2. a **retaliatory** campaign against a political rival   punitive

3. a relaxing **stopover** on a tropical island   sojourn

4. meditated on the possibility of a raise   mused

5. an attempt to **rectify** past mistakes   redress

6. intimidated into making a deal   coerced

7. a graduate of a **cooking** school in Rome   culinary

8. a common **ruse** used to fool unwary customers   artifice

9. a dangerous **rival** who will stop at nothing   adversary

10. became a **model** for future generations   precedent

11. continued the search for a cure   perpetuated

12. a speech that **excited** the crowd   exhilarated

13. removed offensive language from the text   deleted

14. a **fearful** follower of those in power   craven

15. driven apart by a misunderstanding   alienated

Antonyms

*Choose the word from this unit that is **most nearly opposite** in meaning to the **boldface** word or expression in the given phrase. Write the word on the line provided.*

16. a generally **tranquil** climate   inclement

17. a very **crude** performance   urbane

18. the **beginning** of an era of prosperity   demise

19. significant gains in reading scores   negligible

20. a writer's **productive** years   fallow

Choosing the Right Word

*Circle the **boldface** word that more satisfactorily completes each of the following sentences.*

1. We need a supervisor who can maintain good discipline in the shop without (**harassing,** exhilarating) the workers.

2. We must reject the (**craven,** fallow) advice of those who feel we can solve social problems by abandoning our democratic freedoms.

3. Only when the attempt to get the British government to (**redress,** delete) injustices proved unsuccessful did the American colonists resort to arms.

4. Since we are making (**negligible,** craven) progress in our fight against pollution, the time has come for us to adopt completely new methods.

5. It is all very well to (**muse,** perpetuate) on what might have been, but it is far better to take action to make good things happen.

6. The highlight of my trip to Europe came when I (**sojourned,** redressed) in the birthplace of my ancestors.

7. I admit that we did some foolish things after the game, but you must remember how (mused, **exhilarated**) we were by the victory.

8. After a long (urbane, **fallow**) period during which she scarcely touched her brushes, the painter suddenly produced a series of major canvases.

9. The coach ran the risk of (exhilarating, **alienating**) influential graduates of the school when she suspended a star player who had broken training.

10. When he blocked my jump shot, took the rebound, drove down the court, and scored, I realized that I was facing a worthy (artifice, **adversary**).

11. I want to know by whose authority my name was (**deleted,** coerced) from the list of students eligible to take the scholarship examinations.

12. And now I want you all to try my (inclement, **culinary**) masterpiece—a salami soufflé, garnished with sour cream.

13. If we do not take steps now to clear their names, we will be (**perpetuating,** redressing) an injustice that has already lasted far too long.

14. When Washington refused to serve a third term as President, he set a(n) (artifice, **precedent**) that was to last for 150 years.

15. May I remind you that the (**punitive,** urbane) action we are authorized to take does not include physical force of any kind.

16. Our city government needs basic reforms; clever little (sojourns, **artifices**) will not solve our problems.

17. Our history shows how the (**demise,** adversary) of one political party provides an opportunity for the formation of a new one.

18. Do you really expect me to believe that your friends (**coerced,** alienated) you into cutting class to go to the movies?

19. Because of the severe sentences she often handed down, she gained the reputation of being an extremely (**inclement,** negligible) judge.

20. The critics unanimously praised the actor for the (**urbane,** punitive) charm with which he played the well-bred English gentleman.

Read the following passage, in which some of the words you have studied in this unit appear in **boldface** type. Then complete each statement given below the passage by circling the letter of the item that is **the same** or **almost the same** in meaning as the highlighted word.

The First Great American Statesman

(Line)

Benjamin Franklin was the first great American diplomat. His historic **sojourns** in England and France changed the destiny of the thirteen American colonies.

Franklin went to England in 1757 as a representative of the Pennsylvania legislature. The British owners of the colony were proposing to exempt

(5) themselves from any taxes imposed by the colonial legislature, and it was Franklin's mission to **redress** this injustice. In the first of many diplomatic triumphs, Franklin was able to persuade Parliament to adopt a more just

(10) taxation scheme for Pennsylvania. Franklin stayed in England for almost twenty years.

Throughout the 1760s, tensions mounted between the American colonies and Great Britain. Franklin was slow at first to embrace

(15) outright rebellion. He preferred to persuade rather than **coerce**. He even offered to pay the British out of his own pocket for the tea destroyed by the colonists in the Boston Tea Party if Great Britain would repeal its unjust tea

Benjamin Franklin (1706–1790)

(20) tax. When Britain refused, Franklin realized that the time for diplomacy had passed. He returned to Philadelphia in 1775 to help shape the new American nation.

In 1776, Congress sent Franklin to France to seek support against the British. Britain and France were historic **adversaries**. Franklin was an immediate hit with the French people. Both aristocrats and commoners admired his wit, tact,

(25) and shrewdness. Despite his simple dress and manners, he was accepted in the most **urbane** Parisian circles. Making the most of his personal popularity, Franklin secured the alliance in February 1778. When the war ended, Franklin helped draft the Treaty of Paris, which set the terms for an uneasy peace with Great Britain.

---

1. The meaning of **sojourns** (line 1) is
a. speeches
c. stays
b. palaces
d. protests

2. Redress (line 7) most nearly means
a. correct
c. discuss
b. endorse
d. study

3. Coerce (line 16) is best defined as
a. coax
c. confuse
b. pressure
d. surrender

4. The meaning of **adversaries** (line 23) is
a. monarchies
c. neighbors
b. allies
d. antagonists

5. Urbane (line 26) most nearly means
a. elegant
c. radical
b. boorish
d. fussy

Analogies

In each of the following, circle the item that best completes the comparison.

See pages T38–T48 for explanations of answers.

1. smile is to grimace as
a. laugh is to cry
b. sneeze is to yawn
c. weep is to bewail
d. wink is to blink

2. hovel is to poverty as
a. apartment is to artifice
b. palace is to opulence
c. fort is to jeopardy
d. cave is to quintessence

3. gape is to wide as
a. yawn is to narrow
b. frown is to wide
c. squint is to narrow
d. blink is to wide

4. virtue is to extol as
a. accomplishment is to gibe
b. duplicity is to honor
c. right is to redress
d. vice is to deplore

5. flood is to water as
a. avalanche is to wind
b. holocaust is to fire
c. hurricane is to ice
d. tornado is to snow

6. averse is to reluctant as
a. adroit is to dexterous
b. insidious is to benevolent
c. verbatim is to oral
d. culinary is to tepid

7. adversary is to friendly as
a. peacemaker is to belligerent
b. juggler is to ambidextrous
c. orphan is to bereft
d. coward is to craven

8. reiterate is to repeat as
a. extol is to criticize
b. perpetuate is to commit
c. scrutinize is to muse
d. deploy is to arrange

9. dour is to cheery as
a. stolid is to impervious
b. amicable is to pliable
c. fallow is to productive
d. inclement is to belligerent

10. sponge is to impervious as
a. glass is to brittle
b. wall is to rigid
c. umbrella is to porous
d. belt is to pliable

11. precedent is to before as
a. intimation is to after
b. redress is to before
c. consequence is to after
d. retrogression is to before

12. delete is to insert as
a. muse is to ponder
b. decrease is to augment
c. harass is to frighten
d. coerce is to compel

13. lawyer is to legal as
a. sculptor is to naval
b. politician is to punitive
c. athlete is to intellectual
d. chef is to culinary

14. meticulous is to cursory as
a. adulterated is to unkempt
b. warily is to cautiously
c. appreciable is to negligible
d. tentative is to feasible

15. nostalgia is to sad as
a. adversity is to joyful
b. impetus is to sad
c. exhilaration is to joyful
d. guise is to sad

16. unkempt is to appearance as
a. tepid is to height
b. urbane is to manner
c. impervious is to complexion
d. stolid is to weight

17. duplicity is to unfavorable as
a. fortitude is to favorable
b. intimation is to unfavorable
c. demise is to favorable
d. precedent is to unfavorable

18. insidious is to unfavorable as
a. benevolent is to favorable
b. meticulous is to unfavorable
c. craven is to favorable
d. ambidextrous is to unfavorable

Word Associations

In each of the following groups, circle the word that is best defined or suggested by the given phrase.

1. contemplate one's future
a. deploy　　　b. harass　　　c. coerce　　　(d. muse)

2. payment for a scratched fender from the person responsible
(a. redress)　　　b. fortitude　　　c. holocaust　　　d. grimace

3. the purest of the pure
a. nostalgia　　　b. artifice　　　c. intimation　　　(d. quintessence)

4. emphasize by repetition
a. scrutinize　　　(b. reiterate)　　　c. gibe　　　d. muse

5. neither hot nor cold
a. craven　　　b. averse　　　(c. tepid)　　　d. ambidextrous

6. look over carefully and critically
a. perpetuate　　　b. alienate　　　(c. scrutinize)　　　d. reiterate

7. showing extreme attention to details
(a. meticulous)　　　b. adroit　　　c. punitive　　　d. negligible

8. driving force
a. jeopardy　　　b. nostalgia　　　c. grimace　　　(d. impetus)

9. a clever stratagem
a. intimation　　　(b. artifice)　　　c. precedent　　　d. adversary

10. tease with mocking words
a. muse　　　b. delete　　　c. coerce　　　(d. gibe)

11. a facial expression that shows a negative reaction
a. redress　　　(b. grimace)　　　c. artifice　　　d. intimation

12. a deceptive appearance
a. nostalgia　　　b. redress　　　c. craven　　　(d. guise)

13. one step forward, two steps back
a. reiterate　　　b. scrutinize　　　(c. retrogress)　　　d. delete

14. a one-week stay in Athens
(a. sojourn)　　　b. precedent　　　c. nostalgia　　　d. jeopardy

15. harmful, but in a rather attractive way
(a. insidious)　　　b. cursory　　　c. fallow　　　d. dour

16. how one might characterize the prosecution and the defense in a legal suit
a. guises　　　b. intimations　　　c. precedents　　　(d. adversaries)

17. "The King is dead. Long live the King!"
a. jeopardy　　　(b. demise)　　　c. duplicity　　　d. adversary

18. not easily moved by emotion
a. meticulous　　　(b. stolid)　　　c. impervious　　　d. feasible

19. stare at in amazement
(a. gape)　　　b. grimace　　　c. redress　　　d. harass

20. "That guy is chickenhearted."
a. fallow　　　b. stolid　　　c. verbatim　　　(d. craven)

*Read the following passage, in which some of the words you have studied in Units 1–3 appear in **boldface** type. Then complete each statement given below the passage by circling the item that is **the same** or **almost the same** in meaning as the highlighted word.*

In America's Kitchen

(Line)

In the world of the **culinary** arts, probably no one has had a greater influence on Americans than Julia Child. She was born Julia McWilliams
(5) in Pasadena, California, in 1912. Her interest in cooking was **negligible** until she met Paul Cushing Child, an artist, diplomat, and gourmet, in China in the early 1940s. The couple
(10) married in 1946 and moved to Paris in 1948. There Julia studied French and enrolled at the Cordon Bleu, a famous French cooking school. Soon she was an **adroit** cook and an
(15) enthusiast of classical French cuisine. Eager to share her knowledge, Julia opened a cooking school in Paris with two friends. With one of these friends, Simone Beck,
(20) she began writing a cookbook based on their experiences at the school. They continued to work on the book as Julia moved around Europe with her husband.
(25) When Paul retired in 1961, the Childs returned to the United States and settled in Cambridge, Massachusetts. Also in 1961, Julia's first cookbook, *Mastering the Art of*
(30) *French Cooking,* was published in

the United States. It was an immense popular and critical success. Julia Child was immediately **extolled** as an expert on French cuisine and
(35) cooking instruction. Her book was praised for its **meticulous** attention to detail, clear and complete explanations, and straightforward, unpretentious tone.
(40) In 1963, Julia's half-hour cooking program, *The French Chef*, debuted on Boston's public television station. This award-winning show attracted an enthusiastic and ever-growing
(45) audience. Even noncooks enjoyed Julia Child's evident love of fine food, down-to-earth good humor, and easygoing manner. She had the uncommon ability to convince her
(50) viewers that it was **feasible** for them to succeed in the kitchen. She made people realize that cooking is fun.
In new cookbooks and television programs in the 1970s and 1980s,
(55) Julia Child adapted her recipes to accommodate the contemporary desire for low-fat meals that could be prepared quickly. Yet she remained true to what she considered the
(60) essentials of fine French cuisine.

---

1. The meaning of **culinary** (line 1) is
  a. fine   (c. cooking)
  b. literary   d. performing

2. Negligible (line 6) most nearly means
  a. immense   c. sincere
  (b. insignificant)   d. limited

3. Adroit (line 14) is best defined as
  (a. skillful)   c. amateur
  b. inept   d. sloppy

4. The meaning of **extolled** (line 33) is
  a. dismissed   c. trained
  (b. acclaimed)   d. identified

5. Meticulous (line 36) most nearly means
  a. welcome   c. occasional
  b. unnecessary   (d. painstaking)

6. Feasible (line 50) is best defined as
  a. unlikely   (c. possible)
  b. important   d. challenging

Read each sentence carefully. Then circle the item that best completes the statement below the sentence.

See pages T38–T48 for explanations of answers.

In their steep mountain fastnesses, clan leaders were impervious to attack, even from "technologically advanced" enemies such as Rome. (2)

1. In line 1 the phrase **impervious to** most nearly means

(a. safe from)　　b. prepared for　　c. unmoved by　　d. subject to

Only a complete megalomaniac would maintain such an opulent view of his own importance to the order of things. (2)

2. In line 1 the word **opulent** is used to mean

a. wealthy　　(b. grandiose)　　c. progressive　　d. abundant

After years of fallow in his life, a series of brilliant military triumphs catapulted the general into national prominence. (2)

3. The word **fallow** in line 1 can best be defined as

a. unused land　　b. preparation　　(c. inactivity)　　d. a reddish-yellow color

In some ancient societies prisoners of war figured prominently in the elaborate holocausts that marked major religious festivals. (2)

4. The word **holocausts** in line 2 is best described as

a. human sacrifices　　b. religious ceremonies　　c. theological disputes　　(d. burnt offerings)

"The Raven" and "The Tell-Tale Heart" prove that Poe, in T. S. Eliot's memorable phrase, was "ambidextrous in prose and verse." (2)

5. The word **ambidextrous** in line 2 most nearly means

a. twice-told　　(b. equally skilled)　　c. able to use both hands　　d. doubly literate

Antonyms

*In each of the following groups, circle the word or expression that is most nearly the **opposite** of the word in **boldface** type.*

1. inclement
(a. pleasant)
b. strange
c. boring
d. tasty

2. exhilarate
a. accuse
(b. depress)
c. excite
d. worsen

3. pliable
a. consumable
b. straight
c. demanding
(d. rigid)

4. urbane
(a. crude)
b. rural
c. weak
d. irrelevant

5. amicable
(a. quarrelsome)
b. friendly
c. easy
d. intellectual

6. craven
a. stuffed
b. yielding
(c. brave)
d. tidy

7. perpetuate
a. soothe
(b. discontinue)
c. anger
d. commit

8. augment
a. insult
(b. reduce)
c. predict
d. annoy

9. adroit
a. friendly
b. bereft
c. smooth
d. clumsy ⟵

10. feasible
a. cheap
b. glum
c. impractical ⟵
d. delicious

11. adulterate
a. lose
b. harass
c. purify ⟵
d. cheat

12. adversary
a. accuser
b. enemy
c. relative
d. ally ⟵

13. warily
a. rashly ⟵
b. softly
c. quietly
d. angrily

14. verbatim
a. nominal
b. pleasing
c. adapted ⟵
d. delayed

15. extol
a. improve
b. criticize ⟵
c. charge
d. analyze

16. unkempt
a. bound
b. punctual
c. neat ⟵
d. shiny

Word Families

A. On the line provided, write the word you have learned in Units 1–3 that is related to each of the following nouns.

EXAMPLE: insidiousness—**insidious**

1. harassment, harasser — harass
2. coercion, coercivity — coerce
3. exhilaration — exhilarate
4. adulteration, adulterant, adulterator — adulterate
5. feasibleness, feasibility — feasible
6. scrutiny, scrutinizer — scrutinize
7. adroitness — adroit
8. opulence, opulency — opulent
9. deletion — delete
10. benevolence, benevolentness — benevolent
11. alienation, alienator — alienate
12. wariness — warily
13. perpetuator, perpetuation — perpetuate
14. urbanity — urbane
15. tentativeness — tentative

B. On the line provided, write the word you have learned in Units 1–3 that is related to each of the following verbs.

EXAMPLE: precede—**precedent**

16. jeopardize — jeopardy
17. intimate — intimation
18. punish — punitive
19. neglect — negligible
20. bereave — bereft

Two-Word Completions

Circle the pair of words that best complete the meaning of each of the following passages.

See pages T38–T48 for explanations of answers.

1. My first _____ of Nelson's double-dealing came when I discovered him whispering with my opponent. Prior to that, I had no inkling of my so-called friend's _____.

   a. intimation . . . duplicity *(circled)*
   b. scrutiny . . . fortitude
   c. precedent . . . artifice
   d. redress . . . coercion

2. Some people always stick up their noses at food they're not accustomed,to, but I'm not at all _____ to trying something new. Still, experience has taught me to be _____ of such dubious delicacies as chocolate-covered ants, and I usually look before I leap, so to speak.

   a. amicable . . . bereft
   b. tepid . . . negligible
   c. averse . . . wary *(circled)*
   d. impervious . . . craven

3. Because the course of the disease was so _____, we didn't notice at first that the patient's condition was no longer improving but in fact had begun to _____.

   a. tentative . . . adulterate
   b. adroit . . . redress
   c. averse . . . perpetuate
   d. insidious . . . retrogress *(circled)*

4. Tony's general attitude toward people is so _____ that he has _____ absolutely everybody who knows him. If he didn't walk around with such a huge chip on his shoulder, he would have a few friends.

   a. benevolent . . . deployed
   b. impervious . . . exhilarated
   c. belligerent . . . alienated *(circled)*
   d. amicable . . . redressed

5. I want to use an excerpt from the president's inaugural address in my report. Unfortunately, the passage I want is far too long to reproduce _____. To get it down to the size I need, I'll have to _____ part of it.

   a. tentatively . . . augment
   b. stolidly . . . coerce
   c. meticulously . . . reiterate
   d. verbatim . . . delete *(circled)*

6. "I haven't yet had time to give your latest sales report more than a _____ glance," my boss told me. "However, I plan to _____ it carefully before we sit down to discuss it in detail."

   a. verbatim . . . reiterate
   b. cursory . . . scrutinize *(circled)*
   c. meticulous . . . augment
   d. tentative . . . redress

Building with Classical Roots

mis, miss, mit—to send

This root appears in **demise** (page 36). The literal meaning is "a sending down," but the word now suggests a death, especially of a person in an elevated position. Some other words based on the same root are listed below.

commissary	**emit**	**missile**	**premise**
emissary	**manumit**	**permit**	**remission**

From the list of words above, choose the one that corresponds to each of the brief definitions below. Write the word in the blank space in the illustrative sentence below the definition.

1. to release or send forth ("*send out*")

Crickets _____emit_____ a shrill chirp by rubbing their front wings together.

2. an object to be thrown or shot

The new fighter plane can fire a(n) _____missile_____ with deadly accuracy.

3. to consent to formally; to authorize; to allow

The law _____permits_____ a person convicted of a crime to file an appeal.

4. a messenger, agent ("*one sent out*")

The president sent a special _____emissary_____ to discuss the drafting of a peace agreement.

5. a statement or idea upon which a conclusion is based ("*that which is sent before*")

Some members of Congress argued that the budget proposal was based on false _____premises_____.

6. a place where supplies are distributed; a lunchroom

Campers and counselors eat their meals at the _____commissary_____.

7. to free from slavery or bondage

In some ancient societies, it was the custom to _____manumit_____ all children born into slavery.

8. a letup, abatement; a relief from suffering

A patient may need some medication for the _____remission_____ of pain immediately after undergoing major surgery.

From the list of words above, choose the one that best completes each of the following sentences. Write the word in the space provided.

1. The families of the soldiers stationed on the base were able to buy food and clothing at the _____commissary_____.

2. In the hands of the old-time vaudeville comedian, a custard pie became a(n) _____missile_____ that could stop any pursuer in his or her tracks.

3. When he issued the Emancipation Proclamation in 1863, President Abraham Lincoln _____ manumitted _____ four million enslaved human beings.

4. Basing his decision on the _____ premise _____ that some child in the school was carrying an infectious disease, the doctor ordered that all the students be inoculated.

5. Please _____ permit _____ me to offer my congratulations on your well-deserved promotion.

6. The trapped animal _____ emitted _____ a frantic squeal.

7. The doctors had begun to give up hope when the disease suddenly went into _____ remission _____ and the patient began to recover.

8. The secretary of state went to the arms conference being held in a foreign capital as the official _____ emissary _____ of the United States.

---

*Circle the **boldface** word that more satisfactorily completes each of the following sentences.*

1. Within the eye of a hurricane, there is a (**premise,** **remission**) of the storm's high winds and torrential rain.

2. Slaves (**manumitted,** **emitted**) in ancient Rome could become full citizens of the republic.

3. Her job is to supervise the ordering of all the supplies sold at the school (**commissary,** **emissary**).

4. The javelin, discus, and shot are (**remissions,** **missiles**) hurled by athletes in a decathlon.

5. The chemicals used in a photographer's darkroom (**emit,** **permit**) very strong fumes.

6. All too often in life and art, the (**emissary,** **missile**) is unjustly punished for being the bearer of bad news.

7. Over the centuries, some scholars have adhered to the (**commissary,** **premise**) that Shakespeare did not write the plays that bear his name.

8. If only time (**permitted,** **manumitted**), I would explain my brilliant theory to you in great detail.

Writer's Challenge

Read the following sentences, paying special attention to the words and phrases underlined. From the words in the box below, find better choices for these underlined words and phrases. Then use these choices to rewrite the sentences.

		WORD BANK		
adulterate	coerce	extol	impetus	(quintessence)
adversary	(deploy)	fortitude	(opulent)	redress
artifice	duplicity	(gape)	(perpetuate)	scrutinize
(augment)	exhilarate	guise	precedent	(sojourn)

Hearst's Castle

1. Tourists tend to <u>open their mouths wide</u> when they arrive at Enchanted Hill, the magnificent estate built by newspaper tycoon William Randolph Hearst in San Simeon, California.

_____**gape**_____

_____

2. To many people, Enchanted Hill is the <u>most typical example</u> of personal extravagance.

_____**quintessence**_____

_____

3. In 1919, Hearst hired architect Julia Morgan to build and manage his dream castle. For the next twenty-eight years, she would <u>position or arrange</u> thousands of workers to build and maintain the estate.

_____**deploy**_____

_____

4. In its heyday, Enchanted Hill was the destination of choice for the rich and famous to <u>hang out</u> in luxurious surroundings.

_____**sojourn**_____

_____

5. Guests could avail themselves of a private zoo, an airport, a theater, <u>wealthy</u> guest quarters, vast gardens, ballrooms, and enormous swimming pools.

_____**opulent**_____

_____

6. Hearst was an avid collector who never hesitated to <u>make larger</u> his extensive art holdings, regardless of the cost or difficulty.

_____**augment**_____

_____

7. In order to <u>make permanent or long-lasting</u> his idea of the good life, Hearst willed his estate to the people of California. Today it is a popular historical site.

_____**perpetuate**_____

_____

Definitions

Note carefully the spelling, pronunciation, part(s) of speech, and definition(s) of each of the following words. Then write the word in the blank space(s) in the illustrative sentence(s) following. Finally, study the lists of synonyms and antonyms given at the end of each entry.

1. affiliated
(ə fil′ ē āt əd)

(*adj., part.*) associated, connected

Being _____**affiliated**_____ with a well-known law firm is often the first step on the way to a successful political career.

SYNONYMS: attached, related, joined
ANTONYMS: dissociated, unconnected

2. ascertain
(as ər tān′)

(*v.*) to find out

We need to _____**ascertain**_____ what it will cost to remodel our kitchen.

SYNONYMS: discover, determine, establish

3. attainment
(ə tān′ mənt)

(*n.*) an accomplishment, the act of achieving

In addition to his abilities as a leader, Abraham Lincoln was a man of high literary _____**attainment**_____.

SYNONYMS: achievement, fulfillment
ANTONYMS: failure, defeat, frustration

4. bequeath
(bi kwēth′)

(*v.*) to give or pass on as an inheritance

Few people will make enough money in their lifetimes to be in a position to _____**bequeath**_____ a fortune to their heirs.

SYNONYMS: transmit, bestow, hand down

5. cogent
(kō′ jint)

(*adj.*) forceful, convincing; relevant, to the point

A group of legal scholars held a press conference to present a _____**cogent**_____ plea for reform of the state's prison system.

SYNONYMS: persuasive, compelling
ANTONYMS: weak, unconvincing, ineffective, irrelevant

6. converge
(kən verj′)

(*v.*) to move toward one point, approach nearer together

The television coverage resumed as soon as the delegates _____**converged**_____ on the hall to hear the keynote speaker's address.

SYNONYMS: meet, unite, intersect, merge
ANTONYMS: diverge, separate

7. disperse
(di spərs′)

(*v.*) to scatter, spread far and wide

When a scuffle broke out, the commissioner ordered the police to _____**disperse**_____ the crowd.

SYNONYMS: break up, dispel
ANTONYMS: collect, congregate, assemble, muster

8. esteem
(es tēm′)

(*v.*) to regard highly; (*n.*) a highly favorable opinion or judgment

In traditional Native American cultures, young people are taught to _____**esteem**_____ their ancestors.

The Chief Justice of the Supreme Court should be someone whom all parties hold in high _____**esteem**_____.

SYNONYMS: (*v.*) respect, admire, honor, revere
ANTONYMS: (*v.*) disdain, scorn; (*n.*) contempt

9. expunge
(ik spənj′)

(*v.*) to erase, obliterate, destroy

The judge ordered the remarks _____**expunged**_____ from the court record.

SYNONYMS: delete, efface, annihilate
ANTONYMS: insert, mark, imprint, impress

10. finite
(fī′ nīt)

(*adj.*) having limits; lasting for a limited time

There are only a _____**finite**_____ number of possible answers to a multiple-choice question.

SYNONYMS: bounded, measurable
ANTONYMS: unlimited, immeasurable, everlasting, eternal

11. invulnerable
(in vəl′ nər ə bəl)

(*adj.*) not able to be wounded or hurt; shielded against attack

Medieval lords did everything possible to make their castles _____**invulnerable**_____ fortresses.

SYNONYMS: impregnable, impervious, immune
ANTONYMS: exposed, unprotected, defenseless

12. malevolent
(mə lev′ ə lənt)

(*adj.*) spiteful, showing ill will

While pretending to be a loyal friend, Iago told Othello _____**malevolent**_____ lies.

SYNONYMS: malicious, wicked, sinister, malignant
ANTONYMS: kind, benevolent, compassionate

13. nonchalant
(nän shə lant′)

(*adj.*) cool and confident, unconcerned

The elegantly dressed couple strolled down the boulevard with a _____**nonchalant**_____ air.

SYNONYMS: composed, unruffled, indifferent, blasé
ANTONYMS: perturbed, agitated, disconcerted, abashed

14. omniscient
(äm nish' ənt)

(*adj.*) knowing everything; having unlimited awareness or understanding

> Scientists today have so much specialized knowledge that they sometimes seem _____ **omniscient** _____.

SYNONYMS: wise, all-knowing
ANTONYMS: ignorant, unknowing

15. panacea
(pan ə sē' ə)

(*n.*) a remedy for all ills; cure-all; an answer to all problems

> You are mistaken if you think that getting more money will be a _____ **panacea** _____ for all your troubles.

SYNONYMS: universal cure, easy solution

16. scrupulous
(skrü' pyə ləs)

(*adj.*) exact, careful, attending thoroughly to details; having high moral standards, principled

> Scientists are trained to record their observations with _____ **scrupulous** _____ accuracy.

SYNONYMS: painstaking, meticulous, conscientious
ANTONYMS: careless, negligent, remiss, dishonest

17. skulk
(skəlk)

(*v.*) to move about stealthily; to lie in hiding

> The burglar _____ **skulked** _____ in the alley looking for a way to get into the darkened jewelry store without attracting the attention of anyone who might be nearby.

SYNONYMS: lurk, slink, prowl

18. supercilious
(sü pər sil' ē əs)

(*adj.*) proud and contemptuous; showing scorn because of a feeling of superiority

> Their _____ **supercilious** _____ attitude toward their servants was extremely offensive.

SYNONYMS: snobbish, patronizing, overbearing
ANTONYMS: humble, meek, deferential, servile

19. uncanny
(ən kan' ē)

(*adj.*) strange, mysterious, weird, beyond explanation

> It is highly unusual for a beginner to display such an _____ **uncanny** _____ skill at playing bridge.

SYNONYMS: eerie, inexplicable, spooky

20. venial
(vē' nē əl)

(*adj.*) easily excused; pardonable

> Someone whose offense is deemed by the judge to be _____ **venial** _____ may be ordered to perform community service.

SYNONYMS: excusable, forgivable
ANTONYMS: inexcusable, unforgivable, unpardonable

Completing the Sentence

From the words for this unit, choose the one that best completes each of the following sentences. Write the word in the space provided.

1. Though I wanted to "let bygones be bygones," I found that I could not wholly _____ **expunge** _____ the bitter memory of their behavior from my mind.

2. If only parents could _____ **bequeath** _____ their hard-won practical wisdom and experience to their children!

3. Our representative offered one simple but _____ **cogent** _____ argument against the proposal: It would raise the cost of living.

4. In the opening scene of the horror film, a shadowy figure dressed in black _____ **skulked** _____ through the graveyard in the moonlight.

5. Your ability to guess what I am thinking about at any given time is nothing short of _____ **uncanny** _____.

6. As we stood on the railway tracks looking off into the distance, the rails seemed to _____ **converge** _____ and meet at some far-off point.

7. Before making our final plans, we should _____ **ascertain** _____ exactly how much money we will have for expenses.

8. When the candidate admitted openly that he had been mistaken in some of his earlier policies, we _____ **esteemed** _____ him more highly than ever.

9. Because our natural resources are _____ **finite** _____ and by no means inexhaustible, we must learn to conserve them.

10. When I saw the pain he caused others and the pleasure he took in doing so, I realized he was a truly _____ **malevolent** _____ person.

11. So long as we remained indoors, we were _____ **invulnerable** _____ to the arctic blasts that swept down on our snowbound cabin.

12. In a situation that would have left me all but helpless with embarrassment, he remained cool and _____ **nonchalant** _____.

13. Isn't it remarkable how quickly a throng of sunbathers will pick up their belongings and _____ **disperse** _____ when a few drops of rain fall?

14. The screening committee investigated not only the candidates themselves but also the organizations with which they were _____ **affiliated** _____.

15. Is there anyone in the world as _____ **supercilious** _____ as a senior who attends a mere sophomore class dance?

16. The more knowledge and wisdom people acquire, the more keenly they become aware that no one is _____ **omniscient** _____.

17. Only by paying _____ **scrupulous** _____ attention to innumerable details were the investigators able to piece together the cause of the accident.

18. Antibiotics were once considered wonder drugs, but we now know that they are not _____panaceas_____ for all our physical ailments.

19. I knew the dean would accept my apology when she characterized my behavior as thoughtless but _____venial_____.

20. Her election to Congress was the _____attainment_____ of a lifelong ambition.

Synonyms

Choose the word from this unit that is **the same** or **most nearly the same** in meaning as the **boldface** word or expression in the given phrase. Write the word on the line provided.

1. no **remedy** for the problems of aging — panacea

2. an **eerie** tale of the supernatural — uncanny

3. must **determine** who is responsible — ascertain

4. **lurked** in the shadows of the old warehouse — skulked

5. **handed down** their knowledge to their apprentices — bequeathed

6. the **fulfillment** of a cherished dream — attainment

7. a **limited** number of choices — finite

8. an **indifferent** shrug of the shoulders — nonchalant

9. **impervious** to normal wear and tear — invulnerable

0. a **painstaking** restoration of the original — scrupulous

1. the **excusable** flaws in a youthful work — venial

2. does not claim to be **all-knowing** — omniscient

3. a cold front that **dispelled** the heat and humidity — dispersed

4. needed to **delete** out-of-date files — expunge

5. made a **compelling** case for government aid — cogent

Antonyms

Choose the word from this unit that is **most nearly opposite** in meaning to the **boldface** word or expression in the given phrase. Write the word on the line provided.

6. shows **contempt** for the achievements of others — esteem

7. opinions that **diverge** along party lines — converge

8. a statement that revealed their **kind** intentions — malevolent

9. behaves in a **deferential** manner — supercilious

0. **unconnected** with a national organization — affiliated

Choosing the Right Word

*Circle the **boldface** word that more satisfactorily completes each of the following sentences.*

1. When I found myself flushed with anger, I realized that I was not so (**scrupulous, invulnerable**) to their bitter sarcasm as I had thought I was!

2. Lincoln said, "If you once forfeit the confidence of your fellow citizens, you can never regain their respect and (**esteem, attainment**)."

3. Vast wealth, elegant clothes, and a (**finite, supercilious**) manner may make a snob, but they do not of themselves make a person a true gentleman or lady.

4. I found your criticism of my conduct unpleasant, but I had to admit that your remarks were (**venial, cogent**).

5. She is the kind of person who has many (**panaceas, attainments**) but seems unable to put them to any practical use.

6. Her bright, optimistic manner did much to (**ascertain, disperse**) the atmosphere of gloom that had settled over the meeting.

7. Nothing he may (**expunge, bequeath**) to the next generation can be more precious than the memory of his long life of honorable public service.

8. Though the couple have spent years studying African history, they do not claim to be (**omniscient, cogent**) in that field.

9. Scientists have concluded that a sudden catastrophe (**expunged, converged**) dinosaurs from the face of the earth.

10. Instead of blaming a (**malevolent, invulnerable**) fate for your failures, why not look for the causes within yourself?

11. The newspaper revealed that the city's chief building inspector was (**omniscient, affiliated**) with a large construction company.

12. Is it true that some dogs have a(n) (**uncanny, nonchalant**) sense of the approach of death?

13. As a member of the grand jury, it is your duty to be (**supercilious, scrupulous**) in weighing every bit of evidence.

14. The critic recognized the book's faults but dismissed them as (**venial, uncanny**) in view of the author's overall achievement.

15. At first, the two candidates were in disagreement on every issue; but as the campaign went on, their opinions seemed to (**disperse, converge**).

16. When I splattered paint on my art teacher, I tried to appear (**nonchalant, malevolent**) but succeeded only in looking horrified.

17. The reform candidate vowed to root out the corruption that (**bequeathed, skulked**) through the corridors of City Hall.

18. Instead of making an informed guess, why not (**ascertain, esteem**) exactly how many students are going on the trip to Washington?

19. Though the journey seemed interminable, I knew that it was (**cogent, finite**) and that I would soon be home.

20. There are so many different factors involved in an energy crisis that no single measure can be expected to serve as a(n) (**panacea, attainment**).

Vocabulary in Context

Read the following passage, in which some of the words you have studied in this unit appear in **boldface** type. Then complete each statement given below the passage by circling the letter of the item that is **the same** or **almost the same** in meaning as the highlighted word.

Gone Forever?

(Line)

One of the great **attainments** of modern medicine was the eradication of smallpox in the late 1970s. The last naturally occurring case of the disease was found in Somalia in Africa in 1977. The disease was declared eliminated by the World Health Organization (WHO), an agency of the United Nations, in May 1980.

(5) Smallpox is a highly contagious viral disease that is spread when invisible droplets from the nose and mouth of an infected person are **dispersed** through the air. About twenty percent of its victims die, and many who survive it are blinded or permanently scarred.

(10) How was smallpox finally **expunged**? The first vaccine was discovered in 1796 by Edward Jenner, a British physician. However, it was not until the twentieth century that a truly effective vaccine was distributed on a wide

(15) scale. Large-scale vaccination eliminated smallpox in the United States and Europe in the 1940s, but no population was **invulnerable** as long as the disease was still active elsewhere. In 1967, hundreds of doctors,

(20) nurses, and scientists **affiliated** with WHO teamed up with health workers in Africa, Asia, and South America to mount a coordinated assault on smallpox. The teams traveled from village to village, isolating the victims and

(25) vaccinating those who came in contact with them. The effort paid off.

Laboratory technician at work

Mass vaccination seemed to be a true **panacea**. The medical community was so confident smallpox was gone forever that all vaccinations were halted in the 1980s. Stockpiles of the vaccine were

(30) destroyed. Very little vaccine is now available, and immunity is on the decline. Could the deadly smallpox cycle begin again?

. The meaning of **attainments** (line 1) is
a. intentions
(c.) achievements
b. mysteries
d. failures

. Dispersed (line 6) most nearly means
(a.) scattered
c. planted
b. observed
d. collected

. Expunged (line 10) is best defined as
a. spread
c. exported
(b.) erased
d. cured

4. The meaning of **invulnerable** (line 17) is
a. insecure
c. endangered
b. infected
(d.) immune

5. Affiliated (line 20) most nearly means
a. friendly
(c.) associated
b. happy
d. angry

6. Panacea (line 28) is best defined as
a. luxury
c. disaster
(b.) cure-all
d. story

Definitions

Note carefully the spelling, pronunciation, part(s) of speech, and definition(s) of each of the following words. Then write the word in the blank space(s) in the illustrative sentence(s) following. Finally, study the lists of synonyms and antonyms given at the end of each entry.

1. altruistic
(al trü is' tik)

(*adj.*) unselfish, concerned with the welfare of others

Most people support _____ **altruistic** _____ programs to help the less fortunate of this world.

SYNONYM: selfless
ANTONYMS: selfish, self-centered

2. assent
(ə sent')

(*v.*) to express agreement; (*n.*) agreement

Workers hope that the threat of a long strike will force management to _____ **assent** _____ to their demands.

Romeo and Juliet knew they would never gain their feuding families' _____ **assent** _____ to marry.

SYNONYMS: (*v.*) concur, consent, accede
ANTONYMS: (*v.*) disagree, differ, dissent

3. benefactor
(ben' ə fak tər)

(*n.*) one who does good to others

Without the help of many _____ **benefactors** _____, most charities would be unable to carry out their work.

SYNONYMS: patron, humanitarian
ANTONYMS: misanthrope, malefactor

4. chivalrous
(shiv' əl rəs)

(*adj.*) marked by honor, courtesy, and courage; knightly

In today's busy world, where people are often heedless of others, a _____ **chivalrous** _____ act is admired by all.

SYNONYMS: gallant, civil, valiant
ANTONYMS: crude, uncouth, churlish, loutish

5. clemency
(klem' ən sē)

(*n.*) mercy, humaneness; mildness, moderateness

Many judges are willing to show _____ **clemency** _____ to first offenders who express regret for their wrongdoing.

SYNONYMS: leniency, forbearance, gentleness
ANTONYMS: harshness, severity, cruelty, inflexibility

6. dearth
(dərth)

(*n.*) a lack, scarcity, inadequate supply; a famine

An employer may complain of a _____ **dearth** _____ of qualified applicants for available jobs.

SYNONYMS: insufficiency, want, paucity
ANTONYMS: surplus, oversupply, glut, abundance

7. diffident
(dif' ə dənt)

(*adj.*) shy, lacking self-confidence; modest, reserved

Many a _____ **diffident** _____ suitor has lost his beloved to a bold rival.

SYNONYMS: timid, bashful, unassertive, withdrawn
ANTONYMS: bold, brash, audacious, self-confident, jaunty

8. discrepancy
(dis krep' ən sē)

(*n.*) a difference; a lack of agreement

_____ **Discrepancies** _____ in the testimony of witnesses to a crime can have a decisive impact on the outcome of a trial.

SYNONYMS: disagreement, divergence, inconsistency
ANTONYMS: agreement, convergence, consistency

9. embark
(em bärk')

(*v.*) to go aboard; to make a start; to invest

Columbus spent years raising money before he was able to _____ **embark** _____ on his perilous ocean voyage in search of a passage to the Far East.

SYNONYMS: commence, launch, begin, board

10. facile
(fas' əl)

(*adj.*) easily done or attained; superficial; ready, fluent; easily shown but not sincerely felt

Writing is a _____ **facile** _____ process for some authors but a laborious task for others.

SYNONYMS: effortless, assured, poised, specious
ANTONYMS: labored, awkward, halting

11. indomitable
(in däm' ət ə bəl)

(*adj.*) unconquerable, refusing to yield

All who hear of the remarkable deeds of Harriet Tubman admire her _____ **indomitable** _____ courage in the face of grave danger.

SYNONYMS: unbeatable, invincible, unyielding
ANTONYMS: surrendering, submissive, yielding

12. infallible
(in fal' ə bəl)

(*adj.*) free from error; absolutely dependable

Some critics seem convinced that their expert knowledge makes them _____ **infallible** _____ judges of the quality of an artist's work.

SYNONYMS: unerring, certain
ANTONYM: imperfect

13. plod
(pläd)

(*v.*) to walk heavily or slowly; to work slowly

After the blizzard, we had to _____ **plod** _____ through deep snowdrifts to reach the nearest stores.

SYNONYMS: lumber, trudge
ANTONYMS: scamper, skip, prance

14. pungent
(pən' jənt)

(*adj.*) causing a sharp sensation; stinging, biting

The kitchen of the French restaurant was filled with the _____ **pungent** _____ aroma of onion soup.

SYNONYMS: sharp, spicy, piquant, caustic, racy
ANTONYMS: bland, unappetizing, colorless, insipid

15. remiss
(rē mis')

(*adj.*) neglectful in performance of one's duty, careless

When I am _____ **remiss** _____ in doing daily chores, I have to spend a big part of the weekend catching up.

SYNONYMS: negligent, lax, slack
ANTONYMS: scrupulous, dutiful, punctilious

16. repose
(rē pōz')

(*v.*) to rest; lie; place; (*n.*) relaxation, peace of mind, calmness

The mortal remains of thousands who fell in America's wars _____ **repose** _____ in Arlington National Cemetery.

After spending all day with others, you may wish for a period of _____ **repose** _____ before dinner.

SYNONYMS: (*v.*) sleep; (*n.*) tranquillity, respite
ANTONYMS: (*n.*) exertion, wakefulness, tumult, bustle, ado

17. temerity
(tə mer' ə tē)

(*n.*) rashness, boldness

Few of his subordinates had the _____ **temerity** _____ to answer the general back.

SYNONYMS: recklessness, foolhardiness, effrontery
ANTONYMS: timidity, fearfulness, diffidence, humility

18. truculent
(trək' yə lənt)

(*adj.*) fierce and cruel; aggressive; deadly, destructive; scathingly harsh

People with _____ **truculent** _____ dispositions can make life miserable for those who have to work with them.

SYNONYMS: brutal, savage, belligerent, vitriolic
ANTONYMS: gentle, mild, meek, unthreatening

19. unfeigned
(ən fānd')

(*adj.*) sincere, real, without pretense

The novelist won high praise for her ability to portray the _____ **unfeigned** _____ emotions of children.

SYNONYMS: genuine, heartfelt
ANTONYMS: insincere, simulated, phony

20. virulent
(vir' yə lənt)

(*adj.*) extremely poisonous; full of malice; spiteful

The First Amendment protects the right of free speech for everyone, even those with _____ **virulent** _____ views that are repugnant to most people.

SYNONYMS: venomous, noxious, baneful, hateful
ANTONYMS: innocuous, harmless, benign

Completing the Sentence

From the words for this unit, choose the one that best completes each of the following sentences. Write the word in the space provided.

1. Doctors attributed the epidemic to the rampant spread of a particularly __virulent__ strain of influenza virus.

2. My parents will not __assent__ to my going to the dance unless I promise faithfully to be home no later than 1:00 A.M.

3. As a school cafeteria guard, I would be __remiss__ in my duties if I failed to report a serious disturbance.

4. We were all impressed by your __facile__ use of unusual words and expressions that you had learned only a few hours before.

5. Humor should be clever and amusing but never so __pungent__ that it hurts the feelings of other people.

6. The pathetic refugees __plodded__ along the dusty road, hoping to reach the Red Cross camp before nightfall.

7. I rarely join in the discussions, not because I lack information and ideas, but rather because I am __diffident__.

8. History tells us that many men and women regarded as failures in their own lifetimes were really major __benefactors__ of humanity.

9. The principal claimed that there were major __discrepancies__ between what actually happened in the school and the way the incident was reported on TV.

10. What good are __altruistic__ principles if no real attempt is made to help people by putting those principles into practice?

11. I did not realize how beautiful the twins were until they fell asleep and I saw their faces in complete __repose__.

12. In view of the many able people in public life today, I do not agree that we are suffering from a(n) __dearth__ of capable leaders.

13. Do you really think it is __chivalrous__ to give your seat to a pretty young woman when an aged lady is standing nearby?

14. Refusing to admit defeat even when things looked completely hopeless, our __indomitable__ football team drove eighty-five yards in the last few minutes to score the winning touchdown.

15. He is not merely unpleasant but actually dangerous whenever he gets into one of his __truculent__ moods.

16. The rash young lieutenant had the __temerity__ to disregard the express orders of the commanding officer.

17. Emphasizing the youth of the convicted man, the defense attorney pleaded for __clemency__.

18. Your _____unfeigned_____ joy when it was announced that I had won the scholarship meant more to me than all the polite congratulations I received.

19. As soon as the last passenger had _____embarked_____, the captain ordered the ship to get under way.

20. The custom of putting erasers on pencils is one way of recognizing the fact that no one is _____infallible_____.

Synonyms

*Choose the word from this unit that is **the same** or **most nearly the same** in meaning as the **boldface** word or expression in the given phrase. Write the word on the line provided.*

1. trudged slowly up the hill	plodded
2. launch a political campaign	embark on
3. faced with a **paucity** of volunteers	dearth
4. found **respite** in the shade of a tree	repose
5. refused to **accede** to the will of the majority	assent
6. selfless dedication to finding a cure	altruistic
7. a **caustic** response to a hostile question	pungent
8. a **brutal** band of hardened criminals	truculent
9. made allowances for the **recklessness** of youth	temerity
10. the spreading of **venomous** rumors	virulent
11. an **unerring** sense of what the public wants	infallible
12. recognized the **difference** between fact and fiction	discrepancy
13. negligent in paying their taxes	remiss
14. the patient's **unconquerable** desire to live	indomitable
15. moved with **effortless** grace	facile

Antonyms

*Choose the word from this unit that is **most nearly opposite** in meaning to the **boldface** word or expression in the given phrase. Write the word on the line provided.*

16. made a **crude** apology for his behavior	chivalrous
17. harshness in judging others	clemency
18. an obviously **insincere** expression of concern	unfeigned
19. wrote a **bold** letter to the person in charge	diffident
20. discovered the identity of the **malefactor**	benefactor

Choosing the Right Word

*Circle the **boldface** word that more satisfactorily completes each of the following sentences.*

1. American Presidents often point to one of their schoolteachers as the (**discrepancy, benefactor**) who helped shape their character and ideas.

2. We soon learned that behind his retiring and (**truculent, diffident**) manner, there was a keen mind and a strong will.

3. In a grim old joke, a man found guilty of murdering his parents appeals for (**clemency, assent**) because he is an orphan.

4. It would be (**indomitable, remiss**) of me, as editor-in-chief of the school newspaper, not to express appreciation for the help of our faculty advisor.

5. After boasting to me of your family's great wealth, how could you have the (**clemency, temerity**) to ask me for a loan?

6. As a state legislator, you should not give your (**assent, chivalry**) to any measure unless you truly believe in it.

7. We breathed a sigh of relief when we saw the supposedly missing set of keys (**plodding, reposing**) in the desk drawer.

8. I admired the speaker's (**remiss, facile**) flow of words, but they failed to convince me that she had practical ideas to help solve our problems.

9. By 1781, George Washington's green recruits of a few years earlier had been forged into an (**infallible, indomitable**) army.

10. With all the deductions for taxes, there is a substantial (**dearth, discrepancy**) between my official salary and my weekly paycheck.

11. Planet Earth is a sort of spaceship on which billions of human beings have (**reposed, embarked**) on a lifelong voyage.

12. Great political leaders know how to appeal to people not only through self-interest but also through their sense of (**temerity, altruism**).

13. She is a popular young woman because people realize that her interest in them is sympathetic and (**remiss, unfeigned**).

14. The critic's (**pungent, facile**) comments during the TV panel show were not only amusing but also very much to the point.

15. You will surely win more support for your view by quiet discussion than by (**truculent, chivalrous**) attacks on your opponents.

16. He is not too well informed on most matters; but when it comes to big-league baseball, he is all but (**indomitable, infallible**).

17. I had no inkling of your deep-seated aversion to pop music until I overheard your (**altruistic, virulent**) comments about it.

18. In the violent world of today's pro football, good sportsmanship and (**pungent, chivalrous**) behavior still have a place.

19. The lawyer (**plodded, embarked**) through hundreds of pages of the trial record, hoping to find some basis for an appeal.

20. How do you account for the (**clemency, dearth**) of old-fashioned family doctors willing to make house calls?

*Read the following passage, in which some of the words you have studied in this unit appear in **boldface** type. Then complete each statement given below the passage by circling the letter of the item that is **the same** or **almost the same** in meaning as the highlighted word.*

The Legend Lives On

(Line)

The original stories of King Arthur and his **chivalrous** Knights of the Round Table were the imaginative creations of 12th- and 13th-century French writers of verse romances. The first great collection of Arthurian material in English, Sir Thomas Malory's *Le Morte Darthur*, was based on these sources. Written about 1470, Malory's work, like its sources, contains a **dearth** of historical fact but a wealth of romantic detail.   (5)

Although Arthur may have been based on an actual 6th-century Celtic chieftain, the figure of legend is far more than a military hero. In the course of the many works written about him, King Arthur has become a symbol of idealism, loyalty, and **indomitable** courage.

Like many legendary heroes, Arthur is born in   (10) exceptional circumstances and grows up in obscurity. The son of King Uther Pendragon, the infant Arthur is placed in the care of the magician Merlin. Because Merlin is paid for his services, he is not entirely **altruistic** in the earlier versions of   (15) the story. His motives remain unclear in later versions as well. For example, he keeps young Arthur ignorant of his royal origins yet makes sure the child is raised as a nobleman.

When King Uther dies without a clear   (20) successor, confusion reigns until a magic sword embedded in a stone is discovered. An inscription on the stone declares that only the rightful heir shall be able to remove the sword. One after another, the nobles try unsuccessfully   (25) to remove the sword. Arthur, knowing nothing of

Tapestry portrait of King Arthur

his parentage, has the **temerity** to step up to the stone and grasp the sword. To the amazement of all, he removes it easily. The nobles then recognize him as king.

Arthur is mortally wounded in a battle with his enemy Mordred. The dying king is carried off into the mist on a barge to the mysterious island of Avalon. But according to   (30) the legend, Arthur may one day return.

---

1. The meaning of **chivalrous** (line 1) is
a. gallant   c. fierce
b. gentle   d. coarse

2. Dearth (line 5) most nearly means
a. abundance   c. thread
b. scarcity   d. pretense

3. Indomitable (line 9) is best defined as
a. reckless   c. faltering
b. moral   d. unyielding

4. The meaning of **altruistic** (line 15) is
a. ambitious   c. harmless
b. unselfish   d. evil

5. Temerity (line 27) most nearly means
a. strength   c. boldness
b. humility   d. skill

Definitions

Note carefully the spelling, pronunciation, part(s) of speech, and definition(s) of each of the following words. Then write the word in the blank space(s) in the illustrative sentence(s) following. Finally, study the lists of synonyms and antonyms given at the end of each entry.

1. accede
(ak sēd')

(*v.*) to yield to; to assume an office or dignity

Management was not willing to _____ **accede** _____ to labor's initial demands, thus increasing the likelihood of a long and bitter strike.

SYNONYMS: consent, concur, comply, assent
ANTONYMS: demur, balk at

2. brandish
(bran' dish)

(*v.*) to wave or flourish in a menacing or vigorous fashion

I _____ **brandished** _____ my umbrella repeatedly in a vain effort to hail an empty cab.

SYNONYMS: swing, shake

3. comprise
(kəm prīz')

(*v.*) to include or contain; to be made up of

Classical symphonies usually _____ **comprise** _____ three or four movements of varying musical form, tempo, and character.

SYNONYMS: compose, constitute, encompass
ANTONYM: exclude

4. deft
(deft)

(*adj.*) skillful, nimble

The _____ **deft** _____ fingers of Spanish nuns produced some of the finest, most delicate lace ever seen.

SYNONYMS: dexterous, adroit, proficient, clever, masterful
ANTONYMS: clumsy, awkward, bungling, inept

5. destitute
(des' tə tüt)

(*adj.*) deprived of the necessities of life; lacking in

Some people fled their homes so suddenly that they arrived at the refugee camp absolutely _____ **destitute** _____.

SYNONYMS: wanting, devoid, impoverished, penniless
ANTONYMS: rich, wealthy, luxurious, bountiful, full, replete

6. explicit
(ek splis' it)

(*adj.*) definite, clearly stated

The more _____ **explicit** _____ your directions are, the easier it will be for all of us to find our way to the campsite.

SYNONYMS: distinct, forthright, unambiguous, clear
ANTONYMS: vague, ambiguous, implied, implicit

7. extirpate
(ek′ stər pāt)

(v.) to tear up by the roots; to destroy totally

We must do everything we can to _____ extirpate _____ racism from American society.

SYNONYMS: uproot, eradicate, wipe out, excise
ANTONYMS: implant, sow, foster, nourish

8. inopportune
(in äp ər tün′)

(adj.) coming at a bad time; not appropriate

Why do my relatives always seem to turn up at the most _____ inopportune _____ time imaginable?

SYNONYMS: ill-timed, inconvenient, inappropriate, unsuitable
ANTONYMS: timely, convenient, felicitous, opportune

9. ironic
(ī rän′ ik)

(adj.) suggesting an incongruity between what might be expected and what actually happens; given to irony, sarcastic

The short stories of O. Henry are famous for their _____ ironic _____ endings.

SYNONYMS: incongruous, satiric, sardonic, wry
ANTONYMS: straightforward, unequivocal

10. musty
(məs′ tē)

(adj.) stale, moldy; out-of-date

Houses that have been closed up for a very long time often have an unpleasantly _____ musty _____ smell about them.

SYNONYMS: hackneyed, antiquated
ANTONYMS: fresh, sweet-smelling, up-to-date, brand-new

11. officious
(ə fish′ əs)

(adj.) meddling; excessively forward in offering services or assuming authority

The manager of the store warned the entire sales force not to be too _____ officious _____ when helping customers.

SYNONYMS: meddlesome, prying, impertinent, obtrusive
ANTONYMS: reserved, diffident, timid, aloof

12. ominous
(äm′ ən əs)

(adj.) unfavorable, threatening, of bad omen

The _____ ominous _____ sound of distant thunder warned us of the storm's approach.

SYNONYMS: unpropitious, inauspicious, portentous
ANTONYMS: propitious, auspicious, promising

13. pinnacle
(pin′ ə kəl)

(n.) a high peak or point

Some pop musicians reach the _____ pinnacle _____ of their careers comparatively early in life.

SYNONYMS: apex, acme, summit, apogee
ANTONYMS: nadir, low point

14. premeditated
(prē med′ ə tāt id)

(*adj., part.*) considered beforehand, deliberately planned

Some crimes are spontaneous acts of passion; others are quite _____ **premeditated** _____.

SYNONYMS: preplanned, rehearsed, calculated, prearranged
ANTONYMS: unplanned, spontaneous, impromptu

15. rampant
(ram′ pənt)

(*adj.*) growing without check, running wild

All kinds of odd rumors run _____ **rampant** _____ during a political campaign.

SYNONYMS: widespread, unrestrained, extravagant, prevalent
ANTONYMS: controlled, restrained

16. solace
(säl′ əs)

(*n.*) comfort, relief; (*v.*) to comfort, console

Many world leaders seek _____ **solace** _____ from the cares of state in the pages of great literature.

I could find no way to _____ **solace** _____ my deeply troubled conscience.

SYNONYMS: (*v.*) soothe, reassure, cheer up
ANTONYMS: (*v.*) vex, aggravate, upset

17. stately
(stāt′ lē)

(*adj.*) dignified, majestic

The _____ **stately** _____ procession slowly wound its way from the palace to the cathedral.

SYNONYMS: grand, magnificent, imposing
ANTONYMS: lowly, humble, servile, abject

18. supple
(səp′ əl)

(*adj.*) bending easily; bending with agility; readily adaptable; servile

Have you ever read Robert Frost's famous poem about swinging on the _____ **supple** _____ branches of a birch tree?

SYNONYMS: flexible, limber, pliable, pliant
ANTONYMS: stiff, rigid, unbending, hidebound

19. suppress
(sə pres′)

(*v.*) to stop by force, put down

Totalitarian governments usually take strong measures to _____ **suppress** _____ free speech.

SYNONYMS: subdue, crush, stifle, squelch, quash, silence
ANTONYMS: provoke, spur, arouse, incite, instigate

20. venal
(vēn′ əl)

(*adj.*) open to or marked by bribery or corruption

The presence of even one _____ **venal** _____ official may jeopardize the integrity of an entire organization.

SYNONYMS: dishonest, bribable, corruptible, mercenary
ANTONYMS: honest, incorruptible, scrupulous

Completing the Sentence

From the words for this unit, choose the one that best completes each of the following sentences. Write the word in the space provided.

1. How can I ever forget that _____**officious**_____ inspector in the customs office who insisted that I empty every piece of luggage before him!

2. We will never _____**accede**_____ to those selfish and unfair terms.

3. The students couldn't _____**suppress**_____ their groans of dismay when the teacher announced a surprise quiz.

4. It is a truly sobering thought to realize that when one has reached the _____**pinnacle**_____ of a mountain, there is nowhere to go but down.

5. A great dancer, like a great athlete, must have a sharp sense of timing and a highly trained, responsive, and _____**supple**_____ body.

6. Accomplished portrait painters can usually reveal a person's character with a few _____**deft**_____ strokes of a brush.

7. I vowed that I would _____**extirpate**_____ every weed that dared to show itself in our newly seeded lawn.

8. The unruly mob retreated as the line of deputies moved forward slowly, _____**brandishing**_____ their riot sticks.

9. "We could not have chosen a more _____**inopportune**_____ spot for our picnic," she observed as she swept ants off the blanket.

10. Who would have dreamed that the cluttered old attic, with all its darkness, dust, and _____**musty**_____ odor, contained such a treasure!

11. The referee gave a(n) _____**explicit**_____ warning that if either team protested her decisions, she would be forced to call a technical foul.

12. Whether your act was _____**premeditated**_____ or the result of carelessness, the fact remains that you have caused great pain to someone who has always been very good to you.

13. How _____**ironic**_____ that they finally inherited all that money at a time when it could no longer help to solve their problems!

14. The sudden drop in temperature and the unnatural stillness in the air were _____**ominous**_____ signs of an unfavorable change in the weather.

15. Attacking the present administration, the candidate said that crime has been _____**rampant**_____ in the streets of our city.

16. Who can forget the sight of those _____**stately**_____ tall ships with their lofty masts and graceful lines as they sailed past the Statue of Liberty on the Fourth of July?

17. Unfortunately, the so-called recreational facilities _____**comprise(d)**_____ nothing more than a card table and a small-screen TV set.

18. In the mid-1800s, "Boss" Tweed controlled New York City through a(n) _____venal_____ political machine that fed on graft and extortion.

19. Airline companies often call in professional grief counselors to help _____solace_____ the families and friends of crash victims.

20. Even when the economy is strong, there are always a large number of _____destitute_____ families in urgent need of assistance.

Synonyms

*Choose the word from this unit that is **the same** or **most nearly the same** in meaning as the **boldface** word or expression in the given phrase. Write the word on the line provided.*

1. the **dignified** language of the Gettysburg Address _____stately_____

2. triumphantly **flourished** the latest poll results _____brandished_____

3. **contains** bits and pieces of longer works _____comprises_____

4. an **incongruous** conclusion to a promising career _____ironic_____

5. left the orphans totally **impoverished** _____destitute_____

6. at the very **summit** of the social scene _____pinnacle_____

7. the **widespread** lawlessness of the times _____rampant_____

8. actions that were obviously **calculated** _____premeditated_____

9. annoyingly **meddlesome** coworkers _____officious_____

10. an **inappropriate** occasion for a feast _____inopportune_____

11. **uproot** evil from our midst _____extirpate_____

12. **soothe** the troubled spirit of a child _____solace_____

13. **subdued** an impulse to cry _____suppressed_____

14. the **mercenary** atmosphere of the campaign _____venal_____

15. not yet ready to **consent** to the proposal _____accede_____

Antonyms

*Choose the word from this unit that is **most nearly opposite** in meaning to the **boldface** word or expression in the given phrase. Write the word on the line provided.*

16. a **fresh**-tasting loaf of bread _____musty_____

17. made **vague** references to the past _____explicit_____

18. a **clumsy** bid for power _____deft_____

19. an extremely **stiff** fabric _____supple_____

20. an **auspicious** development _____ominous_____

Choosing the Right Word

*Circle the **boldface** word that more satisfactorily completes each of the following sentences.*

1. Was Oscar Wilde being (**ironic,** deft) when he said that he could resist everything except temptation?

2. There's a world of difference between a helpful research assistant and an (**explicit, officious**) one!

3. She has the kind of (**supple,** venal) personality that can easily adapt itself to a wide variety of needs and conditions.

4. During the darkest hours of defeat, their only (**solace,** pinnacle) was the knowledge that they had fought hard to the very end.

5. If the law is intended to limit nonessential use of gasoline and heating oil, it should state this (**explicitly,** ironically).

6. He is in for a rude awakening if he thinks that as the son of a rich family, he will simply (**accede,** suppress) to a position of wealth and power.

7. No matter how ticklish the situation, the hero of the cartoon always devised some (**deft,** rampant) maneuver to avoid capture.

8. The actress felt that she had reached the (**pinnacle,** solace) of fame when the principal of her former school asked for her autograph.

9. They tried to explain away their racial slur as a slip of the tongue, but in my opinion it was deliberate and (**premeditated,** ominous).

10. Coming at a time when I was flat broke, your suggestion that we have a bite to eat and go to the movies was highly (officious, **inopportune**).

11. Even in the concentration camps, some basic feelings of decency and humanity were not completely (brandished, **extirpated**).

12. We were prepared for a sharp scolding but not for the (**ominous,** inopportune) silence with which the principal greeted us.

13. His speech at first seemed highly dramatic and impressive, but we soon realized that he was quite (destitute, **musty**) of new ideas.

14. The way he (**brandishes,** comprises) his facts and figures reminds me of a butcher swinging a meat cleaver.

15. Someone who insists that everyone has a price believes that human beings are (premeditated, **venal**) by nature.

16. No doubt there are some dishonest officials, but it is a gross exaggeration to say that graft and corruption are (**rampant,** explicit) in our government.

17. Eliza Doolittle was a poor flower seller, but she learned to conduct herself with the (supple, **stately**) bearing of a princess.

18. The only sure way to (**suppress,** brandish) social unrest is to make possible a decent, secure life for all the people.

19. Let's prepare a joint statement that will (accede, **comprise**) the various objections of all civic groups to the freeway plan.

20. I have no patience with (**musty,** stately) old ideas about family roles based on gender.

Vocabulary in Context

*Read the following passage, in which some of the words you have studied in this unit appear in **boldface** type. Then complete each statement given below the passage by circling the letter of the item that is **the same** or **almost the same** in meaning as the highlighted word.*

(Line)

The Road to Freedom

The Underground Railroad assisted African American slaves to escape to freedom in the North and Canada. However, it was neither a railroad nor underground. Rather, it was a loose association that **comprised** both blacks and whites in the North and the South. This network secretly aided runaway slaves on their journey north.

(5) The effort began in the early 1800s and reached its **pinnacle** in the 1850s. Slaves were the absolute property of their owners, and owners had the right to use any means to recapture those who tried to flee. The Fugitive Slave Act of 1850 made it a crime to help a

(10) slave to escape. Runaways and their guides had to travel by night through dangerous terrain, often pursued by armed men and dogs.

One of the most famous

(15) "conductors" on the Underground Railroad was a runaway slave herself. Harriet Tubman escaped in 1849. She returned to the South nineteen times to help others flee.

(20) Having been taught about the

Forward by Jacob Lawrence, 1967

woods by her father when she was a child, Harriet Tubman was a **deft** guide. Fearless and determined, she always carried a gun on her missions and was willing to **brandish** it if a frightened runaway tried to turn back. Tubman led about 300 people, including her parents, to freedom and was never caught herself.

(25) The "stations" on the Underground Railroad were houses where fugitive slaves were given food and shelter. There they also found welcome **solace** from their lonely and dangerous journeys. One of the most famous of these safe houses was the Indiana home of a Quaker named Levi Coffin. He aided more than 3,000 men and women. Other frequently traveled routes passed through the state of Ohio, the

(30) city of Philadelphia, and the Great Lakes region into Canada. Before slavery was **extirpated** at the end of the Civil War (1861–1865), an estimated 100,000 African Americans escaped to freedom using the Underground Railroad.

---

1. The meaning of **comprised** (line 3) is
a. hired
b. excluded
c. deprived
d. included

2. Pinnacle (line 5) most nearly means
a. apex
b. start
c. nadir
d. end

3. Deft (line 21) is best defined as
a. clumsy
b. skillful
c. daring
d. willing

4. The meaning of **brandish** (line 23) is
a. fire
b. wave
c. surrender
d. conceal

5. Solace (line 26) most nearly means
a. ammunition
b. advice
c. relief
d. rest

6. Extirpated (line 31) is best defined as
a. modified
b. debated -
c. upheld
d. eradicated

 **Analogies**

In each of the following, circle the item that best completes the comparison.

See pages T38–T48 for explanations of answers.

1. cogent is to **favorable** as
a. venal is to unfavorable
b. officious is to favorable
c omniscient is to unfavorable
d. ominous is to favorable

2. extirpate is to **end** as
a. suppress is to begin
b. plod is to end
c. embark is to begin
d. comprise is to end

3. solace is to **grief** as
a. wound is to bandage
b. bequeath is to property
c. repose is to weariness
d. clemency is to justice

4. officious is to **meddlesome** as
a. virulent is to harmless
b. altruistic is to mercenary
c. stately is to clumsy
d. diffident is to bashful

5. attainment is to **achievement** as
a. panacea is to disease
b. clemency is to cruelty
c. temerity is to cowardice
d. dearth is to scarcity

6. malevolent is to **unfavorable** as
a. supple is to favorable
b. unfeigned is to unfavorable
c. truculent is to favorable
d. deft is to unfavorable

7. plod is to **quick** as
a. trudge is to heavy
b. sprint is to swift
c. scamper is to slow
d. skip is to light

8. snob is to **supercilious** as
a. pauper is to venial
b. benefactor is to malevolent
c. thief is to nonchalant
d. knight is to chivalrous

9. assent is to **reject** as
a. accede is to comply
b. bequeath is to inherit
c. ascertain is to scrutinize
d. expunge is to erase

10. pinnacle is to **high** as
a. strait is to wide
b. plateau is to steep
c. ocean is to shallow
d. abyss is to deep

11. invulnerable is to **wound** as
a. infallible is to collapse
b. indomitable is to conquer
c. inopportune is to risk
d. insidious is to destroy

12. crime is to **premeditated** as
a. purpose is to prevented
b. guilt is to presumed
c. idea is to preconceived
d. discrepancy is to prescribed

13. brandish is to **sword** as
a. string is to kite
b. wave is to flag
c. inflate is to balloon
d. board is to airplane

14. converge is to **together** as
a. esteem is to below
b. disperse is to apart
c. assent is to above
d. skulk is to beyond

15. infallible is to **mistaken** as
a. ominous is to impervious
b. explicit is to finite
c. scrupulous is to remiss
d. stately is to arrogant

16. pungent is to **odor** as
a. vivid is to sound
b. musty is to appearance
c. unkempt is to feeling
d. spicy is to taste

17. destitute is to **wealthy** as
a. altruistic is to self-centered
b. scrupulous is to meticulous
c. supercilious is to energetic
d. cogent is to clever

18. rampant is to **much** as
a. opulence is to none
b. dearth is to much
c. destitute is to none
d. negligible is to much

Word Associations

In each of the following groups, circle the word that is best defined or suggested by the given phrase.

1. someone who contributes to many charities
a. venal
b. diffident
c. cogent
(d. altruistic)

2. What gall!
a. esteem
b. irony
(c. temerity)
d. nonchalance

3. humane treatment of a defeated enemy
a. dearth
(b. clemency)
c. solace
d. irony

4. all-purpose remedy
(a. panacea)
b. pinnacle
c. benefactor
d. clemency

5. carefully planned
(a. premeditated)
b. finite
c. uncanny
d. facile

6. showing good breeding
a. venal
b. supercilious
(c. chivalrous)
d. officious

7. give in to the enemy's demands
a. bequeath
(b. accede)
c. brandish
d. comprise

8. smooth-talking
a. cogent
b. ironic
(c. facile)
d. diffident

9. to include or be made up of
a. plod
b. brandish
(c. comprise)
d. converge

10. two different accounts of the same event
a. dearth
b. assent
c. esteem
(d. discrepancy)

11. Order now! Quantities are limited.
a. venial
(b. finite)
c. venal
d. uncanny

12. abounding
a. scrupulous
b. venial
(c. rampant)
d. nonchalant

13. negligent of one's duty
a. diffident
(b. remiss)
c. omniscient
d. infallible

14. loiter suspiciously
(a. skulk)
b. disperse
c. plod
d. expunge

15. held in high regard
(a. esteem)
b. discrepancy
c. temerity
d. pinnacle

16. plain and clear
a. pungent
(b. explicit)
c. truculent
d. ironic

17. a shortage of supplies
a. clemency
(b. dearth)
c. truculence
d. solace

18. like the air in a room long closed up
a. nonchalant
b. cogent
c. deft
(d. musty)

19. beyond explanation
a. supercilious
(b. uncanny)
c. omniscient
d. infallible

20. how one might describe a harsh and aggressive person
a. altruistic
(b. truculent)
c. musty
d. indomitable

Vocabulary in Context

*Read the following passage, in which some of the words you have studied in Units 4–6 appear in **boldface** type. Then complete each statement given below the passage by circling the item that is **the same** or **almost the same** in meaning as the highlighted word.*

Butterfly Gardening

(Line)

Butterfly populations are on the decline around the world, mainly because of the loss of habitat and the use of pesticides. But there is
(5) something you can do right in your own backyard to help reverse this trend. With a little time and effort, you can create a welcoming environment in which these
(10) beautiful creatures can find food and lay their eggs in safety.

Your first step is to **ascertain** which species of flowers attract the butterflies that are native to your
(15) area. These insects are drawn to brightly colored, nectar-rich flowers that have a strong scent. Butterflies see more color than humans do, and they have a finely tuned sense of
(20) smell. They are said to be able to identify their favorite plants from miles away. They also need trees, shrubs, and leafy green plants on which to lay their eggs and on which
(25) hatched caterpillars can feed.

Next you will want to give some thought to the arrangement of the shrubs and flowers you plant. For example, **stately** trees and shrubs
(30) such as cottonwood, tulip poplar,

lantana, privet, and hibiscus may be combined with shorter, more **supple** flowering plants such as bee balm, borage, and lavender to provide
(35) protection as well as food.

An abundance of varied types of flowering plants is the best possible magnet you can use. But you need not be **scrupulous** about separating
(40) flowers into isolated, symmetrical beds of similar species or colors. Nor do you need to work as hard as other gardeners to **suppress** weeds and wildflowers. Even crabgrass provides
(45) food for some species of caterpillars.

Butterflies cannot regulate their own body temperatures; so be sure to plant your garden in a sunny spot. Include some rocks or other
(50) exposed surfaces on which butterflies can **repose**, with wings outstretched to soak up the sun. Butterflies can also benefit from windbreaks and sheltered places
(55) where they can hide from the elements and sleep at night.

1. The meaning of **ascertain** (line 12) is
a. eliminate　c. memorize
b. discover　d. describe

2. Stately (line 29) most nearly means
a. modest　c. slender
b. imposing　d. colorful

3. Supple (line 32) is best defined as
a. limber　c. commonplace
b. statuesque　d. exotic

4. The meaning of **scrupulous** (line 39) is
a. relaxed　c. timid
b. excited　d. painstaking

5. Suppress (line 43) most nearly means
a. irrigate　c. stifle
b. spread　d. promote

6. Repose (line 51) is best defined as
a. display　c. signal
b. rest　d. flutter

Choosing the Right Meaning

Read each sentence carefully. Then circle the item that best completes the statement below the sentence.

See pages T38–T48 for explanations of answers.

A foreign policy that is truly supple can both defend American interests abroad and respond successfully to unforeseen challenges. (2)

1. The word **supple** in line 1 is best defined as
(a. adaptable)   b. superior   c. farsighted   d. bendable

History will never truly know how many lives were expunged in the intertribal holocaust that overwhelmed Rwanda in the 1990s. (2)

2. The word **expunged** in line 1 most nearly means
a. affected   b. deleted   c. canceled   (d. destroyed)

"No one as scrupulous as she is would ever consent to be party to such an obvious piece of sharp practice," I protested. (2)

3. In line 1 the word **scrupulous** most nearly means
a. religious   (b. principled)   c. finicky   d. knowledgeable

In his student days before World War I, J. R. R. Tolkien embarked on the fantastic literary voyage that produced *The Lord of the Rings*. (2)

4. The words **embarked on** in line 1 most nearly mean
a. got aboard   b. considered   (c. commenced)   d. wound up

At the critical moment the British Empire reposed its entire hope of safety in the abilities of a single one-armed, one-eyed sailor. (2)

5. In line 1 the word **reposed** most nearly means
a. misplaced   b. gambled   (c. put)   d. relaxed

Antonyms

In each of the following groups, circle the word or expression that is most nearly the **opposite** of the word in **boldface** type.

1. accede
(a. demur)
b. brandish
c. suppress
d. bequeath

2. inopportune
a. uncanny
(b. convenient)
c. invulnerable
d. cogent

3. altruistic
a. venial
(b. selfish)
c. false
d. remiss

4. extirpate
a. convene
b. imprison
c. trust
(d. implant)

5. supercilious
a. untimely
b. dormant
(c. humble)
d. stately

6. deft
a. affiliated
b. invulnerable
c. remiss
(d. clumsy)

7. embark
a. suppress
(b. conclude)
c. extirpate
d. accede

8. plod
(a. scamper)
b. assent
c. esteem
d. ascertain

9. ominous
a. indomitable
b. favorable (circled)
c. deft
d. diffident

11. stately
a. disloyal
b. quiet
c. truculent
d. undignified (circled)

13. cogent
a. stately
b. officious
c. explicit
d. unconvincing (circled)

15. unfeigned
a. pretended (circled)
b. lively
c. genuine
d. infallible

10. diffident
a. mild
b. bold (circled)
c. destitute
d. supple

12. nonchalant
a. supple
b. embarrassed (circled)
c. ominous
d. ironic

14. venial
a. incorruptible
b. inexcusable (circled)
c. indomitable
d. unbiased

16. musty
a. valorous
b. explicit
c. pungent
d. fresh (circled)

Word Families

A. On the line provided, write the word you have learned in Units 4–6 that is related to each of the following nouns.

EXAMPLE: embarkation—**embark**

1. destituteness, destitution — destitute
2. malevolence — malevolent
3. bequeathal, bequest — bequeath
4. stateliness — stately
5. chivalrousness, chivalry — chivalrous
6. suppressor, suppression, suppressibility, suppressiveness, suppressant — suppress
7. virulence, virulency — virulent
8. pungency — pungent
9. nonchalance — nonchalant
10. invulnerableness, invulnerability — invulnerable
11. disperser, dispersion, dispersal, dispersant, dispersiveness — disperse
12. ominousness, omen — ominous
13. irony, ironicalness — ironic
14. convergence, convergency — converge
15. omniscience — omniscient

B. On the line provided, write the word you have learned in Units 4–6 that is related to each of the following verbs.

EXAMPLE: attain—**attainment**

16. facilitate — facile
17. feign — feigned
18. scruple — scrupulous
19. premeditate — premeditated
20. affiliate — affiliated

Two-Word Completions

Circle the pair of words that best complete the meaning of each of the following passages.

See pages T38–T48 for explanations of answers.

1. During the long years that the painter struggled to _____ fame, his talents never failed him. However, once he had actually achieved the public _____ that he sought, they began to desert him.

    a. attain . . . esteem *(circled)*
    b. comprise . . . nonchalance
    c. suppress . . . clemency
    d. ascertain . . . pinnacle

2. The salesman pressed me to sign the contract, but I refused to give my _____ to the agreement until all the terms and provisions he so vaguely mentioned were spelled out _____.

    a. discrepancy . . . cogently
    b. esteem . . . officiously
    c. temerity . . . scrupulously
    d. assent . . . explicitly *(circled)*

3. The senator found some _____ after her electoral defeat in the comforting knowledge that she would now be able to enjoy a life of _____, far from the strife of the political arena.

    a. esteem . . . temerity
    b. solace . . . repose *(circled)*
    c. panacea . . . dearth
    d. clemency . . . destitution

4. While it is true that human beings are neither _____ nor _____, they can certainly use what they do know to avoid making foolish or unnecessary mistakes.

    a. diffident . . . supercilious
    b. omniscient . . . infallible *(circled)*
    c. altruistic . . . malevolent
    d. indomitable . . . invulnerable

5. Pundits were quick to note the _____ when the councilman, who had campaigned on a reform platform, was discovered to be every bit as _____ as the corrupt bosses he had railed against.

    a. clemency . . . rampant
    b. discrepancy . . . venial
    c. attainment . . . altruistic
    d. irony . . . venal *(circled)*

6. The school trustees gave up their attempt to _____ the identify of the donor when an intermediary explained that the mysterious _____ wished to remain anonymous.

    a. comprise . . . affiliation
    b. accede . . . attainment
    c. ascertain . . . benefactor *(circled)*
    d. esteem . . . bequest

7. Nineteenth-century hucksters touted their elixirs as _____ for every ailment imaginable. Unfortunately, these concoctions often proved more _____ than the maladies they were supposed to cure.

    a. benefactors . . . musty
    b. pinnacles . . . ominous
    c. panaceas . . . virulent *(circled)*
    d. attainments . . . pungent

Building with Classical Roots

fac, fact—to make or do

This root appears in **facile**, "easily accomplished or done" (page 59). Some other words based on the same root are listed below.

artifact	faction	factor	faculty
facility	factitious	factual	malefactor

From the list of words above, choose the one that corresponds to each of the brief definitions below. Write the word in the blank space in the illustrative sentence below the definition.

1. one who commits a crime, evildoer ("*one who does evil*")

The _____ **malefactors** _____ will stand trial for their terrible deeds.

2. a teaching staff; the ability to act or to do something

A school may be known for its outstanding science _____ **faculty** _____.

3. one of the elements that help to bring about a result; an agent

The ability to work together was a major _____ **factor** _____ in the group's success.

4. based on fact, real

Our assignment is to write a detailed _____ **factual** _____ report on the presidential election.

5. an object of historical or archaeological interest produced by human workmanship ("*something made with skill*")

The museum has an outstanding collection of _____ **artifacts** _____ from the pre-Columbian period.

6. a small group of people within a larger group

The Senate _____ **faction** _____ that opposed the president's budget was soundly defeated.

7. artificial, not natural; sham

The enthusiasm of those cheering infomercial audiences seems to me to be _____ **factitious** _____.

8. ease, skill; that which serves or acts as a convenience or for a specific function

By the time he was five years old, Mozart could play the piano with great _____ **facility** _____.

From the list of words above, choose the one that best completes each of the following sentences. Write the word in the space provided.

1. President Theodore Roosevelt criticized certain rich men as evildoers, calling them " _____ **malefactors** _____ of great wealth."

2. We are dealing not with opinions or interpretations but with a simple matter of _____factual_____ accuracy.

3. What was once a united political party has been splintered into two or three warring _____factions_____.

4. The speaker pointed out a number of ways in which we could raise the money necessary to expand the library _____facilities_____ in our community.

5. His major weakness, which keeps him from a position of leadership, is a complete lack of the _____faculty_____ of self-criticism.

6. What seems to be strong popular support for that program is in reality shallow and _____factitious_____.

7. The _____artifacts_____ of ancient cultures tell us a great deal about the day-to-day life of earlier civilizations.

8. Television has become a key _____factor_____ in determining public opinion and shaping popular tastes.

---

*Circle the **boldface** word that more satisfactorily completes each of the following sentences.*

1. A diplomat must have a(n) (**artifact, faculty**) for communicating tactfully with both allies and enemies.

2. In social situations, politeness may require a (**factitious, factual**) show of interest in the topic of conversation.

3. Some people are able to master foreign languages with remarkable (**facility, faculty**), but others find the process quite difficult.

4. The opposing (**faction, malefactors**) on the city council argued bitterly over a proposed increase in property taxes.

5. Over the centuries, many priceless (**artifacts, facilities**) have been stolen from the tombs of Egypt's pharaohs.

6. The increase in air pollution was a key (**faction, factor**) in the decision to ban automobile traffic from the heart of the downtown shopping district.

7. The jury decided that the prosecution had not presented sufficient (**factual, factitious**) evidence to prove the defendant guilty as charged.

8. Some readers find the (**malefactors, artifacts**) in the novels of Charles Dickens more interesting than the heroes.

Read the following sentences, paying special attention to the words and phrases underlined. From the words in the box below, find better choices for these underlined words and phrases. Then use these choices to rewrite the sentences.

WORD BANK

accede	brandish	deftly	esteem	panacea
assent	comprise	destitute	facile	pinnacle
attainment	converge	discrepancy	invulnerable	plod
bequeath	dearth	embark	ironic	remiss

The Great Wall

1. The Great Wall is considered by some to represent the culminating point of Chinese ingenuity.

  pinnacle _____

_____

2. Chinese emperors believed that the Wall would make their kingdoms indestructible to attacks by northern barbarians.

  invulnerable _____

_____

3. Because there was a scarcity and insufficiency of workers available, thousands of peasants and intellectuals were conscripted as forced labor.

  dearth _____

_____

4. Workers marched steadily and laboriously through inclement weather to compress inches of dirt within wooden frames, layer after layer, until the inches added up to yards

  plodded _____

_____

5. In the second century B.C., merchants from all over the globe moved toward a meeting point on the Great Wall.

  converged _____

_____

6. Though its deep suspicion of foreigners led it to close China off from the West, the Ming Dynasty is generally held in high opinion.

  esteem _____

_____

7. Though it may not have been the remedy for all internal and external problems that the emperors hoped, the Great Wall served its purpose.

  panacea _____

_____

Analogies

In each of the following, circle the item that best completes the comparison.

See pages T38–T48 for explanations of answers.

1. resources are to **destitute** as
a. plots are to insidious
b. bribes are to venal
c. guises are to incognito
d. relatives are to bereft

2. grimace is to **pain** as
a. nod is to assent
b. yawn is to exhilaration
c. wink is to nostalgia
d. squint is to nonchalance

3. indomitable is to **overcome** as
a. infallible is to solace
b. impervious is to penetrate
c. insidious is to coerce
d. invulnerable is to heal

4. eyes are to **scrutinize** as
a. fingers are to redress
b. feet are to plod
c. ears are to brandish
d. toes are to muse

5. cogent is to **force** as
a. opulent is to poverty
b. facile is to effort
c. urbane is to modesty
d. pungent is to bite

6. pliable is to **fold** as
a. remiss is to twist
b. unkempt is to comb
c. supple is to bend
d. uncanny is to explain

7. pinnacle is to **loom** as
a. attainment is to extend
b. chasm is to gape
c. sojourn is to embark
d. path is to converge

8. memory is to **expunge** as
a. artifice is to deceive
b. gibe is to extol
c. sentence is to delete
d. experiment is to retrogress

9. deft is to **adroit** as
a. inclement is to balmy
b. punitive is to punishable
c. truculent is to belligerent
d. omniscient is to infallible

10. wary is to **caution** as
a. stolid is to insight
b. meticulous is to care
c. cursory is to diligence
d. tentative is to firmness

Choosing the Right Meaning

Read each sentence carefully. Then circle the item that best completes the statement below the sentence.

See pages T38–T48 for explanations of answers.

f a piece of evidence is not cogent—that is, if it does not speak to the matter at hand—no court in the land will admit it. (2)

1. The word **cogent** is used in line 1 to mean
a. convincing   b. relevant   c. genuine   d. hearsay

As the heavens poured forth their tears, the bereft parents slowly followed the iny casket through the gates of the cemetery. (2)

2. The word **bereft** in line 1 is best defined as
a. grief-stricken through loss   b. lacking in resources   c. financially embarrassed   d. deprived of strength

His only reply to my suggestion was an ironic smile that made me feel slightly oolish and very uncomfortable. (2)

3. The word **ironic** in line 1 most nearly means

    a. witty   (b. sarcastic)   c. remarkable   d. poignant

"No matter how you cut it," Sancho Panza replied, "a chivalrous enterprise does
not normally end in a joust with windmills."   (2)

4. The item that best defines the word **chivalrous** in line 1 is

    a. civil   b. gracious   c. courteous   (d. knightly)

As his troops deployed, Wellington noticed a gap opening on his left flank and
quickly gave orders to close it.   (2)

5. In line 1 the word **deployed** most nearly means

    a. prepared for a   b. marched briskly   (c. formed up for   d. stood at
       fight   past   battle)   attention

Two-Word Completions

Circle the pair of words that best complete the meaning of each of the following sentences.

See pages T38–T48 for explanations of answers.

1. Most dictators eventually resort to open violence and _____ in their
relentless attempts to root out resistance or _____ opposition to
their regimes.

    a. nostalgia . . . harass   c. quintessence . . . suppress
    b. artifice . . . adulterate   (d. coercion . . . extirpate)

2. Though few panaceas work all the time, a trip to the barber is an _____
remedy for the great _____ of this world.

    a. indomitable . . . unfeigned   (c. infallible . . . unkempt)
    b. inopportune . . . uncanny   d. invulnerable . . . unpremeditated

3. In a(n) _____ gesture of reconciliation reminiscent of the
magnanimous knights of old, Abraham Lincoln declared that the federal
government would take no _____ or retaliatory measures against
former supporters of the Confederacy.

    a. ironic . . . venial   c. craven . . . inopportune
   (b. chivalrous . . . punitive)   d. altruistic . . . tentative

4. The famous chef often spoke of his truly prodigious _____
knowledge as a precious heirloom that he wished to _____
somehow to future generations of cooks all over the world.

   (a. culinary . . . bequeath)   c. opulent . . . perpetuate
    b. omniscient . . . accede   d. cursory . . . deploy

5. For the umpteenth time the speaker wearily _____ her reasons for
running as an independent candidate who is in no way _____ any
organized political party in this country.

    a. ascertained . . . jeopardized by   c. brandished . . . extirpated from
    b. augmented . . . alienated from   (d. reiterated . . . affiliated with)

Enriching Your Vocabulary

Read the passage below. Then complete the exercise at the bottom of the page.

Thanks to the French

Modern English is sprinkled with words that have their origins in other languages. The word *adroit* (Unit 2), for example, comes virtually unchanged from the French *a droit*, which literally means "according to the right." The French word in turn stems from the Latin *dexter*, which is also the root from which *ambidextrous* (Unit 1) derives. (Note that one of the synonyms given for *adroit* is *dexterous*.) It is also interesting to note that from the French word for left comes the English word *gauche*, which means "blundering or tactless." In many languages, words associated with left are unfavorable in connotation. The Latin word *sinister*, for example, originally meant "left"; but it also came to mean, as the same word now does in English, "evil" or "ominous." Why? Probably because in Ancient Rome an omen seen from the left was thought to be unlucky.

The Louvre Museum is on the right bank, or *rive droite*, of the Seine.

When it entered the English language in the seventeenth century, *adroit* was probably pronounced as the French would pronounce it. But over the centuries its pronunciation has been anglicized; and if heard today on the streets of Paris, it would not be recognized by most Parisians as a word "borrowed" from their native tongue.

In Column A below are 10 more words for which we have to thank the French. With or without a dictionary, match each of these words with its meaning in Column B.

Column A

_i_	**1.**	verve
_d_	**2.**	boutique
_f_	**3.**	rendezvous
_e_	**4.**	etiquette
_g_	**5.**	penchant
_a_	**6.**	hors d'oeuvres
_j_	**7.**	nuance
_b_	**8.**	fracas
_h_	**9.**	charade
_c_	**10.**	rapport

Column B

a. appetizers
b. a noisy quarrel
c. harmony and good will
d. a small specialty store
e. correct behavior
f. a meeting or meeting place
g. a liking or inclination
h. a pretense
i. enthusiasm and spirit
j. a subtle difference or quality

Note carefully the spelling, pronunciation, part(s) of speech, and definition(s) of each of the following words. Then write the word in the blank space(s) in the illustrative sentence(s) following. Finally, study the lists of synonyms and antonyms given at the end of each entry.

1. abhor
(ab hôr′)

(*v.*) to regard with horror or loathing; to hate deeply

A pacifist is someone who _____ **abhors** _____ violence in all its forms.

SYNONYMS: detest, despise, abominate
ANTONYMS: admire, cherish, respect, relish

2. amend
(ə mend′)

(*v.*) to change in a formal way; to change for the better

If you are not doing well in a particular subject, you may want to _____ **amend** _____ your way of studying it.

SYNONYMS: modify, improve, correct

3. buffet
(bəf′ ət)

(*v.*) to slap or cuff; to strike repeatedly; to drive or force with blows; to force one's way with difficulty; (*n.*) a slap, blow

Blinding snowstorms _____ **buffet** _____ the barren landmass of Antarctica for months on end.

Few figures in history or literature are as severely tested by fortune's _____ **buffets** _____ as Job in the Old Testament.

SYNONYMS: (*v.*) batter, sock, thump, pummel, toss about

4. chaos
(kā′ äs)

(*n.*) great confusion, disorder

A great many people lost their fortunes and even their lives in the _____ **chaos** _____ brought on by the French Revolution.

SYNONYMS: anarchy, turmoil, pandemonium
ANTONYMS: order, regularity, tranquillity

5. commodious
(kə mō′ dē əs)

(*adj.*) roomy, spacious

No one would expect a tiny studio apartment to have particularly _____ **commodious** _____ closets.

SYNONYMS: comfortable, ample, capacious
ANTONYMS: cramped, claustrophobic, insufficient

6. corrosive
(kə rō′ siv)

(*adj.*) eating away gradually, acidlike; bitterly sarcastic

Sulfuric acid is one of the most _____ **corrosive** _____ substances known to chemistry.

SYNONYMS: caustic, mordant, acidulous, spiteful
ANTONYMS: bland, mild, benign, amiable

7. discern
(di sərn′)

(v.) to see clearly, recognize

It is a jury's job to _____ discern _____ the truth by carefully evaluating all the evidence presented at trial.

SYNONYMS: perceive, detect, distinguish
ANTONYM: overlook

8. extant
(ek′ stənt)

(adj.) still existing; not exterminated, destroyed, or lost

The paintings of animals and human hands in Spain's Altamira caves are among the oldest _____ extant _____ specimens of Stone Age art.

SYNONYMS: surviving, in existence
ANTONYMS: extinct, defunct, vanished

9. implicate
(im′ plə kāt)

(v.) to involve in; to connect with or be related to

The suspects never stood trial because there was no solid evidence to _____ implicate _____ them in the daring series of robberies.

SYNONYMS: incriminate, entangle
ANTONYMS: absolve, exculpate

0. inter
(in tər′)

(v.) to bury, commit to the earth; to consign to oblivion

Jewels and other objects once _____ interred _____ with Egypt's pharaohs can now be seen in numerous museums all over the world.

ANTONYMS: unearth, exhume

1. martinet
(mär tə net′)

(n.) a strict disciplinarian; a stickler for the rules

When it came to drilling troops, the Revolutionary War general Baron Friedrich von Steuben was something of a _____ martinet _____ .

SYNONYMS: taskmaster, slave driver

2. obviate
(äb′ vē āt)

(v.) to anticipate and prevent; to remove, dispose of

Vaccinations can do much to _____ obviate _____ the dangers of childhood illnesses.

SYNONYMS: preclude, forestall, ward off

3. renegade
(ren′ ə gād)

(n.) one who leaves a group; a deserter, outlaw; (adj.) traitorous; unconventional, unorthodox

Many a writer has been labeled a _____ renegade _____ for refusing to conform to society's conventions.

_____ Renegade _____ senators from the President's own party joined the opposition to defeat the bill.

SYNONYMS: (n.) turncoat, defector, heretic
ANTONYMS: (n.) loyalist, patriot

14. reprehensible
(rep rē hen′ sə bəl)

(*adj.*) deserving blame or punishment

Stalin eliminated many potential rivals by accusing them of all sorts of _____ **reprehensible** _____ acts that they did not commit.

SYNONYMS: objectionable, blameworthy, culpable, odious
ANTONYMS: commendable, blameless, meritorious

15. somber
(säm′ bər)

(*adj.*) dark, gloomy; depressed or melancholy in spirit

The atmosphere in the locker room of the losing team could best be described as _____ **somber** _____.

SYNONYMS: mournful, dismal
ANTONYMS: bright, sunny, lighthearted, cheerful, jaunty

16. squalid
(skwäl′ id)

(*adj.*) filthy, wretched, debased

Many laws prohibit the types of _____ **squalid** _____ working conditions found in sweatshops.

SYNONYMS: dingy, sordid, foul, vile, abject
ANTONYMS: neat, spruce, exalted, lofty

17. turbulent
(tər′ byə lənt)

(*adj.*) disorderly, riotous, violent; stormy

Letters and diary entries may reveal a person's lifelong struggle to gain some control over _____ **turbulent** _____ emotions.

SYNONYMS: tumultuous, unruly, agitated
ANTONYMS: calm, placid, tranquil, still

18. vociferous
(vō sif′ ə rəs)

(*adj.*) loud and noisy; compelling attention

Relief agencies regularly make _____ **vociferous** _____ appeals for aid for victims of war, terrorism, and natural disasters.

SYNONYMS: clamorous, uproarious, blustering
ANTONYMS: quiet, soft-spoken, muted, subdued

19. voluminous
(və lü′ mə nəs)

(*adj.*) of great size; numerous; writing or speaking at great length

The task of summarizing the _____ **voluminous** _____ reports issued by government agencies may fall to members of a legislator's staff.

SYNONYMS: bulky, massive, copious, plentiful
ANTONYMS: scant, meager, brief, succinct

20. waive
(wāv)

(*v.*) to do without, give up voluntarily; to put off temporarily, defer

The senator agreed to _____ **waive** _____ opposition to the proposed bill if some of its more controversial provisions were substantially modified.

SYNONYMS: decline, relinquish, forgo
ANTONYMS: claim, accept

Completing the Sentence

From the words for this unit, choose the one that best completes each of the following sentences. Write the word in the space provided.

1. A person who has been _____ **buffeted** _____ about by many dreadful misfortunes will either become stronger or suffer a complete breakdown.

2. In a natural history museum, we can see physical remains of many species of animals that are no longer _____ **extant** _____ .

3. In our frantic search for the missing papers, we overturned everything in the room, leaving it in complete _____ **chaos** _____ .

4. Shakespeare tells us that "the evil that men do lives after them; the good is oft _____ **interred** _____ with their bones."

5. Let me say frankly that I _____ **abhor** _____ prejudice in anyone, even a member of my own family.

6. It is particularly _____ **reprehensible** _____ for citizens to fail to vote in national elections and then complain about the government.

7. We are petitioning the council to _____ **amend** _____ its procedures so that all citizens will have a chance to express their opinions.

8. The American writer Dorothy Parker was celebrated for her sharp tongue and _____ **corrosive** _____ wit.

9. Are we justified in showing visitors only the most attractive and interesting sections of our cities, towns, or villages while keeping them away from the _____ **squalid** _____ neighborhoods where so many people live?

10. Getting a good education will do much to _____ **obviate** _____ the problem of finding a job that pays well.

11. Those accused of crimes are sometimes willing to _____ **implicate** _____ their accomplices in return for immunity from prosecution.

12. Who would not feel depressed on entering that _____ **somber** _____ old courtroom, with its dim lighting and dark, massive furnishings!

13. Confident that she could present the case effectively to a judge, the lawyer advised her client to _____ **waive** _____ his right to a jury trial.

14. A person who changes from one political party to another on the basis of honest conviction should not be regarded as a(n) _____ **renegade** _____ .

15. The trunk of the car was so _____ **commodious** _____ that it held all our skiing equipment as well as our other luggage.

16. The records of the school board meeting on the proposed bond issue are so _____ **voluminous** _____ that it would take me a week to read them.

17. One of the signs of maturity is the ability to _____ **discern** _____ the difference between things that are secondary and things that are truly important.

18. We Americans are proud that each change of the national administration, far from being _____ turbulent _____ , is carried out in a peaceful and friendly manner.

19. I didn't expect you to like my suggestion, but I was shocked by your bitter and _____ vociferous _____ criticism of it.

20. Although our drill instructor went by the book, he was by no means an overbearing _____ martinet _____ .

Synonyms

Choose the word from this unit that is **the same** or **most nearly the same** in meaning as the **boldface** word or expression in the given phrase. Write the word on the line provided.

1. battered by fluctuations in the stock market _____ buffeted _____

2. a **spacious** and elegant hotel lobby _____ commodious _____

3. detected a change in public opinion _____ discerned _____

4. a cold and heartless **taskmaster** _____ martinet _____

5. willing to **modify** long-standing company policy _____ amend _____

6. precludes further debate _____ obviates _____

7. clamorous objections to the plan _____ vociferous _____

8. condemned by all as a **turncoat** _____ renegade _____

9. disorder in the courtroom _____ chaos _____

10. found in appallingly **dingy** surroundings _____ squalid _____

11. entangled in a web of deceit _____ implicated _____

12. the **mournful** tolling of church bells _____ somber _____

13. detested all snobbery and conceit _____ abhorred _____

14. forgo payment for their services _____ waive _____

15. letters containing **spiteful** remarks _____ corrosive _____

Antonyms

Choose the word from this unit that is **most nearly opposite** in meaning to the **boldface** word or expression in the given phrase. Write the word on the line provided.

16. a prolonged period of **calm** weather _____ turbulent _____

17. exhumed the victim's body _____ interred _____

18. took **brief** notes during the meeting _____ voluminous _____

19. a truly **meritorious** policy _____ reprehensible _____

20. an **extinct** flightless bird _____ extant _____

Choosing the Right Word

Circle the **boldface** word that more satisfactorily completes each of the following sentences.

1. At lunchtime, the room rang with the sound of (**reprehensible, vociferous**) debates between the fans of rival teams.

2. The Tech team was offside on the play; but since we had thrown them for an eight-yard loss, we (**waived, abhorred**) the five-yard penalty.

3. Which great poet said that his head was "bloody but unbowed" under the (**buffeting, chaos**) of fate?

4. Even in his old age, Thomas Jefferson kept up a (**voluminous, turbulent**) correspondence with important people in America and abroad.

5. The Founding Fathers set up a method of (**amending, obviating**) the Constitution that is neither too easy nor too difficult to use.

6. We can expect (**chaos, martinets**) in the years ahead if we do not develop a tough, realistic conservation policy.

7. If you examine the evidence carefully, you will soon (**discern, amend**) the contradictions in the witness's story.

8. I don't know which was more (**somber, reprehensible**)—making improper use of the money or lying about it later.

9. The time has come for us to (**implicate, inter**) our ancient disputes and go forward as a truly united people.

10. In 1940, Winston Churchill conveyed to the British people the (**somber, voluminous**) truth that they were fighting for their national existence.

11. A compromise agreement reached in the judge's chambers would clearly (**discern, obviate**) the need for a long, costly lawsuit.

12. When he accused me of playing fast and loose with the rules, I lost my temper and called him an officious (**renegade, martinet**).

13. I'm not so sure that I want to rent a bungalow so (**commodious, squalid**) that I'll have room for guests every weekend.

14. I wouldn't say that I (**inter, abhor**) housework, but I must admit that I avoid it whenever I can.

15. Instead of trying to help the people who had elected him, he became involved in a (**squalid, extant**) little quarrel about handing out jobs.

16. It is hard for us to realize that the great men who led our revolution were considered (**renegades, buffets**) by the British king.

17. History gives us many examples of how the (**vociferous, corrosive**) effects of religious hatred can weaken the entire social structure.

18. Didn't it occur to them that by signing the letter "Sophomores of Central High," they would (**implicate, waive**) the entire class in the protest?

19. Some people prefer the (**discernment, turbulence**) of life in a big city to the more placid atmosphere of a small town.

20. The custom by which a young man buys his bride through a payment to her father is still (**commodious, extant**) in some parts of the world.

Vocabulary in Context

*Read the following passage, in which some of the words you have studied in this unit appear in **boldface** type. Then complete each statement given below the passage by circling the letter of the item that is **the same** or **almost the same** in meaning as the highlighted word.*

Sail On!

(Line)

For over 5,000 years, wind and water have **buffeted** boats propelled by sails. The Egyptians were the first to use sails to power wooden boats. Over the centuries, European shipbuilders constructed bigger and stronger wooden ships with **voluminous** sails and increasingly intricate rigging. In the 1400s and 1500s, a type of (5) sailing ship called a *galleon* was used both to make war and to carry cargo. As guns grew heavier and cargoes more precious, the design of warships and merchant ships diverged.

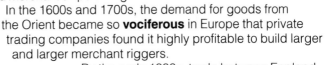

In the 1600s and 1700s, the demand for goods from the Orient became so **vociferous** in Europe that private trading companies found it highly profitable to build larger (10) and larger merchant riggers.

By the early 1800s, trade between England and the United States was booming. There was an increasing demand for more **commodious** accommodations for passengers who wanted to (15) cross the Atlantic. To meet these demands, American shipowners came up with something entirely new: packet service. The *packets* were the first ships to sail on a regular schedule regardless of weather or the size of their cargo. (20) By catering to passenger comfort and convenience, they became immensely successful. However, the packets needed to travel very fast to meet their schedules. As a result, many of the captains drove their ships (25) unmercifully, even in the most **turbulent** weather.

The most beautiful of the sailing ships—and the crowning glory of the age of sail—were the American *clippers*. These ships had slender hulls and many sails, and they were built for speed. They "clipped off" the miles. In (30) their heyday in the mid-1800s, the clippers could make the trip from New York City to San Francisco, around the tip of South America, in under one hundred days.

American clipper ship in full sail

---

1. The meaning of **buffeted** (line 1) is
a. soaked   c. aided
b. pummeled   d. lulled

2. Voluminous (line 4) most nearly means
a. fragile   c. sturdy
b. colorful   d. numerous

3. Vociferous (line 9) is best defined as
a. loud   c. annoying
b. common   d. limited

4. The meaning of **commodious** (line 14) i
a. inexpensive   c. comfortable
b. luxurious   d. cramped

5. Turbulent (line 26) most nearly means
a. stormy   c. calm
b. sunny   d. unpredictable

Definitions

Note carefully the spelling, pronunciation, part(s) of speech, and definition(s) of each of the following words. Then write the word in the blank space(s) in the illustrative sentence(s) following. Finally, study the lists of synonyms and antonyms given at the end of each entry.

1. animosity
(an ə mäs' ə tē)

(*n.*) strong dislike; bitter hostility

The deep _____animosity_____ between the Montagues and Capulets could not prevent Romeo and Juliet from falling in love.

SYNONYMS: enmity, rancor, antipathy
ANTONYMS: affection, fondness, rapport, amity

2. apathy
(ap' ə thē)

(*n.*) a lack of feeling, emotion, or interest

I was horrified when the sales force greeted my great idea for an ad campaign with total _____apathy_____.

SYNONYMS: indifference, disinterest, detachment
ANTONYMS: enthusiasm, fervor, ardor, concern

3. apprehensive
(ap rē hen' siv)

(*adj.*) fearful or anxious, especially about the future

As the hurricane approached, _____apprehensive_____ residents all along the coast prepared for the worst.

SYNONYMS: worried, nervous, fretful, jittery
ANTONYMS: unworried, assured, confident, certain

4. commend
(kə mend')

(*v.*) to praise, express approval; to present as worthy of attention; to commit to the care of

The mayor _____commended_____ the young people for their volunteer work at local hospitals and soup kitchens.

SYNONYM: applaud; entrust
ANTONYMS: abhor, loathe

5. compatible
(kəm pat' ə bəl)

(*adj.*) able to get along or work well together; capable of use with some other model or system

Eyewitness accounts of an accident rarely are totally _____compatible_____.

SYNONYMS: harmonious, in agreement, like-minded
ANTONYMS: mismatched, incongruous, antagonistic

6. condolence
(kən dō' ləns)

(*n.*) an expression of sympathy

A few well-chosen words of _____condolence_____ can be a great comfort to someone who has lost a loved one.

SYNONYMS: commiseration, solace, sympathy

7. consecrate
(kän' sə krāt)

(*v.*) to make sacred, hallow; to set apart for a special purpose
Traditionally most religious denominations hold special ceremonies to _____ **consecrate** _____ a new house of worship.
SYNONYMS: devote, dedicate, sanctify
ANTONYMS: desecrate, defile, profane, dishonor

8. decrepit
(di krep' it)

(*adj.*) old and feeble; worn-out, ruined
"I may be aging," the famous movie star replied, "but I am hardly _____ **decrepit** _____ ."
SYNONYMS: infirm, broken-down, rickety, dilapidated
ANTONYMS: vigorous, robust, sturdy

9. deride
(de rīd')

(*v.*) to ridicule, laugh at with contempt
Most people find jokes that _____ **deride** _____ somebody's national origin or social background extremely offensive.
SYNONYMS: mock, scorn, disparage, jeer at
ANTONYMS: praise, extol, acclaim, applaud

10. ingenuous
(in jen' yü əs)

(*adj.*) innocent, simple; frank, sincere
In his novels, Dickens has harsh words for those who take cruel advantage of _____ **ingenuous** _____ young people.
SYNONYMS: naive, artless, guileless, candid
ANTONYMS: artful, crafty, worldly, sophisticated

11. multifarious
(məl tə far' ē əs)

(*adj.*) having great variety; numerous and diverse
Leonardo da Vinci's notebooks reveal that he was a man of _____ **multifarious** _____ interests.
SYNONYMS: varied, manifold, heterogeneous
ANTONYMS: unvaried, uniform, homogeneous

12. obsolete
(äb sə lēt')

(*adj.*) out-of-date, no longer in use
In order to remain competitive, manufacturing companies periodically replace _____ **obsolete** _____ machinery.
SYNONYMS: outmoded, antiquated, passé, old hat
ANTONYMS: current, up-to-date, brand-new

13. omnivorous
(äm niv' ə rəs)

(*adj.*) eating every kind of food; eagerly taking in everything, having a wide variety of tastes
An _____ **omnivorous** _____ animal has a greater chance of survival than one that depends on a single food source.
SYNONYMS: all-devouring, voracious

14. parsimonious
(pär sə mō′ nē əs)

(*adj.*) stingy, miserly; meager, poor, small

Many people who lost money in the Great Depression later adhered to a _____**parsimonious**_____ lifestyle, even during more prosperous times.

SYNONYMS: frugal, niggardly, penny-pinching, cheap
ANTONYMS: generous, openhanded

15. quandary
(kwän′ drē)

(*n.*) a state of perplexity or doubt

Try as I might, I could see no way out of the ethical _____**quandary**_____ in which I found myself.

SYNONYMS: confusion, dilemma, predicament

16. recalcitrant
(ri kal′ sə trənt)

(*adj.*) stubbornly disobedient, resisting authority

A _____**recalcitrant**_____ individual may have great difficulty adjusting to a job that requires a good deal of teamwork.

SYNONYMS: unruly, obstinate, contrary, ornery
ANTONYMS: obedient, docile, cooperative, compliant

17. reprisal
(ri prī′ zəl)

(*n.*) an injury done in return for injury

The Highland clans of Scotland engaged in cattle rustling in _____**reprisal**_____ for real or imagined injuries.

SYNONYMS: retaliation, revenge, retribution

18. revel
(rev′ əl)

(*v.*) to take great pleasure in; (*n.*) a wild celebration

Some movie stars do not _____**revel**_____ in the attention their fans and the media pay them.

All around the world, the new millennium was ushered in with both prayers and _____**revels**_____.

SYNONYMS: (*v.*) relish, savor, bask in, carouse
ANTONYMS: (*v.*) abhor, loathe

19. stultify
(stəl′ tə fī)

(*v.*) to make ineffective or useless, cripple; to have a dulling effect on

Oppressive heat may _____**stultify**_____ the mind and spirit as well as the body.

SYNONYMS: smother, stifle, neutralize, negate
ANTONYMS: arouse, excite, inspire, stimulate

20. suave
(swäv)

(*adj.*) smoothly agreeable or polite; pleasing to the senses

Nick Charles, the clever detective in the *Thin Man* movies, is a _____**suave**_____ man-about-town.

SYNONYMS: sophisticated, urbane, polished
ANTONYMS: crude, clumsy, unpolished, oafish, loutish

Completing the Sentence

From the words for this unit, choose the one that best completes each of the following sentences. Write the word in the space provided.

1. It is surprising how often people with very different personalities turn out to be _____**compatible**_____ when they get to know one another.

2. It was difficult for us to believe that such a _____**suave**_____ and cultured gentleman was a member of a gang of international jewel thieves.

3. In spite of all the elaborate safety precautions, I couldn't help feeling a little _____**apprehensive**_____ as I set out for my first skydiving lesson.

4. Political candidates who do nothing but _____**deride**_____ their opponents' character and abilities may alienate voters.

5. The _____**multifarious**_____ problems that will face America's Presidents in the twenty-first century will make their job one of the most demanding in the world.

6. So there I was, having accepted invitations to two different parties on the same evening. What a(n) _____**quandary**_____ to be in!

7. Simple _____**apathy**_____ seems to be the main reason such a large percentage of those eligible to vote fail to cast ballots in any election.

8. I think that the phrase "on its last legs" is an apt description of that _____**decrepit**_____ old house down the block.

9. I trust you will never have the experience of trying to cross the desert with a(n) _____**recalcitrant**_____ mule that wants to remain where it is.

10. From all his growling and snapping, you would think our beagle felt a personal _____**animosity**_____ toward every other dog on the block.

11. Although I was unable to visit my old friend's widow in person, I offered my _____**condolences**_____ in a heartfelt letter.

12. If you think of all the different kinds of food that human beings are able to consume, you will realize that we are truly a(n) _____**omnivorous**_____ species.

13. Struggling to overcome her _____**parsimonious**_____ inclinations, she finally reached into her pocket and handed me one thin dime!

14. The board of directors voted to _____**commend**_____ him for the skill and enthusiasm with which he had managed the charity drive.

15. "Today," said the speaker, "we _____**consecrate**_____ this monument to the memory of all those who fought and died in defense of their country."

16. Now that I am a senior, it is hard to believe that I was ever as innocent and _____**ingenuous**_____ as the members of the new freshman class.

17. Technology changes so rapidly that a particular computer may be state-of-the-art one day and _____**obsolete**_____ the next.

18. If we increase our tariff rates on the goods of other countries, we can be sure that they will raise their own rates in _____reprisal_____ .

19. Throughout the hot, dusty journey, we _____reveled_____ in the thought that soon we would be swimming in the cool lake.

20. In totalitarian regimes, censorship and violence are often employed to suppress criticism and _____stultify_____ dissent.

Synonyms

*Choose the word from this unit that is **the same** or **most nearly the same** in meaning as the **boldface** word or expression in the given phrase. Write the word on the line provided.*

1. an **all-devouring** sense of curiosity — omnivorous
2. cruel acts of **revenge** — reprisal
3. **entrusted** to the care of friends — commended
4. caught in a hopeless **predicament** — quandary
5. welcome expressions of **sympathy** — condolence
6. **jeered at** by the protesters — derided
7. surrounded by **like-minded** friends — compatible
8. too **naive** to question others' motives — ingenuous
9. rejected the author's **outmoded** theories — obsolete
10. a shocking display of **rancor** — animosity
11. blocked by a **penny-pinching** legislature — parsimonious
12. a climate of public **indifference** — apathy
13. an old house with a **dilapidated** porch — decrepit
14. **dedicated** themselves to healing the sick — consecrated
15. **basked** in the approval of friends and family — reveled

Antonyms

*Choose the word from this unit that is **most nearly opposite** in meaning to the **boldface** word or expression in the given phrase. Write the word on the line provided.*

16. a person with **unpolished** manners — suave
17. an atmosphere that **stimulates** inquiry — stultifies
18. a **homogeneous** society — multifarious
19. a thoroughly **cooperative** individual — recalcitrant
20. behaved in a very **confident** manner — apprehensive

*Circle the **boldface** word that more satisfactorily completes each of the following sentences.*

1. Can you be so (**apprehensive, ingenuous**) that you don't realize she is paying us all those phony compliments to get something out of us?

2. Yes, there is some (**apathy, animosity**) between different racial and ethnic groups, but it can be overcome by education and experience.

3. He is so absorbed in himself that he has become (**parsimonious, suave**) in the normal expression of human sympathy and affection.

4. I think we should offer congratulations rather than (**revels, condolences**) for the disappearance of that battered old heap you called a car.

5. In this third century of our nation's life, let us (**stultify, consecrate**) ourselves anew to the ideals of human freedom.

6. Some people are (**omnivorous, parsimonious**) readers, with a lively appetite for all types of fiction and nonfiction.

7. Two of the chief strengths of modern American society are the variety and vitality that arise from its (**multifarious, obsolete**) cultures.

8. Those students who have been doing their work all term need not feel (**apprehensive, recalcitrant**) about the final examination.

9. The headwaiter was so (**suave, ingenuous**) and self-assured in his manner that we took him for a diplomat.

10. Your unwillingness to study foreign languages is in no way (**compatible, omnivorous**) with your ambition to get a job in the foreign service.

11. Our Constitution is more than 200 years old; but far from being (**suave, decrepit**), it is still a vital, dynamic, and highly practical plan of government.

12. Many stand-up comedians regularly (**revel, deride**) popular fads and fashions.

13. So we are faced with that old (**quandary, reprisal**)—an income that simply can't be stretched to cover the things that we simply must have.

14. The address was so dull and long-winded that it seemed to (**consecrate, stultify**) rather than inspire the audience.

15. When my friends appeared with a stack of CDs, I realized that our crash study session might become an all-day (**reprisal, revel**).

16. I must give you the sad news that correct spelling and good grammar are not, and never will be, (**obsolete, decrepit**).

17. If you can't (**deride, commend**) me for my efforts to help you, at least don't criticize me for not doing everything you want.

18. Her moods seem to go from one extreme to the other—from deepest (**apathy, animosity**) to unlimited enthusiasm.

19. The handful of (**recalcitrant, compatible**) students who refuse to obey study hall regulations are violating the rights of the majority.

20. Although our society must punish criminals, I don't think we should do so simply as a (**reprisal, quandary**) for the wrongs they have committed.

Vocabulary in Context

*Read the following passage, in which some of the words you have studied in this unit appear in **boldface** type. Then complete each statement given below the passage by circling the letter of the item that is **the same** or **almost the same** in meaning as the highlighted word.*

Thriving Coyotes

(Line)

Most people probably associate coyotes with the American West. Indeed, these handsome and adaptable animals are native to that part of the world. However, over the past hundred years, the species has greatly enlarged its territory. It has moved steadily eastward and into areas that are more densely populated. Today
(5) the melodious howls of coyotes can be heard throughout the United States and in parts of Canada and Central America.

Why have coyotes been so successful? Their **omnivorous** eating habits certainly have helped them. They are known to eat just about anything, including insects, snakes, frogs, porcupines, grass, apples,
(10) cactus fruit, and even watermelon. Yet coyotes also prey on livestock. For this reason, some people seek to reduce their numbers or even eliminate them altogether. Ranchers in the western United States have long felt **animosity** toward coyotes because
(15) the animals kill hundreds of thousands of sheep each year. In turn, ranchers, hunters, and government workers kill hundreds of thousands of coyotes annually. The methods used are **multifarious**, ranging from poisoning and trapping to aerial
(20) shooting.

Urban and suburban residents may also feel **apprehensive** about the presence of coyotes. A hungry coyote may attack and kill a pet cat or dog.

Coyotes communicate by howling.

Yet there is also reason to **commend** coyotes. They play an important role in
(25) maintaining the balance of nature. Their preferred foods are mice, gophers, and other small rodents. Without coyotes to keep their numbers down, these rodents would do enormous damage to crops.

Can humans and coyotes be **compatible**? Whether they will be able to live in some measure of harmony remains to be seen. Meanwhile, this wily animal that
(30) Native Americans call the Trickster continues to thrive.

---

1. The meaning of **omnivorous** (line 7) is
a. peculiar
c. voracious
b. appealing
d. finicky

2. Animosity (line 14) most nearly means
a. kindness
c. affection
b. enmity
d. respect

3. Multifarious (line 18) is best defined as
a. uniform
c. wicked
b. effective
d. varied

4. The meaning of **apprehensive** (line 22) is
a. worried
c. excited
b. certain
d. annoyed

5. Commend (line 24) most nearly means
a. loathe
c. praise
b. avoid
d. study

6. Compatible (line 28) is best defined as
a. on time
c. able to get along
b. sympathetic
d. antagonistic

 **Definitions**

Note carefully the spelling, pronunciation, part(s) of speech, and definition(s) of each of the following words. Then write the word in the blank space(s) in the illustrative sentence(s) following. Finally, study the lists of synonyms and antonyms given at the end of each entry.

1. allocate
(al′ ə kāt)

(*v.*) to set apart or designate for a special purpose; to distribute
In their wills many people _____**allocate**_____ a portion of their wealth to favorite charities or educational institutions.
SYNONYMS: assign, allot, apportion

2. ardent
(är′ dənt)

(*adj.*) very enthusiastic, impassioned
The members of the winning team acknowledged the cheers of their _____**ardent**_____ fans.
SYNONYMS: intense, zealous, fervent, avid
ANTONYMS: indifferent, stolid, phlegmatic, apathetic

3. assiduous
(ə sij′ ü əs)

(*adj.*) persistent, attentive, diligent
Workers who are conscientious in the performance of their duties are, by definition, _____**assiduous**_____.
SYNONYMS: industrious, unremitting, sedulous
ANTONYMS: lazy, lackadaisical, shiftless

4. brash
(brash)

(*adj.*) prone to act in a hasty manner; impudent
Successful political candidates soon learn how to handle tough questions fired at them by _____**brash**_____ newspaper and TV reporters.
SYNONYMS: rash, impetuous, brazen, impertinent
ANTONYMS: prudent, wary, cautious, circumspect

5. capricious
(kə prish′ əs)

(*adj.*) subject to whims or passing fancies
Our constitutional system of checks and balances is designed to prevent the _____**capricious**_____ use of power by any branch of the federal government.
SYNONYMS: impulsive, fickle, unpredictable, mercurial
ANTONYMS: constant, steady, steadfast, unwavering

6. chastise
(chas tīz′)

(*v.*) to inflict physical punishment as a means of correction; to scold severely
State and federal laws now forbid the use of corporal punishment to _____**chastise**_____ prisoners.
SYNONYMS: discipline, censure
ANTONYMS: commend, reward

7. copious
(kō′ pē əs)

(*adj.*) abundant; plentiful; wordy, verbose

The _____ **copious** _____ and detailed footnotes found in most scholarly books are designed to document the authors' sources.

SYNONYMS: ample, profuse, bountiful
ANTONYMS: inadequate, meager, scanty, concise

8. deviate
(*v.*, dē′ vē āt;
n., *adj.*, dē′ vē ət)

(*v.*) to turn aside; to stray from a norm; (*n.*) one who departs from a norm; (*adj.*) differing from a norm, heterodox, unconventional

Try not to _____ **deviate** _____ from the directions given in the owner's manual.

Those who disagreed with the Soviet form of government were often branded as _____ **deviates** _____ and imprisoned.

Under our system of justice, the mentally ill cannot be held responsible for their _____ **deviate** _____ behavior.

SYNONYMS: (*v.*) diverge, veer, swerve
ANTONYMS: (*v.*) conform to, abide by; (*adj.*) orthodox

9. emaciated
(i mā′ shē ā tid)

(*adj.*, *part.*) unnaturally thin

People who suffer from serious eating disorders may soon become woefully _____ **emaciated** _____.

SYNONYMS: gaunt, withered, shriveled
ANTONYMS: plump, fat, obese, corpulent

10. exult
(eg zəlt′)

(*v.*) to rejoice greatly

The campaign workers _____ **exulted** _____ in the unexpected victory of their candidate.

SYNONYMS: revel, glory
ANTONYMS: mope, sulk, regret, rue, lament

11. gnarled
(närld)

(*adj.*) knotted, twisted, lumpy

The _____ **gnarled** _____ limbs of cypresses dominate many of the landscapes painted by the Dutch artist Vincent van Gogh.

SYNONYMS: knotty, misshapen, contorted
ANTONYMS: smooth, unblemished, straight

12. indemnity
(in dem′ nə tē)

(*n.*) a payment for damage or loss

A certain type of life insurance contract provides double _____ **indemnity** _____ for the accidental death of the policyholder.

SYNONYMS: compensation, restitution, reparation

13. inkling
(iŋk′ liŋ)

(*n.*) a hint; a vague notion

I had absolutely no _____inkling_____ of what to expect as I entered the room.

SYNONYMS: clue, intimation, suggestion

14. limpid
(lim′ pid)

(*adj.*) clear, transparent; readily understood

Snorklers flock to the _____limpid_____ waters of the Caribbean to view schools of brightly colored fish.

SYNONYMS: lucid, intelligible
ANTONYMS: clouded, murky, opaque

15. omnipotent
(äm nip′ ə tənt)

(*adj.*) almighty, having unlimited power or authority

Many of the heroes of ancient myths and legends appear to be all but _____omnipotent_____.

SYNONYM: all-powerful
ANTONYMS: powerless, impotent, feeble, weak

16. palatable
(pal′ ə tə bəl)

(*adj.*) agreeable to the taste or one's sensibilities; suitable for consumption

The addition of some seasonings will usually make even the blandest of dishes _____palatable_____.

SYNONYMS: edible, appetizing, attractive
ANTONYMS: inedible, distasteful, disagreeable

17. poignant
(poin′ yənt)

(*adj.*) deeply affecting, touching; keen or sharp in taste or smell

There is something truly _____poignant_____ about the sight of falling leaves in autumn.

SYNONYMS: heartrending, bittersweet, melancholy
ANTONYMS: unaffecting, bland, vapid, insipid, funny

18. rancor
(raŋ′ kər)

(*n.*) bitter resentment or ill-will

An unusual degree of _____rancor_____ may creep into the tone of the political debate in an election year.

SYNONYMS: animosity, enmity, bitterness
ANTONYMS: goodwill, harmony, rapport, amity

19. sophomoric
(säf ə môr′ ik)

(*adj.*) immature and overconfident; conceited

Adolescents aren't the only people whose behavior might at times be considered a bit _____sophomoric_____.

SYNONYMS: pretentious, superficial, fatuous
ANTONYMS: mature, judicious, sage, knowledgeable

20. spontaneous
(spän tā′ nē əs)

(*adj.*) arising naturally; not planned or engineered in advance

Actors try to make their performances seem as _____spontaneous_____ as possible.

SYNONYMS: unpremeditated, unplanned, impromptu
ANTONYMS: premeditated, planned, contrived, rehearsed

Completing the Sentence

From the words for this unit, choose the one that best completes each of the following sentences. Write the word in the space provided.

1. The teacher decided to _____**allocate**_____ a corner of the classroom for an exhibition of student science projects.

2. Some of my friends are mentally rather mature for their age; others are of a decidedly _____**sophomoric**_____ turn of mind.

3. The Bible tells us that the Lord will _____**chastise**_____ the wicked, but our student dean is trying very hard to help him out.

4. Nothing can arouse _____**poignant**_____ memories of long ago and far away like an old, well-loved song!

5. General Grant accepted Lee's surrender with quiet dignity, refusing to _____**exult**_____ over the defeat of a worthy foe.

6. If you wish to recover quickly, you must not _____**deviate**_____ in the slightest from the doctor's instructions.

7. Remembering my old friend as a robust 200-pounder, I was shocked to see how _____**emaciated**_____ he had become during his long illness.

8. My travels have shown me that many exotic foods I once considered disgusting are really quite _____**palatable**_____.

9. If you were as _____**assiduous**_____ in studying foreign affairs as you are in memorizing batting averages, you would have known how to reply to her comments on the situation in the Middle East.

10. Under the American system of separation of powers, no government official or agency can ever become _____**omnipotent**_____.

11. As the speaker's voice droned on endlessly in the hot, crowded room, I suddenly realized that I hadn't the slightest _____**inkling**_____ of what he was saying.

12. _____**Rancor**_____ is never so bitter as when it arises among people who were once close friends.

13. There can be no _____**indemnity**_____ for the pain and suffering that your carelessness has caused me!

14. When he told me that he was reading *Huckleberry Finn* for the ninth time, I realized that he was indeed a(n) _____**ardent**_____ admirer of the novel.

15. We were fascinated to see the consummate grace and skill with which the _____**gnarled**_____ hands of the old carpenter manipulated his tools.

16. Friends and relatives can be counted on to give _____**copious**_____ amounts of advice on child rearing to the parents of a new baby.

17. Wasn't it rather _____**brash**_____ of you to offer the soccer coach advice on your very first day as a candidate for the team?

*Unit 9 ■ 101*

18. How can you say that the audience's reaction was _____spontaneous_____ when the director held up a sign reading "Applause"?

19. Somewhere in a(n) _____limpid_____ pool in the Canadian Rockies is the large trout that will someday grace the wall of my den.

20. Far from being _____capricious_____, the director's casting choices were based on a solid appreciation of each actor's abilities and limitations.

Synonyms

*Choose the word from this unit that is **the same** or **most nearly the same** in meaning as the **boldface** word or expression in the given phrase. Write the word on the line provided.*

1. had no **clue** that a storm was approaching — inkling

2. **compensation** equal to our loss — indemnity

3. a **bittersweet** tale of love and loss — poignant

4. **apportioned** supplies to each member of the group — allocated

5. **rejoiced** in the news from the front — exulted

6. **misshapen** and weather-beaten fingers — gnarled

7. **zealous** supporters of liberty — ardent

8. the survivors' **gaunt** faces — emaciated

9. a **pretentious** literary style — sophomoric

10. could find nothing **appetizing** on the menu — palatable

11. asked **impertinent** questions — brash

12. **ample** proof of the defendant's innocence — copious

13. a history of **animosity** between the two countries — rancor

14. an **impromptu** celebration — spontaneous

15. a **lucid** explanation of the issues — limpid

Antonyms

*Choose the word from this unit that is **most nearly opposite** in meaning to the **boldface** word or expression in the given phrase. Write the word on the line provided.*

16. **rewarded** for their behavior — chastised

17. known to be a **lackadaisical** student — assiduous

18. **abide by** the rules of the game — deviate from

19. **steadfast** in one's affections — capricious

20. ruled by **feeble** monarchs — omnipotent

Choosing the Right Word

*Circle the **boldface** word that more satisfactorily completes each of the following sentences.*

1. The lecturer explained that the UN is not (**palatable, omnipotent**) and that it can do only what the member states allow it to do.

2. The tastes of the TV audience are so (**gnarled, capricious**) that no one can predict in advance which programs will be successful.

3. What she lacks in skill, she makes up for in (**assiduous, spontaneous**) attention to every last detail and requirement of the job.

4. George Gershwin's early songs gave only a dim (**inkling, deviation**) of the genius that was to express itself in *Porgy and Bess.*

5. Your (**ardent, brash**) interest in ecology shows that you care deeply about the welfare of this planet.

6. The entire student body (**exulted, allocated**) when our team finally won the citywide basketball championship after years of losing to our bitter rivals.

7. Tennyson speaks of "sorrow's crown of sorrow," by which he means the (**copious, poignant**) experience of remembering happier times.

8. In the concentration camps, the liberating troops found thousands of victims horribly (**ardent, emaciated**) as the result of starvation diets.

9. Perhaps you have been treated unfairly, but what good will it do to allow your sense of (**indemnity, rancor**) to control your mood and behavior?

10. Our meeting last week was marred by a heated debate over how to (**allocate, chastise**) the funds in this year's budget.

11. Far from being effortless, her simple, (**limpid, capricious**) writing style is the result of the most painstaking effort.

12. He tries hard to sound well-informed, but his superficial answers only betray his (**poignant, sophomoric**) knowledge of world affairs.

13. We must show understanding and acceptance of those who (**deviate, exult**) somewhat from our own standards of what is appropriate.

14. She was (**assiduous, brash**) enough to tell her mother she was going to the dance in spite of the doctor's orders.

15. During the depression of the 1930s, the entire nation seemed to take new strength from Roosevelt's (**poignant, copious**) energy and enthusiasm.

16. He seems to feel that it is his mission in life to (**exult, chastise**) all those who fail to live up to his standards.

17. Since their loud talk and crude manners were anything but (**palatable, limpid**) to me, I politely declined their invitation to dine with them.

18. The destruction wrought by a nuclear war would be so vast that any form of (**inkling, indemnity**) to the injured would be impossible.

19. I spent the better part of an hour trying to untangle my badly (**gnarled, assiduous**) telephone cord.

20. Your simple, (**spontaneous, capricious**) expression of appreciation meant more to me than all the elaborate, carefully phrased tributes I received.

*Read the following passage, in which some of the words you have studied in this unit appear in **boldface** type. Then complete each statement given below the passage by circling the letter of the item that is **the same** or **almost the same** in meaning as the highlighted word.*

Light on the Land

(Line)

Until the late 1820s, few American painters chose landscapes as a subject. Those who did paint landscapes did not **deviate** much from European models. In 1825, however, the course of American painting changed dramatically when a young English-born painter named Thomas Cole (1801–1848) took a trip to hike and sketch in the upper Hudson River Valley. (5)

Cole was deeply affected by the natural beauty of the Catskill Mountains. The area was still wilderness, and Cole **exulted** in its unspoiled splendor. He immediately began

sketching the **limpid** streams, majestic waterfalls, sunlit valleys, and rugged stone (10) outcroppings that he saw there. Back in his studio in New York City, he produced paintings based on these sketches.

A group of younger (15) painters eagerly followed in Cole's footsteps. The paintings of Cole and his followers exhibited an **ardent** idealization of nature. After (20) Cole's death, John Frederick Kensett (1816–1872) became one of the leaders of

Autumn Afternoon on Lake George
by John Frederick Kensett

the movement that Cole had started (now known as the Hudson River School). These painters concentrated on light-filled landscapes. (25)

Artists working in other settings also showed the influence of the Hudson River School. For example, Frederic Edwin Church (1826–1900) journeyed to Ecuador. There he captured on canvas the **capricious** moods of nature in the Andes and the tropical forests. Albert Bierstadt (1830–1902) stressed the awesome grandeur of the mountains and valleys of the American West in his paintings. By the 1870s, the Hudson River (30) School had become the first truly national school of American landscape painting.

---

1. The meaning of **deviate** (line 2) is
  a. imitate   c. learn
  (b.) diverge   d. celebrate

2. Exulted (line 7) most nearly means
  (a.) reveled   c. dwelled
  b. dabbled   d. trekked

3. Limpid (line 8) is best defined as
  a. muddy   (c.) clear
  b. bubbling   d. peaceful

4. The meaning of **ardent** (line 19) is
  a. innocent   c. impetuous
  b. active   (d.) intense

5. Capricious (line 28) most nearly means
  a. exotic   (c.) mercurial
  b. somber   d. familiar

Analogies

In each of the following, circle the item that best completes the comparison.

See pages T38–T48 for explanations of answers.

1. stultify is to **stifle** as
a. allocate is to waive
b. obviate is to commend
c. consecrate is to profane
d. implicate is to incriminate ✓

2. martinet is to **discipline** as
a. renegade is to loyalty
b. miser is to poverty
c. scholar is to ignorance
d. aesthete is to beauty ✓

3. chastise is to **commend** as
a. deviate is to veer
b. amend is to deride
c. inter is to consecrate
d. abhor is to relish ✓

4. copious is to **quantity** as
a. multifarious is to duration
b. vociferous is to range
c. commodious is to capacity ✓
d. voluminous is to application

5. pool is to **limpid** as
a. explanation is to lucid ✓
b. quandary is to compatible
c. combustion is to spontaneous
d. apathy is to assiduous

6. assiduous is to **favorable** as
a. palatable is to unfavorable
b. recalcitrant is to favorable
c. reprehensible is to unfavorable ✓
d. squalid is to favorable

7. extant is to **extinct** as
a. chaotic is to orderly ✓
b. poignant is to sad
c. spontaneous is to obsolete
d. somber is to corrosive

8. thin is to **emaciated** as
a. ingenuous is to dishonest
b. mercenary is to compatible
c. decrepit is to sickly
d. tired is to exhausted ✓

9. ardent is to **apathy** as
a. apprehensive is to anxiety
b. brash is to audacity
c. somber is to levity ✓
d. suave is to polish

10. decrepit is to **vigor** as
a. apprehensive is to confidence ✓
b. recalcitrant is to obstinacy
c. parsimonious is to thrift
d. ingenuous is to ignorance

11. quandary is to **perplex** as
a. deviation is to conform
b. riddle is to stump ✓
c. dilemma is to solve
d. predicament is to escape

12. indemnity is to **loss** as
a. condolence is to sympathy
b. reprisal is to injury ✓
c. apathy is to triumph
d. rancor is to spite

13. vengeful is to **reprisals** as
a. timid is to quandaries
b. contrite is to amends ✓
c. somber is to revels
d. callous is to condolences

14. palatable is to **taste** as
a. gnarled is to shape ✓
b. vociferous is to appearance
c. commodious is to sound
d. brash is to sight

15. exult is to **triumphant** as
a. inter is to vociferous
b. despair is to vanquished ✓
c. spend is to parsimonious
d. obey is to recalcitrant

16. omnipotent is to **power** as
a. omnivorous is to appetite
b. ominous is to wisdom
c. omniscient is to knowledge ✓
d. omnipresent is to skill

17. inkling is to **intimation** as
a. buffet is to quandary
b. condolence is to animosity
c. rancor is to resentment ✓
d. chaos is to indemnity

18. suave is to **boorish** as
a. turbulent is to peaceful ✓
b. voluminous is to copious
c. capricious is to brash
d. limpid is to transparent

Word Associations

In each of the following groups, circle the word that is best defined or suggested by the given phrase.

1. economical to the point of stinginess
   a. apprehensive   b. suave   c. parsimonious   d. ingenuous

2. straying from the straight and narrow
   a. deviate   b. ingenuous   c. ardent   d. spontaneous

3. numerous and diverse
   a. assiduous   b. multifarious   c. poignant   d. extant

4. lay to rest
   a. stultify   b. obviate   c. deviate   d. inter

5. divvy up the chores
   a. implicate   b. waive   c. allocate   d. deride

6. state of complete disorder
   a. reprisal   b. inkling   c. rancor   d. chaos

7. feeling of ill will or resentment
   a. indemnity   b. animosity   c. reprisal   d. buffet

8. all skin and bones
   a. suave   b. corrosive   c. emaciated   d. squalid

9. said of an act that is done hastily, without regard for consequences
   a. ardent   b. corrosive   c. brash   d. turbulent

10. how one might describe a lengthy set of notes
    a. omnivorous   b. somber   c. limpid   d. voluminous

11. said of a lawn mower that is difficult to start
    a. compatible   b. recalcitrant   c. somber   d. ardent

12. on its last legs
    a. capricious   b. decrepit   c. gnarled   d. renegade

13. on the spur of the moment
    a. spontaneous   b. reprehensible   c. extant   d. turbulent

14. said of a tearjerker
    a. capricious   b. ingenuous   c. multifarious   d. poignant

15. an expression of sympathy
    a. indemnity   b. reprisal   c. condolence   d. inkling

16. out-of-date
    a. gnarled   b. reprehensible   c. turbulent   d. obsolete

17. a candid remark
    a. brash   b. poignant   c. omnipotent   d. ingenuous

18. avoid the necessity for doing something
    a. obviate   b. inter   c. chastise   d. discern

19. noisy celebration
    a. allocation   b. revel   c. consecration   d. deviate

20. state of uncertainty or puzzlement
    a. condolence   b. apathy   c. rancor   d. quandary

Vocabulary in Context

Read the following passage, in which some of the words you have studied in Units 7–9 appear in **boldface** type. Then complete each statement given below the passage by circling the item that is **the same** or **almost the same** in meaning as the highlighted word.

Rush to Riches

(Line)

In 1848, a few nuggets of gold were discovered near a sawmill in the Sacramento Valley. News of this discovery set off a rush of gold seekers

(5) to the thinly populated California territory.

As the word of gold spread, **brash** individuals began arriving from all over the globe. Known as

(10) *forty-niners* because most of them arrived in 1849, these immigrants left homes, families, and jobs in hopes of staking a claim to a piece of California that would yield gold.

(15) They came by ship, landing in the port of San Francisco, and by covered wagon across the Oregon and California trails. Few had any **inkling** of the difficulties they would

(20) face. Yet no amount of hardship seemed to dim their dreams. By the end of 1849, this **spontaneous** influx of people had increased California's population from about

(25) 15,000 to 100,000. The territory was admitted to the Union in 1850.

Such rapid growth brought **chaos** as well as prosperity to the new state. Once-small towns such

(30) as San Francisco and Sacramento suddenly grew large and wealthy by catering to the needs of the prospectors. It took a while for this newfound wealth to be put to good

(35) civic use. Numerous camp towns also grew up overnight near the mines. These were generally **squalid**, lawless settlements that often disappeared as quickly as

(40) they appeared if the veins of gold went dry.

Although some forty-niners did strike it rich, the majority found themselves with small holdings that

(45) yielded a **parsimonious** living in return for very hard labor. Many would-be gold miners also ended up working for small wages in large mines owned by others. Still others

(50) had to turn to farming or ranching to support themselves. For many individuals, the California gold rush was a disappointment or a disaster. But for California itself, it was a

(55) boon, providing the fledgling state with new sources of wealth, transportation, and political influence.

---

1. The meaning of **brash** (line 8) is
a. rash
c. hopeful
b. young
d. brave

2. Inkling (line 19) most nearly means
a. news
c. notion
b. theory
d. map

3. Spontaneous (line 22) is best defined as
a. gigantic
c. memorable
b. unplanned
d. desperate

4. The meaning of **chaos** (line 28) is
a. civilization
c. turmoil
b. peace
d. poverty

5. Squalid (line 38) most nearly means
a. sordid
c. ordinary
b. small
d. temporary

6. Parsimonious (line 45) is best defined as
a. lavish
c. average
b. welcome
d. meager

Read each sentence carefully. Then circle the item that best completes the statement below the sentence.

See pages T38–T48 for explanations of answers.

Unfortunately, the software program I wanted was not compatible with the brand of personal computer I had bought. (2)

1. The word **compatible** in line 1 most nearly means

(a. usable)   b. sympathetic   c. cooperative   d. harmonious

I was in the midst of the usual explanation of the poem when a renegade thought crossed my mind and stopped me dead in my tracks. (2)

2. In line 1 the word **renegade** is best defined as

a. brilliant   (b. unorthodox)   c. unworthy   d. outlawed

Listening to overblown soapbox oratory has made me appreciate just how apt Dr. Johnson's phrase "copious without order" still is. (2)

3. The word **copious** in line 2 is best defined as

a. generous   b. abounding   c. disorganized   (d. wordy)

Let us waive judgment until all the facts of the matter are in and we can better assess the merits of the case. (2

4. The word **waive** in line 1 is best defined as

a. relinquish permanently   b. refuse absolutely   (c. postpone temporarily)   d. rush hastily to

"O Lord," the chaplain said softly, "we commend the body of our fallen comrade to the deep and his soul to thy eternal care." (2

5. In line 1 the word **commend** is used to mean

a. praise   (b. entrust)   c. approve   d. surrender

Antonyms

In each of the following groups, circle the word or expression that is most nearly the **opposite** of the word in **boldface** type.

1. vociferous
a. convincing
b. energetic
(c. soft-spoken)
d. eloquent

2. consecrate
a. obviate
b. amend
c. precede
(d. profane)

3. stultify
(a. excite)
b. chatter
c. inter
d. cooperate

4. squalid
a. decrepit
(b. opulent)
c. poignant
d. intense

5. ardent
a. brash
b. chaotic
(c. indifferent)
d. turbulent

6. deride
a. ridicule
b. discern
(c. praise)
d. waive

7. extant
(a. defunct)
b. recalcitrant
c. gnarled
d. omnipotent

8. capricious
a. unselfish
(b. steady)
c. impulsive
d. limpid

9. reprehensible
(a. blameless)
b. renegade
c. uncaptured
d. implicated

11. limpid
(a. clouded)
b. gnarled
c. emaciated
d. squalid

13. waive
(a. claim)
b. reject
c. brandish
d. buffet

15. copious
a. plentiful
b. squalid
(c. in short supply)
d. well-planned

10. assiduous
a. compatible
(b. lazy)
c. somber
d. chaotic

12. suave
a. spontaneous
b. multifarious
c. omnipotent
(d. crude)

14. animosity
a. rancor
b. derision
(c. affection)
d. weariness

16. commodious
a. out of tune
(b. cramped)
c. agreeable
d. voluminous

Word Families

A. On the line provided, write the word you have learned in Units 7-9 that is related to each of the following nouns.
EXAMPLE: assiduousness—**assiduous**

1. turbulence, turbulency — turbulent

2. caprice, capriciousness — capricious

3. sophomore — sophomoric

4. spontaneity, spontaneousness — spontaneous

5. chastisement, chastiser — chastise

6. discernment, discernibleness, discerner — discern

7. poignancy, poignance — poignant

8. exultation, exultance, exultancy — exult

9. compatibility, compatibleness — compatible

10. implication, implicativeness — implicate

11. apprehension, apprehensiveness — apprehensive

12. amends, amendment, amender — amend

13. abhorrence, abhorrer — abhor

14. deviation, deviator, deviant, deviance — deviate

15. squalor, squalidness — squalid

B. On the line provided, write the word you have learned in Units 7-9 that is related to each of the following verbs.
EXAMPLE: accommodate—**commodious**

16. condole — condolence

17. corrode — corrosive

18. renege — renegade

19. gnarl — gnarled

20. indemnify — indemnity

Two-Word Completions

Circle the pair of words that best complete the meaning of each of the following passages.

See pages T38–T48 for explanations of answers.

1. "My years of foreign service have taught me to be as _____ as possible," the veteran diplomat observed, his tongue firmly in his cheek. "These days, turning up one's nose at another country's national dish, no matter how

   _____, might just trigger a very unpleasant international incident."
   a. recalcitrant . . . disingenuous
   b. suave . . . chaotic
   c. compatible . . . squalid
   d. omnivorous . . . unpalatable

2. As the storm increased in intensity, the normally calm waters of the lake became more and more _____. Strong gusts of wind slapped at our sails, and our tiny craft was _____ about like a golf ball in an electric blender.
   a. turbulent . . . buffeted
   b. voluminous . . . deviated
   c. vociferous . . . waived
   d. capricious . . . derided

3. Infuriated by their treacherous behavior, the enraged party leader severely _____ the _____ who had unexpectedly bolted to the opposition during the crucial vote.
   a. chastised . . . renegades
   b. consecrated . . . deviates
   c. implicated . . . martinets
   d. derided . . . revelers

4. Though I am perfectly willing to give praise where I feel praise is due, I refuse to _____ an action that I consider underhanded and

   _____.
   a. abhor . . . extant
   b. commend . . . reprehensible
   c. deride . . . sophomoric
   d. amend . . . apprehensive

5. The soldiers who fell in the engagement were _____ in a portion of the battlefield on which they had fought. The spot where they were laid to rest was not technically "hallowed ground." Still, it was considered appropriate because they had, in effect, _____ it with their blood.
   a. discerned . . . commended
   b. chastised . . . waived
   c. interred . . . consecrated
   d. implicated . . . buffeted

6. I hoped that my project proposal would be hailed by my classmates with _____ enthusiasm. Instead, it was greeted with "deafening"

   _____.
   a. sophomoric . . . indemnity
   b. compatible . . . animosity
   c. vociferous . . . apathy
   d. copious . . . chaos

Building with Classical Roots

voc, vok—to call

This root appears in **vociferous**, "loud or noisy" (page 86). Some other words based on the same root are listed below.

advocate	convocation	evoke	revoke
avocation	equivocal	invoke	vocalize

From the list of words above, choose the one that corresponds to each of the brief definitions below. Write the word in the blank space in the illustrative sentence below the definition.

1. an occupation or activity pursued for enjoyment, in addition to one's regular work; a hobby

Birdwatching can be a lifelong _____**avocation**_____.

2. to call forth; bring to mind ("*to call out*")

The tone poem *La Mer* _____**evokes**_____ the sounds of the sea.

3. to bring or call back; to annul by recalling

A judge can _____**revoke**_____ the license of a driver who has a record of repeated violations.

4. a meeting, especially of members of a college or clergy ("*a calling together*")

The president will attend the _____**convocation**_____ of world leaders.

5. to give voice to; to sing without words

Therapists encourage patients to _____**vocalize**_____ their hopes and fears.

6. open to two or more interpretations, ambiguous; uncertain or doubtful in nature

The reporter's pointed question drew an _____**equivocal**_____ response from the candidate.

7. to plead in favor of; one who defends a cause; one who pleads the cause of another

Our senators _____**advocate**_____ reform of the tax code.

8. to call in for help or support; to appeal to as an authority; to put into effect; to make an earnest request for ("*to call on*")

The lawyer tried to _____**invoke**_____ the sympathy of the jurors.

From the list of words above, choose the one that best completes each of the following sentences. Write the word in the space provided.

1. To warm up their voices, opera singers will _____**vocalize**_____ for a short time before going on the stage.

2. Medical specialists from all over the world have been invited to attend a _____**convocation**_____ of experts on problems in the field of public health.

3. The new ordinance restricting bicycle traffic during rush hours proved to be so unpopular that it was _____revoked_____.

4. The officer's _____equivocal_____ remarks suggested that he was of two minds about the enemy's will to resist.

5. A chemist by profession, Sarah has for many years pursued landscape painting as a(n) _____avocation_____.

6. The mayor has always _____advocated_____ strict government regulation of building codes.

7. To prevent the complete disruption of the city's transportation system, the governor threatened to _____invoke_____ the law that would send the union's leaders to jail for contempt.

8. As if by magic, the actors on the bare stage _____evoked_____ the sights and sounds of life in a small New England town.

---

*Circle the **boldface** word that more satisfactorily completes each of the following sentences.*

1. Elizabeth Cady Stanton was a leading nineteenth-century (**convocation**, **advocate**) of a woman's right to vote.

2. During a raging storm, the mad King Lear (**invokes**, **revokes**) the wrath of the gods and the elements on his ungrateful daughters.

3. Although coin collecting is only his (**convocation**, **avocation**), he devotes as much time to it as he does to his career.

4. A club may reserve the right to (**revoke**, **evoke**) the privileges of a member who violates its rules.

5. A (**convocation**, **avocation**) of distinguished scholars was held to honor the university's new president.

6. There was nothing (**evocative**, **equivocal**) about the critic's scathingly negative review of the new film.

7. Just a few bars of an old song can (**evoke**, **invoke**) fond memories of people and places from long ago.

8. The collective bargaining process allows both labor and management to (**vocalize**, **advocate**) their grievances and demands.

Writer's Challenge

Read the following sentences, paying special attention to the words and phrases underlined. From the words in the box below, find better choices for these underlined words and phrases. Then use these choices to rewrite the sentences.

WORD BANK

(allocate)	compatible	exult	obsolete	(somber)
amend	(consecrate)	gnarled	obviate	stultify
(apathy)	copious	ingenuous	recalcitrant	turbulent
ardent	emaciated	limpid	(reprehensible)	(voluminous)

Yad Vashem

1. In 1953, the Israeli *Knesset* (legislature) voted to <u>set apart or designate for a special purpose</u> funds and land for a "monument to a nation's grief . . . a landmark of moral history" (Abba Eban).

　　allocate

2. The Yad Vashem Holocaust Memorial opened in Jerusalem in 1957 to <u>make sacred</u> the memory of the millions who died during the Holocaust.

　　consecrate

3. Evidence of the innumerable <u>rotten</u> acts perpetrated upon innocent victims is displayed at Yad Vashem not only to shock and sadden but also to educate people so that such cruelty shall never happen again.

　　reprehensible

4. Yad Vashem houses <u>really big</u> collections of books, films, photographs, public and personal documents, and artifacts that provide proof of what happened between 1933 and 1945.

　　voluminous

5. Yad Vashem's Children's Memorial is set in a(n) <u>depressed or melancholy</u> underground cavern, where tiny memorial candles flicker continually to keep alive the memory of all the young lives that were lost.

　　somber

6. After visiting Yad Vashem, people who may once have felt <u>a lack of feeling, emotion, or interest</u> toward that terrible period of human history find themselves changed forever.

　　apathy

Analogies

In each of the following, circle the item that best completes the comparison.

See pages T38–T48 for explanations of answers.

1. negligible is to **little** as
a. bereft is to much
b. commodious is to little
c. copious is to much ⟵
d. rampant is to little

2. gibes are to **deride** as
a. panaceas are to injure
b. mistakes are to amend
c. condolences are to solace ⟵
d. attainments are to obviate

3. shanty is to **squalid** as
a. bungalow is to stately
b. palace is to opulent ⟵
c. cottage is to decrepit
d. condominium is to obsolete

4. abhor is to **esteem** as
a. attire is to redress
b. chastise is to commend ⟵
c. delete is to excise
d. implicate is to suppress

5. omniscient is to **know** as
a. omnipotent is to subject
b. infallible is to think
c. omnivorous is to eat ⟵
d. invulnerable is to wound

6. corrosive is to **burn** as
a. poignant is to pinch
b. limpid is to bite
c. cogent is to scratch
d. pungent is to sting ⟵

7. somber is to **mood** as
a. ambidextrous is to temperament
b. facile is to effort
c. vociferous is to noise
d. dour is to disposition ⟵

8. recalcitrant is to **mule** as
a. stolid is to cow ⟵
b. ironic is to weasel
c. supercilious is to pig
d. ingenuous is to sheep

9. skinflint is to **parsimonious** as
a. busybody is to officious ⟵
b. renegade is to loyal
c. craven is to emaciated
d. deviate is to capricious

10. brash is to **temerity** as
a. fervent is to apathy
b. chivalrous is to artifice
c. hard-hearted is to clemency
d. ardent is to enthusiasm ⟵

Choosing the Right Meaning

Read each sentence carefully. Then circle the item that best completes the statement below the sentence.

See pages T38–T48 for explanations of answers.

The book claims to be an "impartial analysis of the issue," but its unkempt prose shows it to be the work of a fanatic. (2)

1. In line 1 the word **unkempt** most nearly means
a. uncombed   b. lucid   c. wordy   d. sloppy ⟵

Facile solutions to complex problems do not impress me, nor do those who put forward such ideas to attain their own ends. (2)

2. In line 1 the word **Facile** most nearly means
a. Spurious ⟵   b. Modest   c. Weird   d. Fluent

It is horrifying to think that centuries after the war, so many of the animosities that produced it have still not been interred. (2)

3. The word **interred** in line 2 is best defined as

a. consigned to the earth   b. laid to rest   c. put on the back burner   d. engraved in our hearts

Slowly but surely the grand old frigate buffeted its way through the turbulent seas off that storm-tossed coast.   (2)

4. The word **buffeted** in line 1 is best defined as

a. threaded   b. pushed   c. sought   d. pummeled

Our tradition of academic freedom allows all views, orthodox and deviate alike, to be heard unmolested.   (2)

5. The word **deviate** in line 1 is best defined as

a. straying   b. commonplace   c. unconventional   d. substandard

Two-Word Completions

Circle the pair of words that best complete the meaning of each of the following sentences.

See pages T38–T48 for explanations of answers.

1. It was one of life's little _____ that the implacable judge who had so _____ condemned others to the gallows should himself die by the noose.

a. quandaries . . . scrupulously
b. ironies . . . assiduously
c. discrepancies . . . meticulously
d. artifices . . . warily

2. In his will, the philanthropist _____ a sizable portion of his great fortune to such _____ endeavors as sheltering the homeless and feeding the hungry.

a. allocated . . . altruistic
b. deployed . . . virulent
c. commended . . . diffident
d. consecrated . . . obsolete

3. In a truly eerie opening scene, the _____ sight of the ghost of Hamlet's father walking on the battlements fills three very superstitious mortals with fear and _____.

a. poignant . . . animosity
b. ominous . . . temerity
c. somber . . . nostalgia
d. uncanny . . . apprehension

4. The _____ old house, a hoary relic of a bygone era, had been closed up for so many years that a _____ odor permeated the atmosphere of every room like an evil yellow fog.

a. stately . . . tepid
b. malevolent . . . suave
c. decrepit . . . musty
d. squalid . . . limpid

5. Though I love to _____ in a friend's success, I have never been able to take delight in the discomfiture of a(n) _____.

a. revel . . . adversary
b. accede . . . martinet
c. converge . . . craven
d. exult . . . benefactor

Enriching Your Vocabulary

Read the passage below. Then complete the exercise at the bottom of the page.

A Crop of Words

People everywhere—in cities, suburbs, small towns, and rural areas—depend on farmers for food.

It is not surprising, therefore, that English is a language that is rich in words related to farming. Many of these words come from Middle and Old English. Over the centuries,

Combine harvester at work

a number of farming words have taken on figurative as well as literal meanings. For example, *fallow* (Unit 3) refers to land that is not actively being farmed, but it can also be used to describe a mind that is inactive. A *crop* is the result of a harvest, but it is also a batch or collection of something, such as a *crop* of new students or a *crop* of movies based on computer games. The effort to achieve a goal, often an intellectual one, is sometimes likened to the progress of a crop from planting to harvest.

Many common expressions have their origins in farming. Someone who reverses the natural or proper order of doing something is said to *put the cart before the horse*. When you begin a task in earnest, you *put your hand to the plow*. Another expression using *plow* is a wish for success: *Speed the plow*.

In Column A below are 8 crop words that have both literal and figurative meanings. With or without a dictionary, match each word with its meanings in Column B.

Column A

<u> e </u> **1.** sow

<u> g </u> **2.** reap

<u> a </u> **3.** fodder

<u> f </u> **4.** drought

<u> c </u> **5.** winnow

<u> b </u> **6.** grind

<u> d </u> **7.** chaff

<u> h </u> **8.** plow

Column B

a. food for animals; material that is readily available

b. to crush into powder; to oppress, weaken, or destroy

c. to remove by a current of air; to get rid of something unwanted

d. seed coverings and other debris separated from seed; something relatively worthless

e. to plant seeds for growth; to put something in motion

f. a prolonged period of dryness; a chronic shortage or lack

g. to cut grain or gather a crop; to obtain or win

h. to break up or turn over soil; to proceed steadily and with much effort

Definitions

Note carefully the spelling, pronunciation, part(s) of speech, and definition(s) of each of the following words. Then write the word in the blank space(s) in the illustrative sentence(s) following. Finally, study the lists of synonyms and antonyms given at the end of each entry.

1. acquiesce
(ak wē es')

(*v.*) to accept without protest; to agree or submit

Management is not likely to _____ **acquiesce** _____ to union demands for raises because the company's profits have recently been on the decline.

SYNONYMS: comply with, accede, consent, yield
ANTONYMS: resist, protest

2. allure
(a lür')

(*v.*) to entice, tempt; to be attractive to; (*n.*) a strong attraction; the power to attract, charm

Dreams of stardom _____ **allure** _____ many gifted young performers from all over the country to the bright lights of Broadway.

The _____ **allure** _____ of get-rich-quick schemes may lead people down the road to financial ruin.

SYNONYMS: (*v.*) beguile, tantalize; (*n.*) temptation, enticement
ANTONYMS: (*v.*) repel, turn off; (*n.*) repellent

3. askew
(ə skyü')

(*adj., adv.*) twisted to one side, crooked; disapprovingly

Some people cannot refrain from straightening lampshades that are a little _____ **askew** _____.

All our plans for a picnic on the beach went suddenly _____ **askew** _____ when it began to rain very heavily.

SYNONYMS: awry, lopsided, cockeyed
ANTONYMS: straight, symmetrical

4. blithe
(blīth)

(*adj.*) cheerful, lighthearted; casual, unconcerned

It is difficult to deflate the _____ **blithe** _____ optimism of the young.

SYNONYMS: carefree, nonchalant, indifferent
ANTONYMS: glum, morose, despondent, depressed

5. contentious
(kən ten' shəs)

(*adj.*) quarrelsome, inclined to argue

The members of the on-line discussion group were annoyed by the newcomer's _____ **contentious** _____ and rude remarks.

SYNONYMS: argumentative, disputatious, combative
ANTONYMS: agreeable, amiable, affable, pacific

6. covet
(kəv' ət)

(*v.*) to desire something belonging to another

Those who _____ covet _____ the good fortune of others are likely to be unhappy with their own lot in life.

SYNONYMS: crave, yearn for, hunger for
ANTONYMS: disdain, scorn, despise

7. crestfallen
(krest' fô lən)

(*adj.*) discouraged, dejected, downcast

Despite the loss of an important labor endorsement, the candidate appeared in no way _____ crestfallen _____.

SYNONYMS: despondent, disconsolate
ANTONYMS: elated, cheerful, self-satisfied, cocky

8. disheveled
(di shev' əld)

(*adj.*) rumpled, mussed; hanging in disorder

Most people look a little bit _____ disheveled _____ when they get up in the morning.

SYNONYMS: untidy, disarranged, tousled, unkempt
ANTONYMS: tidy, neat, orderly, well-groomed

9. exponent
(ek spō' nənt)

(*n.*) one who advocates, speaks for, explains, or interprets; (*math*) the power to which a number, symbol, or expression is to be raised

President Theodore Roosevelt was one of the first _____ exponents _____ of conservation.

In the equation $x^2 + y^2 = z^2$, the small raised 2s are all _____ exponents _____.

SYNONYMS: defender, champion, interpreter
ANTONYMS: critic, adversary, faultfinder, detractor

10. garrulous
(gar' ə ləs)

(*adj.*) given to much talking, tediously chatty

If you are conversing with a _____ garrulous _____ individual, you may find it hard to get a word in edgewise.

SYNONYMS: talkative, loquacious, long-winded
ANTONYMS: reticent, mum, taciturn, laconic, reserved

11. insuperable
(in sü' pər ə bəl)

(*adj.*) incapable of being overcome

To the composer Ludwig van Beethoven, increasing deafness was not an _____ insuperable _____ handicap.

SYNONYMS: invincible, insurmountable
ANTONYMS: surmountable, conquerable

12. lamentable
(lam' ən tə bəl)

(*adj.*) to be regretted or pitied

After a long, hard winter, city streets may be in a truly _____ lamentable _____ state of disrepair.

SYNONYMS: deplorable, regrettable, distressing
ANTONYMS: praiseworthy, commendable, laudable

13. misnomer
(mis nō′ mər)

(*n.*) an unsuitable or misleading name

The term *World Series* is a _____ **misnomer** _____ because only North American teams participate in this annual event.

SYNONYMS: misnaming, malapropism

14. profess
(prə fes′)

(*v.*) to affirm openly; to state belief in; to claim, pretend

My music teacher _____ **professed** _____ herself satisfied with my technical progress so far this year.

SYNONYMS: assert, declare, proclaim, purport
ANTONYMS: disclaim, disavow, repudiate

15. respite
(res′ pit)

(*n.*) a period of relief or rest

A vacation provides a _____ **respite** _____ from the worries and responsibilities of everyday life.

SYNONYMS: interval, intermission, lull, breather

16. retribution
(re trə byü′ shən)

(*n.*) a repayment; a deserved punishment

In most ancient societies _____ **retribution** _____ was swiftly visited on those who broke their promises.

SYNONYMS: recompense, requital, just deserts

17. sinuous
(sin′ yü əs)

(*adj.*) winding, having many curves; lithe and flexible

The trunk of the tree was almost completely encased by _____ **sinuous** _____ wisteria vines.

SYNONYMS: twisting, convoluted, serpentine, supple
ANTONYMS: direct, straight, unbending, stiff, rigid

18. sonorous
(sə nōr′ əs)

(*adj.*) full, deep, or rich in sound; impressive in style

The _____ **sonorous** _____ tolling of church bells announced the passing of the monarch.

SYNONYMS: resonant, resounding, grandiloquent
ANTONYMS: tinny, reedy, harsh, grating

19. vanguard
(van′ gärd)

(*n.*) the foremost part of an army; the leading position in any field

If a high-tech company is to survive in today's marketplace, it must remain in the _____ **vanguard** _____ of innovation.

SYNONYMS: forefront, cutting edge, trailblazers
ANTONYMS: rear guard, stragglers, laggards

20. wastrel
(wās′ trəl)

(*n.*) a wasteful person, spendthrift; a good-for-nothing

Many a novel has told the sorry tale of a charming but self-destructive _____ **wastrel** _____.

SYNONYMS: loafer, idler, squanderer, profligate
ANTONYMS: skinflint, tightwad, miser

Completing the Sentence

From the words for this unit, choose the one that best completes each of the following sentences. Write the word in the space provided.

1. In spite of her rain-soaked clothing and _____ **disheveled** _____ appearance, it seemed to me that she had never looked lovelier.

2. I confess I suffered a twinge of envy when I learned that my rival had won the prize I had _____ **coveted** _____ so dearly.

3. Retailers who seek to _____ **allure** _____ unwary consumers with false claims should feel the full penalties of the law.

4. The body of the slain hero was accompanied to its final resting place by the _____ **sonorous** _____ strains of a funeral march.

5. You certainly have a right to your opinions, but you have become so _____ **contentious** _____ that you immediately challenge opinions expressed by anyone else.

6. Excessively _____ **garrulous** _____ people usually don't have the imagination to realize that their endless chatter is boring everyone else.

7. "The blinds are hanging _____ **askew** _____ because the pull cord is all knotted and tangled," I said.

8. With the publication of her famous book *Silent Spring*, Rachel Carson moved into the _____ **vanguard** _____ of those seeking to protect our natural environment.

9. Driving a car along those _____ **sinuous** _____ mountain roads at a height of ten thousand feet calls for stronger nerves than I have.

10. After all my high hopes, I was utterly _____ **crestfallen** _____ when the notice arrived that I had failed my driver's test.

11. It isn't likely that the school administration will _____ **acquiesce** _____ to your recommendation to do away with all examinations and grades.

12. I do not _____ **profess** _____ to be heroic, but I hope I have the nerve to stand up for unpopular ideas that I believe are right.

13. The _____ **blithe** _____ personality that had made her so charming and popular was unaffected by the passage of the years.

14. For the innumerable crimes and cruelties he had committed, the tyrant had good reason to fear human, if not divine, _____ **retribution** _____.

15. Now that the football season has ended, don't you think our school's athletes deserve a brief _____ **respite** _____ before beginning basketball practice?

16. After I heard my new parrot's harsh call, I decided that "Melody," the name I had planned for it, was something of a _____ **misnomer** _____.

17. A staunch believer in the equality of the sexes, Susan B. Anthony was one of the most effective _____ **exponents** _____ of women's rights.

18. The pioneers succeeded in settling the West because they refused to admit that any obstacle, however formidable, was _____insuperable_____.

19. We can all agree that the crime situation in this community is truly _____lamentable_____, but what are we going to do about it?

20. He says that he is spending the family fortune "to promote the art of good living," but I consider him no more than a(n) _____wastrel_____.

Synonyms

*Choose the word from this unit that is **the same** or **most nearly the same** in meaning as the **boldface** word or expression in the given phrase. Write the word on the line provided.*

1. constitutes a bit of a **misleading name**   _____misnomer_____

2. **just deserts** for a life of crime   _____retribution_____

3. a welcome **relief** from pain   _____respite_____

4. the **cutting edge** of medical science   _____vanguard_____

5. proved to be something of a **spendthrift**   _____wastrel_____

6. the **resonant** quality of their voices   _____sonorous_____

7. **despondent** at the news of their misfortune   _____crestfallen_____

8. **proclaimed** their allegiance to the new government   _____professed_____

9. a **long-winded** talk show host   _____garrulous_____

10. faced **insurmountable** odds   _____insuperable_____

11. failed to **comply with** the UN resolution   _____acquiesce to_____

12. realized something had gone **awry**   _____askew_____

13. a very **argumentative** meeting   _____contentious_____

14. calculated to **tempt** big spenders   _____allure_____

15. a lifelong **champion** of higher education   _____exponent_____

Antonyms

*Choose the word from this unit that is **most nearly opposite** in meaning to the **boldface** word or expression in the given phrase. Write the word on the line provided.*

16. a **glum** outlook on life   _____blithe_____

17. one who **scorns** worldly possessions   _____covets_____

18. a **straight** path through the forest   _____sinuous_____

19. the **tidy** state of the room   _____disheveled_____

20. the company's **praiseworthy** financial condition   _____lamentable_____

Choosing the Right Word

*Circle the **boldface** word that more satisfactorily completes each of the following sentences.*

1. The intently longing gaze that he fixed upon my plate told me that Rover (**professed, coveted**) my lunch.

2. Since Ben was confident he could play varsity ball, he was extremely (**blithe, crestfallen**) when the coach cut him from the squad.

3. After we had been playing our favorite CDs at top volume for several hours, Mother entered the room and begged for some (**respite, allure**).

4. Although we really don't agree with Mother's musical taste, we decided to (**profess, acquiesce**) to her appeal.

5. His willingness to experiment with interesting new ideas clearly put him in the (**vanguard, retribution**) of social reform in his time.

6. The poet Shelley, entranced by the joyous song of the skylark, addressed the bird as "(**garrulous, blithe**) spirit."

7. The wicked may seem to prosper, but I am convinced that sometime, somehow, in this life or the next, there will be (**exponents, retribution**).

8. He is so (**contentious, sinuous**) that if someone says "Nice day," he'll start a full-scale debate on the weather.

9. Wasteful use of energy at a time when there is a critical shortage of such resources is indeed (**lamentable, sonorous**).

10. It would be a (**misnomer, respite**) to label as biography a book that is clearly a work of fiction, even though its main character is historical.

11. Because it was the duty of town criers to deliver public proclamations, they were often chosen for their (**sonorous, contentious**) voices.

12. With her lipstick smeared, her hair disarranged, and her hat (**askew, crestfallen**), she certainly was a strange sight.

13. Anyone who spends hours, days, and weeks just hanging around is a (**wastrel, vanguard**) with the most precious thing we have—*time*.

14. When we ended up in the lake, we realized that the skipper was not the expert boatman he (**acquiesced, professed**) to be.

15. With hair styles what they are these days, many men now seem to look somewhat (**disheveled, garrulous**) when they come fresh from the barber.

16. The (**vanguard, allure**) of "gold in them thar hills" brought many immigrants to California in 1849.

17. Marshall McLuhan, a leading (**wastrel, exponent**) of TV's importance in modern life, coined the phrase "the medium is the message."

18. Walking out on the empty stage and speaking the opening lines of the play seemed a(n) (**covetous, insuperable**) difficulty to the young actors.

19. The taxi driver was so (**lamentable, garrulous**) during the long trip that it was a relief to return to my silent hotel room.

20. As I watched the gymnastic meet on TV, nothing impressed me more than the incredibly graceful and (**askew, sinuous**) movements of the athletes.

Vocabulary in Context

Read the following passage, in which some of the words you have studied in this unit appear in **boldface** type. Then complete each statement given below the passage by circling the letter of the item that is **the same** or **almost the same** in meaning as the highlighted word.

Kicking Up Her Heels

(Line)

American dancer, choreographer, and director Agnes de Mille (1905–1993) was born into a theatrical family. Her father was a playwright and a director; her uncle was Cecil B. DeMille, the director and producer of movie extravaganzas. As a youngster in California, Agnes was captivated by the **allure** of the dance
(5) and **professed** a desire to become a ballerina. However, her family did not encourage her ambition. Agnes herself was all too aware that she lacked the ideal ballerina's long, **sinuous** limbs and compact torso.
(10) **Crestfallen**, she gave up dancing and studied English, graduating with honors from the University of California in Los Angeles.

When Agnes returned to New York in
(15) the late 1920s, she was drawn again to the dance. She began her career as a performer and then became a choreographer as well, creating and staging works for European and
(20) American ballet companies. These early dances were largely in the classical tradition of European ballet, but in 1942 de Mille broke new ground with *Rodeo*. This **blithe** look at courtship

Agnes de Mille (*center*) working with dancers in rehearsal.

(25) in the American West was a ballet, but it also included square dancing and tap dancing. Its success led Agnes de Mille directly to Broadway.

In 1943, de Mille composed and staged the dances for the Rodgers and Hammerstein musical *Oklahoma*. The show was a triumph, and it put her in the **vanguard** of the American musical theater. *Oklahoma* was the first musical to make
(30) dance a part of the dramatic action. De Mille's choreography, which included ballet and modern dance forms, revolutionized the function of dance in the musical theater.

---

1. The meaning of **allure** (line 4) is
a. rigor   c. excitement
b. charm   d. challenge

2. Professed (line 5) most nearly means
a. feigned   c. renounced
b. denied   d. declared

3. Sinuous (line 9) is best defined as
a. supple   c. thin
b. strong   d. sturdy

4. The meaning of **Crestfallen** (line 10) is
a. Downcast   c. Determined
b. Worried   d. Enthusiastic

5. Blithe (line 24) most nearly means
a. authentic   c. lighthearted
b. unusual   d. solemn

6. Vanguard (line 29) is best defined as
a. tradition   c. center
b. forefront   d. ranks

Definitions

Note carefully the spelling, pronunciation, part(s) of speech, and definition(s) of each of the following words. Then write the word in the blank space(s) in the illustrative sentence(s) following. Finally, study the lists of synonyms and antonyms given at the end of each entry.

1. allude
(ə lüd′)

(*v.*) to refer to casually or indirectly

In his speech, the candidate _____ **alluded** _____ to his opponent's lack of military experience.

SYNONYMS: suggest, insinuate, hint at, intimate

2. clairvoyant
(klâr voi′ ənt)

(*adj.*) supernaturally perceptive; (*n.*) one who possesses extrasensory powers, seer

Few people are taken in by the _____ **clairvoyant** _____ pronouncements of fortune-tellers and mediums.

The police sometimes use _____ **clairvoyants** _____ to help them solve difficult missing-person cases.

SYNONYMS: (*adj.*) insightful, discerning, uncanny; (*n.*) visionary
ANTONYMS: (*adj.*) blind, unseeing, myopic, dense, imperceptive

3. conclusive
(kən klü′ siv)

(*adj.*) serving to settle an issue; final

When they weighed all the evidence in the case, the members of the jury found the testimony of the expert witness to be _____ **conclusive** _____.

SYNONYMS: decisive, indisputable, convincing, definitive
ANTONYMS: unsettled, provisional, indefinite

4. disreputable
(dis rep′ yə tə bəl)

(*adj.*) not respectable, not esteemed

Supermarket tabloids frequently publish stories about the _____ **disreputable** _____ behavior of celebrities.

SYNONYMS: disgraceful, discreditable, shady
ANTONYMS: honest, aboveboard, respectable, creditable

5. endemic
(en dem′ ik)

(*adj.*) native or confined to a particular region or people; characteristic of or prevalent in a field

Scientists have yet to identify many plant and animal species _____ **endemic** _____ to the rain forests.

SYNONYMS: indigenous, restricted to
ANTONYMS: alien, foreign, extraneous

6. exemplary
(eg zem′ plə rē)

(*adj.*) worthy of imitation, commendable; serving as a model

The Medal of Freedom is awarded to U.S. civilians for _____ **exemplary** _____ achievements in various fields.

SYNONYMS: praiseworthy, meritorious, sterling, illustrative
ANTONYMS: infamous, notorious, scandalous, disreputable

7. fathom
(fath' əm)

(v.) to understand, get to the bottom of; to determine the depth of; (n.) a measure of depth in water

It is sometimes difficult to _____**fathom**_____ the motives behind another person's actions.

The great passenger liner *Titanic* still lies buried several thousand _____**fathoms**_____ beneath the ocean's surface.

SYNONYMS: (v.) grasp, comprehend, figure out, plumb

8. guile
(gīl)

(n.) treacherous cunning, deceit

Folklore has it that a serpent's most outstanding trait is _____**guile**_____, just as a fox's is craftiness.

SYNONYMS: trickery, duplicity, chicanery
ANTONYMS: candor, artlessness, naïveté, plain dealing

9. integrity
(in teg' rə tē)

(n.) honesty, high moral standards; an unimpaired condition, completeness, soundness

Scholars debated the _____**integrity**_____ of the text of a newly discovered poem attributed to Shakespeare.

SYNONYMS: rectitude, probity
ANTONYMS: dishonesty, corruption, turpitude

10. itinerary
(ī tin' ə rer ē)

(n.) a route of travel; a record of travel; a guidebook

Tour companies regularly provide potential customers with detailed _____**itineraries**_____ of the trips they offer.

SYNONYMS: schedule, program

11. misconstrue
(mis kən strü')

(v.) to interpret wrongly, mistake the meaning of

Young children sometimes _____**misconstrue**_____ their parents' motives.

SYNONYMS: misjudge, misinterpret

12. obnoxious
(äb näk' shəs)

(adj.) highly offensive, arousing strong dislike

The speeches Hitler delivered at the Nuremberg rallies were full of racial slurs and other _____**obnoxious**_____ language.

SYNONYMS: disagreeable, repugnant, hateful, odious
ANTONYMS: agreeable, pleasing, engaging, personable

13. placate
(plā' kāt)

(v.) to appease, soothe, pacify

Sponsors of the controversial bill modified some of its original provisions in order to _____**placate**_____ the opposition.

SYNONYMS: satisfy, mollify, allay, conciliate
ANTONYMS: vex, irk, provoke, exasperate, annoy

14. placid
(plas' id)

(*adj.*) calm, peaceful

There was no wind to disturb the _____ **placid** _____ surface of the lake.

SYNONYMS: undisturbed, tranquil, quiet, serene
ANTONYMS: stormy, agitated, turbulent, tempestuous

15. plagiarism
(plā' jə riz əm)

(*n.*) passing off or using as one's own the writing (or other materials) of another person

Theft of an author's ideas is far more difficult to prove in court than word-for-word _____ **plagiarism** _____.

SYNONYMS: piracy, theft

16. potent
(pōt' ənt)

(*adj.*) powerful; highly effective

Music has been called the most _____ **potent** _____ agent for inducing people to forget their differences and live in harmony.

SYNONYMS: mighty, formidable, forceful
ANTONYMS: weak, inept, feckless, powerless, ineffective

17. pretext
(prē' tekst)

(*n.*) a false reason, deceptive excuse

I sought some _____ **pretext** _____ for excusing myself from the weekly staff meeting I did not want to attend.

SYNONYMS: pretense, cover story, rationale, evasion

18. protrude
(prō trüd')

(*v.*) to stick out, thrust forth

Dentists commonly use various kinds of braces to correct the alignment of teeth that _____ **protrude** _____ or are crooked.

SYNONYMS: project, jut out, bulge

19. stark
(stärk)

(*adj.*) harsh, unrelieved, desolate; (*adv.*) utterly

Many a young idealist has found it difficult to accept the _____ **stark** _____ realities of life.

By the end of his brief reign, the Roman emperor Caligula was clearly _____ **stark** _____ raving mad.

SYNONYMS: (*adj.*) sheer, downright, grim, bleak; (*adv.*) absolutely
ANTONYMS: (*adj.*) bright, cheerful, embellished, ornate

20. superficial
(sü pər fish' əl)

(*adj.*) on or near the surface; concerned with or understanding only what is on the surface, shallow

A _____ **superficial** _____ analysis of a complex problem is not likely to produce a viable or long-lasting solution.

SYNONYMS: skin-deep, insubstantial, cursory, slapdash
ANTONYMS: deep, profound, thorough, exhaustive

Completing the Sentence

From the words for this unit, choose the one that best completes each of the following sentences. Write the word in the space provided.

1. It is quite useless to try to __placate__ dissatisfied customers who actually enjoy being angry and making complaints.

2. Phyllis was too polite to mention John's crude behavior at the party, but she certainly __alluded__ to it when she spoke of "unnecessary unpleasantness."

3. His skillful use of flattery and double-talk to persuade us to agree to his scheme was a typical example of his __guile__.

4. Neither misfortunes nor happy events seem to have the slightest effect on my friend's __placid__ disposition.

5. America's most __potent__ weapon in the struggle for world influence is its great tradition of democracy and freedom.

6. Although the cut on my arm was bleeding quite heavily, it proved to be quite __superficial__ and required only a tight bandage.

7. The tapes of the conversations were regarded as __conclusive__ proof that the official had been aware of the crime.

8. We spent many pleasant hours poring over all kinds of maps and guidebooks, planning the __itinerary__ for our trip across the United States.

9. Their idea of a(n) __exemplary__ student is someone so perfect in so many ways that he or she would be too good to exist.

10. Sherlock Holmes assured Dr. Watson that it was simple deduction, not some __clairvoyant__ faculty, that led him to the document's hiding place.

11. When we consider the __stark__ misery of the last years of his life, we must conclude that he paid in full for all his offenses.

12. The brilliant essay for which the writer received so much lavish praise has been exposed as a skillful act of __plagiarism__.

13. I selected them as my business partners not only because I respect their ability but also because I have unlimited confidence in their character and __integrity__.

14. Blue jeans, once __endemic__ to the cowboys of the American West, are now a familiar part of the whole world's wardrobe.

15. By disregarding the flood of excuses, explanations, and justifications, we were able to __fathom__ the true reasons for her actions.

16. Legally a defendant is innocent until proven guilty, so do not __misconstrue__ a refusal to testify as an admission of guilt.

17. If you allow your foot to __protrude__ into the aisle, someone may trip over it.

Unit 11 ■ 127

18. In 1722, Daniel Defoe published his famous account of the somewhat _____disreputable_____ history of Moll Flanders.

19. His conceit and his cold disregard of other people's feelings make him utterly _____obnoxious_____!

20. On the _____pretext_____ of delivering a package, the burglar sought to gain entrance to the house.

 **Synonyms**

*Choose the word from this unit that is **the same** or **most nearly the same** in meaning as the **boldface** word or expression in the given phrase. Write the word on the line provided.*

1. failed to **comprehend** the severity of the situation _____ fathom

2. deliberately **misinterpreted** my words _____ misconstrued

3. a hectic **schedule** with no time for relaxation _____ itinerary

4. signs that **jut out** from the front of the building _____ protrude

5. wholesale **piracy** of another's work _____ plagiarism

6. **hinted at** the existence of embarrassing secrets _____ alluded to

7. could find no plausible **excuse** to stay _____ pretext

8. never claimed to be **supernaturally perceptive** _____ clairvoyant

9. an advantage gained by **trickery** _____ guile

10. shellfish **indigenous** to the cape _____ endemic

11. **mollified** critics of the plan _____ placated

12. a **bleak** and barren landscape _____ stark

13. led a **tranquil** existence _____ placid

14. **disagreeable** attempts to get attention _____ obnoxious

15. the **decisive** battle in the war _____ conclusive

 **Antonyms**

*Choose the word from this unit that is **most nearly opposite** in meaning to the **boldface** word or expression in the given phrase. Write the word on the line provided.*

16. **scandalous** conduct _____ exemplary

17. **weak** claims on our affections _____ potent

18. a well-deserved reputation for **corruption** _____ integrity

19. a **respectable** way to earn a living _____ disreputable

20. a **thorough** examination of the issues _____ superficial

Choosing the Right Word

*Circle the **boldface** word that more satisfactorily completes each of the following sentences.*

1. In that neighborhood of small homes, a few massive apartment buildings (**allude, protrude**) like giants set down in a community of dwarfs.

2. Tom Sawyer used (**guile, pretext**) to get the other boys to do his work by convincing them that whitewashing a fence was fun.

3. The spectacular remains of that brilliant period stand in (**disreputable, stark**) contrast to the poverty of archaeological finds from previous eras.

4. Instead of (**alluding, fathoming**) so often to your own achievements and successes, why not wait for other people to mention them?

5. Although most of us cannot hope to match Mother Teresa's pure idealism, we may regard her noble life as inspiring and (**exemplary, endemic**).

6. In times of crisis, the utmost care must be taken to prevent ordinary military maneuvers from being (**placated, misconstrued**) as hostile acts.

7. A candidate for the highest office in the land should be, above all, a person of unshakable (**guile, integrity**).

8. Is it any wonder that your parents are worried, knowing that you are associating with such a (**placid, disreputable**) group of people?

9. The prospect of extremely high starting salaries is a (**stark, potent**) argument for pursuing a career in computer science.

10. Do not be taken in by any (**superficial, conclusive**) resemblances between their half-baked ideas and the sensible program we proposed.

11. With some psychics it is difficult to tell where the (**clairvoyant, itinerary**) leaves off and the con artist begins.

12. Mother was as upset as any of us, but she managed to conceal her fears so that she looked positively (**obnoxious, placid**).

13. It was clear that the student's book review was so similar to a review in a newspaper that it constituted outright (**integrity, plagiarism**).

14. Marge produced a convenient headache as her (**pretext, itinerary**) for having to leave early.

15. I find no one more (**obnoxious, clairvoyant**) than a person who insists on talking instead of listening to the brilliant and important things I have to say.

16. If the British government had made a sincere effort to (**misconstrue, placate**) the colonists, would the American Revolution have occurred?

17. Modern scientists use all kinds of high-tech gadgetry to (**fathom, allude**) the depths of the ocean.

18. Why not include Mount Vernon in the (**plagiarism, itinerary**) of our spring vacation?

19. It is all very well for science fiction writers to speculate, but is there any (**exemplary, conclusive**) evidence that UFOs exist?

20. Some people maintain that intelligent life must exist elsewhere in the universe, but I firmly believe that it is (**endemic, potent**) to Earth.

Vocabulary in Context

*Read the following passage, in which some of the words you have studied in this unit appear in **boldface** type. Then complete each statement given below the passage by circling the letter of the item that is **the same** or **almost the same** in meaning as the highlighted word.*

A Man of Mystery

(Line)

Scholars will probably never fully **fathom** the relationship between the troubled life of the nineteenth-century American writer Edgar Allan Poe and his poems,

The Raven, 1959. Antonio Frasconi. National Gallery of Art, Washington, DC.

short stories, and literary criticism. Poe was born in Boston in 1809. After the death of his mother when he was only two, he was taken into the home of John Allan, a wealthy Virginia merchant. Unfortunately, Poe seemed unable to live up to his guardian's standards of **integrity**. While still a student, he accumulated gambling debts that Allan refused to pay. (10)

Poe began to publish poetry and short fiction in the 1820s and 1830s while also working as an editor at various literary magazines. Yet he was always in financial difficulty. He continually failed to **placate** John Allan, who eventually cut the (15) young writer out of his will.

Poe's literary output was highly original. His poems and stories range from expressions of longing for idealized beauty to grotesque tales of horror. His 1845 poem "The Raven" won him (20) fame. His story "The Murders in the Rue Morgue" (1841) is considered the first modern detective story. His tales of horror, such as "The Fall of the House of Usher" and "The Tell-Tale Heart," are regarded as classics.

Poe's life, however, was less **exemplary** than his work. In 1836, he scandalized many by marrying his young cousin Virginia Clemm. He also had a reputation for (25) being quarrelsome. He started an uproar, for example, when he accused the American poet Henry Wadsworth Longfellow of **plagiarism**. Personal tragedy dogged him. After Virginia died of tuberculosis in 1847, Poe spiraled downward into depression, ill health, and perhaps drunkenness. In 1849, Poe was found semiconscious in the street outside a tavern in Baltimore. He died four days later (30) of causes that have never been satisfactorily explained.

---

1. The meaning of **fathom** (line 1)
 a. admire   c. describe
 (b.)understand   d. condemn

2. Integrity (line 8) most nearly means
 a. scholarship   c. civility
 b. etiquette   (d.)rectitude

3. Placate (line 15) is best defined as
 (a.)appease   c. impress
 b. enrage   d. defeat

4. The meaning of **exemplary** (line 24) is
 a. infamous   (c.)sterling
 b. celebrated   d. intense

5. Plagiarism (line 27) most nearly means
 a. pride   (c.)theft
 b. sloppiness   d. insanity

Definitions

Note carefully the spelling, pronunciation, part(s) of speech, and definition(s) of each of the following words. Then write the word in the blank space(s) in the illustrative sentence(s) following. Finally, study the lists of synonyms and antonyms given at the end of each entry.

1. abjure
(ab jür')

(*v.*) to renounce, repudiate under oath; to avoid, shun

Toward the end of Shakespeare's last play, *The Tempest*, the magician Prospero _____ **abjures** _____ his powers over nature.

SYNONYMS: forswear, retract, recant, abstain from
ANTONYMS: affirm, avow, aver, profess

2. acrid
(ak' rid)

(*adj.*) harsh in taste or odor; sharp in manner or temper

The _____ **acrid** _____ stench of a fire lingers in the air long after the flames have been extinguished.

SYNONYMS: irritating, stinging, bitter, caustic
ANTONYMS: gentle, soothing, mild

3. august
(ô gəst')

(*adj.*) majestic, inspiring admiration and respect

The _____ **august** _____ visages of four of America's great presidents are carved on the face of Mount Rushmore.

SYNONYMS: stately, dignified, exalted, venerable
ANTONYMS: humble, base, mean, lowly, abject

4. callous
(ka' ləs)

(*adj.*) emotionally hardened, unfeeling

Protesters accused the mayor of _____ **callous** _____ indifference to the plight of the homeless.

SYNONYMS: insensitive, unsympathetic, thick-skinned
ANTONYMS: sensitive, compassionate, tenderhearted

5. clandestine
(klan des' tən)

(*adj.*) secret, concealed; underhanded

During the early stages of the American Revolution, _____ **clandestine** _____ colonial printing presses churned out quantities of anti-British propaganda.

SYNONYMS: covert, furtive, surreptitious, stealthy
ANTONYMS: open, overt, undisguised, aboveboard

6. compunction
(kəm pəŋk' shən)

(*n.*) remorse, regret

In some religious writings _____ **compunction** _____ is used as a synonym for *contrition* to express profound regret for one's sins.

SYNONYMS: scruple, qualm, misgiving, contrition
ANTONYMS: shamelessness, insouciance, nonchalance

7. conflagration
(kän flə grā′ shən)

(*n.*) a large destructive fire

A large number of wooden structures quite literally added fuel to the _____conflagration_____ that swept through San Francisco in 1906.

SYNONYMS: holocaust, wildfire
ANTONYMS: deluge, flood

8. elated
(i lā′ tid)

(*adj., part.*) in high spirits, jubilant; extremely pleased

_____Elated_____ fans lined the city's streets to cheer the World Series champions.

SYNONYMS: overjoyed, ecstatic, tickled pink
ANTONYMS: depressed, crestfallen, despondent, blue

9. indelible
(in del′ ə bəl)

(*adj.*) not able to be erased or removed; memorable

The brutal crimes against humanity committed by the Nazis left an _____indelible_____ stain on the history of the twentieth century.

SYNONYMS: lasting, permanent, unforgettable
ANTONYMS: erasable, impermanent, ephemeral

10. indulgent
(in dəl′ jənt)

(*adj.*) yielding to the wishes or demands of others

A heightened sense of compassion has induced the federal government to adopt a more _____indulgent_____ policy toward illegal aliens.

SYNONYMS: lenient, permissive, tolerant, liberal
ANTONYMS: strict, severe, inflexible, hard-nosed

11. inveterate
(in vet′ ər ət)

(*adj.*) firmly established, long-standing; habitual

It has been claimed that many writers and artists have an _____inveterate_____ hostility to criticism.

SYNONYMS: persisting, chronic, dyed-in-the-wool
ANTONYMS: sporadic, intermittent, occasional

12. irrelevant
(i rel′ ə vənt)

(*adj.*) not to the point, not applicable or pertinent

When you take notes, it's best to record only the main ideas and eliminate all _____irrelevant_____ details.

SYNONYMS: inapplicable, immaterial, beside the point
ANTONYMS: pertinent, material, apropos, germane

13. nocturnal
(näk tər′ nəl)

(*adj.*) of or occurring in the night; under cover of darkness

Most _____nocturnal_____ creatures have keen eyesight and acute hearing.

SYNONYM: nighttime
ANTONYMS: daytime, diurnal

14. platitude
(plat′ ə tüd)

(*n.*) a commonplace, stale, or trite remark

The sentiments expressed in most greeting cards seldom rise above the level of timeworn _____ **platitudes** _____.

SYNONYMS: cliché, truism, bromide
ANTONYMS: epigram, quip, witticism, bon mot

15. quell
(kwel)

(*v.*) to subdue, put down forcibly

The English poet John Dryden believed that music has the power either to arouse or to _____ **quell** _____ strong emotions.

SYNONYMS: suppress, pacify, squelch, quash, crush
ANTONYMS: incite, provoke, arouse, foment, stir up

16. quiescent
(kwī es′ ənt)

(*adj.*) inactive; at rest

Although some volcanoes are believed to be truly extinct, many are merely _____ **quiescent** _____.

SYNONYMS: still, inert, motionless, dormant, tranquil
ANTONYMS: active, thriving, lively, bustling, volatile

17. ruminate
(rü′ mə nāt)

(*v.*) to meditate, think about at length; to chew the cud

In old age many people sadly _____ **ruminate** _____ on mistakes made and opportunities missed.

SYNONYMS: ponder, reflect, mull over, muse

18. tacit
(tas′ it)

(*adj.*) unspoken, silent; implied, inferred

The neighbors had a _____ **tacit** _____ understanding that they would help each other in an emergency.

SYNONYMS: unexpressed, unvoiced, understood, implicit
ANTONYMS: explicit, express, specific

19. tangible
(tan′ jə bəl)

(*adj.*) capable of being touched; real, concrete

After months of intensive negotiation, diplomats reported that they had made _____ **tangible** _____ progress toward reaching a settlement of the bitter dispute.

SYNONYMS: perceptible, actual, evident, palpable
ANTONYMS: immaterial, imperceptible, insubstantial

20. trenchant
(tren′ chənt)

(*adj.*) incisive, keen; forceful, effective; cutting, caustic; distinct, clear-cut

Scholars consider the _____ **trenchant** _____ satires of Jonathan Swift to be the greatest works of their kind in the English language.

SYNONYMS: penetrating, cutting, telling, acute
ANTONYMS: dull, bland, insipid, vapid, imperceptive

Completing the Sentence

From the words for this unit, choose the one that best completes each of the following sentences. Write the word in the space provided.

1. Abraham Lincoln's plan for reconstruction simply had the former rebels __**abjure**__ allegiance to the Confederacy and vow to support the Union.

2. Their behavior was so rude and offensive that I had no __**compunction**__ about telling them to leave the house.

3. Some people are so completely wrapped up in their own concerns that they often seem to be __**callous**__ about the feelings of others.

4. I stretched out under the old maple tree in the backyard and began to __**ruminate**__ on the strange events of that remarkable day.

5. Although the disease had been __**quiescent**__ for several years, the doctors warned her that its symptoms could appear again at any time.

6. How can we possibly accept the testimony of someone who is known to be a(n) __**inveterate**__ liar?

7. Who wouldn't be __**elated**__ at winning a huge prize on a television quiz show?

8. In the presence of such a(n) __**august**__ assemblage of religious leaders representing all the major faiths, I felt very humble.

9. The streets seemed safe and familiar during the day, but now we had to face unknown __**nocturnal**__ dangers.

10. The years of close association with outstanding teachers had left a(n) __**indelible**__ mark on the students' characters.

11. I have no patience with a(n) __**indulgent**__ parent who gives in to every whim and demand of an undisciplined child.

12. There was no __**tangible**__ evidence of his sincerity, but somehow we were confident that he would do all he could to help us.

13. The documents showed that, years before, the companies had made a(n) __**clandestine**__ agreement to divide the market among them.

14. According to legend, Mrs. O'Leary's cow kicked over an oil lamp and started the __**conflagration**__ that consumed four square miles of Chicago in 1871.

15. Your statement may be correct, but since it has no bearing on the point now under discussion, I must reject it as __**irrelevant**__.

16. I tried to __**quell**__ my feeling of panic by assuring myself that there is simply no such thing as a ghost.

17. The audience seemed to be stirred by the speaker's remarks, but in my opinion they were no more than a series of __**platitudes**__.

18. Though we were angry with each other, we had a(n) _____tacit_____ agreement to act politely in front of our parents.

19. The fumes released by the volcano were so _____acrid_____ that they caused great discomfort among people in the nearby villages.

20. The debate was decided in our favor when Carole's _____trenchant_____ rebuttal tore the other side's arguments to pieces.

Synonyms

*Choose the word from this unit that is **the same** or **most nearly the same** in meaning as the **boldface** word or expression in the given phrase. Write the word on the line provided.*

1. a **wildfire** that destroyed thousands of acres _____conflagration_____

2. **reflected** on the consequences of their actions _____ruminated_____

3. just one **bromide** after another _____platitude_____

4. tried to **suppress** their fears _____quell_____

5. saw the actor's **memorable** performance _____indelible_____

6. lacking any sense of **remorse** _____compunction_____

7. **overjoyed** by the day's events _____elated_____

8. evidence ruled **immaterial** to the case _____irrelevant_____

9. **palpable** signs of long neglect _____tangible_____

10. willingly **recanted** their old beliefs _____abjured_____

11. the lawyer's **incisive** summation to the jury _____trenchant_____

12. an extremely **caustic** denunciation _____acrid_____

13. in the emperor's **stately** presence _____august_____

14. the **secret** world of intelligence agents _____clandestine_____

15. when nature is at its most **dormant** _____quiescent_____

Antonyms

*Choose the word from this unit that is **most nearly opposite** in meaning to the **boldface** word or expression in the given phrase. Write the word on the line provided.*

16. an **occasional** reader of mysteries _____inveterate_____

17. the city's **daytime** noises _____nocturnal_____

18. a reputation for being **tenderhearted** _____callous_____

19. ignored the **explicit** warning _____tacit_____

20. **inflexible** in matters of discipline _____indulgent_____

Choosing the Right Word

*Circle the **boldface** word that more satisfactorily completes each of the following sentences.*

1. The judge has a reputation for being generally (**indulgent,** trenchant), but not when confronting an individual convicted of drunken driving.

2. Because their misconduct was clearly deliberate, we have no feelings of (**compunction,** platitude) in sentencing them to ten days of detention.

3. Millions of Americans were thrilled as they witnessed on TV the simple but (**august,** quiescent) ceremony of the presidential inauguration.

4. We should seek not to (**quell,** elate) the idealism and enthusiasm of youth but, rather, to direct those impulses into useful channels.

5. The major powers intervened to prevent the brushfire war from engulfing the entire region in a full-scale (**conflagration,** compunction).

6. Since my parents offered no objections, I felt that I had their (acrid, **tacit**) consent to go ahead with my plans for a summer trip to California.

7. The deep-seated resentment of the populace, which had long been (**quiescent,** irrelevant), suddenly blossomed into open rebellion.

8. In these days of presidential primaries, candidates can no longer be chosen at (**clandestine,** august) meetings of a few powerful politicians.

9. After listening to the senator's (**trenchant,** tacit) analysis, I have a clearer idea of what is involved and where I should stand on the issue.

10. We may criticize Americans for many things, but they are never (elated, **callous**) when appeals for help come from distressed people.

11. As part of the settlement, the company must henceforth (quell, **abjure**) unsubstantiated claims for its product.

12. Like so many (clandestine, **inveterate**) smokers, she has found that great self-discipline is needed to break the cigarette habit.

13. An insightful writer usually has no need to rely on hollow generalities or threadbare (ruminations, **platitudes**).

14. His invariably (**acrid,** indulgent) remarks on the state of the world soon earned him the nickname of "Old Sourpuss."

15. Just before going to sleep, we set traps to discourage the (indelible, **nocturnal**) raids of the raccoons on our food supply.

16. Though the anecdote was amusing, it was totally (callous, **irrelevant**) to the matter we were discussing at the moment.

17. Your (**ruminations,** compunctions) on the meaning of life will be just a waste of time unless they lead to some plans for rational behavior.

18. Although there was no (**tangible,** inveterate) reason for my alarm, I could not shake off the feeling that something terrible was about to happen.

19. Alexander the Great's meteoric career of world conquest made an (**indelible,** indulgent) impression on the thought and institutions of antiquity.

20. Taking third place in the hundred-meter dash in the intramural track meet left me satisfied but scarcely (callous, **elated**).

Vocabulary in Context

*Read the following passage, in which some of the words you have studied in this unit appear in **boldface** type. Then complete each statement given below the passage by circling the letter of the item that is **the same** or **almost the same** in meaning as the highlighted word.*

Owl Wisdom

(Line)

For most people, the sight of an owl, with its wings outstretched, swooping swiftly and silently down on its prey is an **indelible** experience. Equally impressive is the sight of an owl sitting virtually motionless on a tree limb with its large, fixed eyes wide open. It may be this wide-eyed

(5) look of exceptional awareness that inspired the **platitude** "the wise old owl." Contrary to appearances, however, owls are not exceptionally intelligent, certainly not when

(10) compared with highly trainable birds such as parrots and parakeets.

Owls are birds of prey, hunters that kill and eat mostly small mammals. Large owls hunt rabbits

(15) and squirrels, and smaller owls catch rodents, such as mice and shrews, or large insects. A few owls eat other

Northern saw-whet owl hunting at night

birds, skim fish out of shallow water, or pick up and eat something that they did not kill themselves. For the most part, owls are **nocturnal** hunters, but a few species

(20) hunt by day and are **quiescent** by night.

It is not only the size of owls' eyes but also their ability, unusual among birds, to see objects with both eyes that make them such effective hunters in the dark. Keen hearing also enables some owls to catch small animals without seeing them. These owls can find their prey by tracking the sounds the animals make while moving on

(25) the forest floor or even under snow.

Night-hunting owls are difficult to locate and observe in the forest by day, as any birdwatcher will tell you. There may be few **tangible** signs that owls are present. Since owls wish to sleep in undisturbed safety, they choose a perch deep in the foliage or on a trunk or branch with coloring similar to their own rather dull-colored

(30) plumage. Daytime hunters, such as the short-eared owl, are easier to spot because they can be seen catching their prey in broad daylight in open country. One thing is certain, however: The person who is lucky enough to see an owl in the wild, whether during the day or at night, will feel **elated**.

. The meaning of **indelible** (line 2) is
a. alarming   c. exciting
b. unusual   (d.) unforgettable

. Platitude (line 6) most nearly means
(a.) cliché   c. phrase
b. classification   d. nickname

. Nocturnal (line 19) is best defined as
a. occasional   c. excellent
(b.) nighttime   d. twilight

4. The meaning of **quiescent** (line 20) is
a. blind   (c.) inactive
b. industrious   d. sociable

5. Tangible (line 27) most nearly means
a. insubstantial   c. confusing
b. identifiable   (d.) perceptible

6. Elated (line 33) is best defined as
a. privileged   c. despondent
(b.) jubilant   d. annoyed

Analogies

In each of the following, circle the item that best completes the comparison.

See pages T38–T48 for explanations of answers.

1. **guile** is to **unfavorable** as
   a. integrity is to favorable
   b. clairvoyance is to unfavorable
   c. plagiarism is to favorable
   d. itinerary is to unfavorable

2. **clairvoyant** is to **insight** as
   a. potent is to power
   b. garrulous is to silence
   c. callous is to sympathy
   d. indulgent is to harshness

3. **fathom** is to **depth** as
   a. width is to meter
   b. bushel is to height
   c. knot is to speed
   d. inch is to yard

4. **exemplary** is to **favorable** as
   a. disreputable is to unfavorable
   b. obnoxious is to favorable
   c. august is to unfavorable
   d. garrulous is to favorable

5. **exponent** is to **pro** as
   a. advocate is to con
   b. opponent is to pro
   c. adversary is to con
   d. critic is to pro

6. **impostor** is to **guile** as
   a. swindler is to integrity
   b. peacemaker is to contentious
   c. wastrel is to thrift
   d. siren is to allure

7. **crestfallen** is to **down** as
   a. lamentable is to up
   b. blithe is to down
   c. elated is to up
   d. nocturnal is to down

8. **acrid** is to **smell** as
   a. disheveled is to hear
   b. tacit is to see
   c. callous is to taste
   d. tangible is to touch

9. **platitude** is to **trite** as
   a. respite is to arduous
   b. pretext is to contentious
   c. misnomer is to erroneous
   d. vanguard is to tacit

10. **quell** is to **quash** as
    a. covet is to shun
    b. fathom is to dive
    c. acquiesce is to comply
    d. protrude is to abjure

11. **conflagration** is to **brush fire** as
    a. blizzard is to avalanche
    b. deluge is to monsoon
    c. tornado is to drought
    d. hurricane is to shower

12. **sonorous** is to **sound** as
    a. august is to season
    b. aromatic is to smell
    c. sinuous is to curve
    d. callous is to touch

13. **august** is to **abject** as
    a. callous is to insensitive
    b. placid is to tempestuous
    c. tacit is to verbatim
    d. clandestine is to furtive

14. **blithe** is to **glum** as
    a. garrulous is to talkative
    b. pertinent is to irrelevant
    c. august is to clandestine
    d. sinuous is to quiescent

15. **placate** is to **provoke** as
    a. profess is to avow
    b. profess is to disclaim
    c. profess is to lament
    d. profess is to allure

16. **miser** is to **amass** as
    a. exponent is to allude
    b. vanguard is to conclude
    c. wastrel is to squander
    d. dent is to protrude

17. **cow** is to **ruminate** as
    a. mammal is to crawl
    b. rodent is to gnaw
    c. amphibian is to fly
    d. reptile is to hibernate

18. **indelible** is to **erase** as
    a. insuperable is to conquer
    b. indulgent is to pamper
    c. inveterate is to refine
    d. unfathomable is to misconstrue

Word Associations   *In each of the following groups, circle the word that is best defined or suggested by the given phrase.*

1. ears that stand out conspicuously
a. protrude   b. placate   c. abjure   d. allude

2. said of a chatterbox
a. garrulous   b. lamentable   c. alluring   d. sonorous

3. bats and other such creatures
a. quiescent   b. nocturnal   c. crestfallen   d. sinuous

4. "The early bird gets the worm."
a. compunction   b. platitude   c. allure   d. respite

5. get to the bottom of the situation
a. protrude   b. fathom   c. quell   d. covet

6. an awe-inspiring religious ceremony
a. crestfallen   b. trenchant   c. elated   d. august

7. unsympathetic to the plight of the needy
a. callous   b. contentious   c. sinuous   d. superficial

8. behavior that is repugnant
a. crestfallen   b. obnoxious   c. nocturnal   d. trenchant

9. a "cover" story
a. plagiarism   b. pretext   c. retribution   d. irrelevancy

10. a time-out in a hotly contested basketball game
a. respite   b. misnomer   c. pretext   d. wastrel

11. a sense of guilt or uncertainty about some action
a. compunction   b. retribution   c. vanguard   d. guile

12. a style that is utterly simple and unadorned
a. placid   b. nocturnal   c. stark   d. tangible

13. the fire that destroyed Chicago in 1871
a. wastrel   b. conflagration   c. pretext   d. allure

14. put down a disturbance
a. allure   b. ruminate   c. acquiesce   d. quell

15. interpret a question incorrectly
a. plagiarize   b. acquiesce   c. misconstrue   d. allude

16. secret meetings
a. callous   b. stark   c. disheveled   d. clandestine

17. "I take it all back."
a. covet   b. ruminate   c. profess   d. abjure

18. spends like there's no tomorrow
a. integrity   b. guile   c. wastrel   d. itinerary

19. an eye for an eye
a. pretext   b. clairvoyant   c. retribution   d. plagiarism

20. artists experimenting with new forms and techniques
a. platitude   b. vanguard   c. itinerary   d. exponent

Vocabulary in Context

*Read the following passage, in which some of the words you have studied in Units 10–12 appear in **boldface** type. Then complete each statement given below the passage by circling the item that is **the same** or **almost the same** in meaning as the highlighted word.*

Harnessing the River

(Line)

The Colorado River rises in the Rocky Mountains of Colorado and runs southwest through five states and part of Mexico. The river travels

(5) through a varied and often **stark** landscape that is notable for many deep gorges and canyons. The longest of these is the Grand Canyon. The Colorado has many

(10) rapids and waterfalls along its course. It is prone to periodic flooding and steady erosion of its banks and riverbed.

In the early 1900s, the Colorado's

(15) floods caused severe damage to agriculture in the Palo Verde and Imperial valleys of California. Many people regarded the river as their enemy. The need to control and

(20) harness this **potent** force of nature was clear, and the federal government responded. In 1928, Congress passed the Boulder Canyon Project Act. The centerpiece of this ambitious plan was

(25) the massive Hoover Dam, which also included a hydroelectric power plant and a huge reservoir.

The 726-foot Hoover Dam **protrudes** high above the surface of

(30) the river between Nevada and

Arizona. Completed in 1936, it contains 4.5 million cubic yards of concrete, enough to build a two-lane highway between New York City and

(35) San Francisco. The harnessed energy of the water flowing through the turbines of the dam generates millions of kilowatts of electricity. The **placid** waters of Lake Mead, the

(40) huge reservoir created by the dam, are used to irrigate the region. They also provide a variety of recreational opportunities.

Altogether, more than twenty huge

(45) dams have been built along the Colorado River system. However, evidence that further intervention in the river's natural cycle is needed is no longer **conclusive**. Proponents of

(50) dams make a strong case for the continuing need to control the power of the Colorado and other rivers. Opponents offer equally **trenchant** arguments for setting rivers free.

---

1. The meaning of **stark** (line 5) is
a. scenic
(c. harsh)
b. lush
d. exotic

2. Potent (line 20) most nearly means
a. beneficial
c. dangerous
b. mysterious
(d. mighty)

3. Protrudes (line 29) is best defined as
a. sits
c. roars
(b. juts out)
d. stands

4. The meaning of **placid** (line 39) is
a. clear
(c. tranquil)
b. turbulent
d. polluted

5. Conclusive (line 49) most nearly means
a. reliable
c. available
b. understandable
(d. indisputable)

6. Trenchant (line 53) is best defined as
(a. forceful)
c. vague
b. inflexible
d. interesting

Choosing the Right Meaning

Read each sentence carefully. Then circle the item that best completes the statement below the sentence.

See pages T38–T48 for explanations of answers.

Since the middle class barely existed in tsarist Russia, the division between haves and have-nots was always trenchant. (2)

1. The word **trenchant** in line 2 most nearly means

a. caustic   b. forceful   c. incisive   (d. clear-cut)

In order to protect the integrity of the museum's collection of Scythian gold, the curator refused to part with even one small treasure—and died in Stalin's purges for his pains. (2)

2. In line 1 the word **integrity** is best defined as

a. uniqueness   (b. completeness)   c. brilliance   d. probity

For a time she settled down; but soon the allure of the open road proved irresistible, and she was off on her travels again. (2)

3. In line 1 the word **allure** most nearly means

a. vitality   (b. appeal)   c. wanderlust   d. rewards

To determine the value of the expression $(x + y)^3$, multiply the sum of the variables x and y by the exponent 3. (2)

4. The word **exponent** in line 2 is best defined as

(a. power)   b. interpreter   c. advocate   d. number

When I checked the printed itinerary, I was astonished to find that we had been allowed exactly one hour to "do" the British Museum. (2)

5. The word **itinerary** in line 1 is used to mean

a. train schedule   b. account of a trip   (c. guidebook for a tour)   d. route of the journey

Antonyms

In each of the following groups, circle the word or expression that is most nearly the **opposite** of the word in **boldface** type.

1. covet
a. release
b. hide
c. disdain
d. desire

2. sinuous
a. clean
b. curved
c. straight
d. open

3. crestfallen
a. brave
b. disappointed
c. neat
d. joyful

4. conclusive
a. contentious
b. final
c. doubtful
d. important

5. lamentable
a. praiseworthy
b. unfortunate
c. carefree
d. honest

6. disreputable
a. angry
b. respected
c. organized
d. extreme

7. quiescent
a. deafening
b. inactive
c. bustling
d. certain

8. indelible
a. sad
b. temporary
c. forceful
d. certain

9. callous
a. sensitive
b. hidden
c. tight
d. curved

11. inveterate
a. foolish
b. closed
c. ungainly
d. occasional

13. tacit
a. cheap
b. expressed
c. undamaged
d. talkative

15. contentious
a. difficult
b. twisted
c. small
d. agreeable

10. guile
a. affluence
b. frankness
c. fraud
d. sweetness

12. irrelevant
a. concerned
b. prompt
c. appropriate
d. ugly

14. placate
a. destroy
b. vex
c. calm
d. enlarge

16. endemic
a. native
b. healthy
c. alien
d. superficial

Word Families

A. On the line provided, write the word you have learned in Units 10–12 that is related to each of the following nouns.

EXAMPLE: tangibility—**tangible**

1. quiescence — quiescent

2. elatedness, elation — elated

3. exemplar, exemplariness, exemplarity, example, exemplification — exemplary

4. ruminator, ruminant, rumination — ruminate

5. conclusiveness, conclusion — conclusive

6. allusion, allusiveness — allude

7. protrusion, protrusiveness — protrude

8. placidity, placidness — placid

9. superficiality — superficial

10. profession, professor, professional — profess

11. irrelevance, irrelevancy — irrelevant

12. potency, potence, potentness, potentate — potent

13. clairvoyance — clairvoyant

14. sinuousness, sinuosity — sinuous

15. sonorousness, sonority — sonorous

B. On the line provided, write the word you have learned in Units 10–12 that is related to each of the following verbs.

EXAMPLE: conclude—**conclusive**

16. plagiarize — plagiarism

17. waste — wastrel

18. indulge — indulgent

19. lament — lamentable

20. contend — contentious

Two-Word Completions

Circle the pair of words that best complete the meaning of each of the following passages.

See pages T38–T48 for explanations of answers.

1. The trail known as "Dead Man's Curves" is so steep and _____ that even the most proficient and experienced skiers often must stop for a brief _____ before completing the course.

a. sinuous . . . respite
b. disreputable . . . pretext
c. stark . . . itinerary
d. clandestine . . . compunction

2. During the evening, Ned must have _____ to his close acquaintance with at least a dozen celebrities. Afterward, we all agreed that his nickname, "Name-dropper Ned," was no _____.

a. protruded . . . plagiarism
b. alluded . . . misnomer
c. misconstrued . . . pretext
d. protruded . . . platitude

3. In view of the countless crimes the dictator had committed while in power, the revolutionary tribunal expressed no _____ in seeking the sternest _____ on behalf of the people.

a. guile . . . conflagration
b. integrity . . . respite
c. compunction . . . retribution
d. pretext . . . vanguard

4. Utterly _____ at their upset defeat, the Belleville squad looked on dismally as the trophy they had so much _____ was awarded to their archrivals from Henderson.

a. lamentable . . . abjured
b. crestfallen . . . coveted
c. disheveled . . . ruminated
d. blithe . . . professed

5. High winds fanned the flames; and in no time at all, the _____ had spread to a nearby tire factory. Clouds of thick black smoke billowed up into the sky, and the _____ stench of burning rubber filled the air.

a. contention . . . obnoxious
b. retribution . . . indelible
c. compunction . . . potent
d. conflagration . . . acrid

6. I had hoped that the candidates would make a few _____ observations during the course of the debate. All I got, however, were the same tired old _____ that politicians have been mouthing for decades.

a. irrelevant . . . plagiarisms
b. exemplary . . . pretexts
c. trenchant . . . platitudes
d. superficial . . . ruminations

7. After romping around with my six-year-old nephew all afternoon, I had become woefully _____. My trousers were rumpled, my shirttails were hanging out, and my tie was all _____.

a. disheveled . . . askew
b. disreputable . . . crestfallen
c. garrulous . . . acrid
d. lamentable . . . sinuous

Building with Classical Roots

dem—people; **pan**— all, every

The root **dem** appears in **endemic**, "native or confined to a particular region or people" (page 124). The root **pan** appears in **panacea**, "a remedy for all ills" (page 53).Some other words based on these roots are listed below.

demagogue	demographics	demotic	pandemic
pandemonium	panoply	panorama	pantheon

From the list of words above, choose the one that corresponds to each of the brief definitions below. Write the word in the blank space in the illustrative sentence below the definition.

1. relating to the common people, especially the language of the people; connected with the colloquial form of Greek spoken in modern times

Homer's epic poems *The Iliad* and *The Odyssey* are written in classical, rather than _____**demotic**_____, Greek.

2. statistics on human populations, such as number of people, location, migration, age, and income

The U.S. Census, which is taken every ten years, is an important source of ___**demographics**___.

3. a wild uproar, din, or commotion; literally, the dwelling place of all demons

At midnight on New Year's Eve, ___**pandemonium**___ breaks out among the revelers in Times Square.

4. a full suit of armor; ceremonial attire; any splendid or impressive array

Figures of knights and horses in full _____**panoply**_____ make up one of the museum's most popular exhibits.

5. taking place over a wide area and affecting a very large number of people

Twenty-one million people died worldwide in the influenza _____**pandemic**_____ of 1918.

6. an unlimited view of an area in every direction; a comprehensive presentation of a subject

The _____**panorama**_____ from the rim of the Grand Canyon is truly awe-inspiring.

7. a temple or building dedicated to all the heroes or other illustrious persons; all the gods of a people

In the Greek _____**pantheon**_____, Zeus is the father of the gods.

8. a leader who gains or holds power by appealing to the emotions or prejudices of the populace and by making false claims

_____**Demagogues**_____ may cloak their true motives in the guise of patriotism.

From the list of words on page 144, choose the one that best completes each of the following sentences. Write the word in the space provided.

1. Many scientists believe that jet travel has increased the likelihood that newly emerging viruses will become ___**pandemic**___.

2. The writer was praised for having a keen ear for the rhythms of ___**demotic**___ speech.

3. At her coronation, Elizabeth II was attired in the gorgeous ___**panoply**___ of crown and royal robes.

4. When planning a political campaign, strategists pay close attention to local and national voter ___**demographics**___.

5. The generals positioned on the crest of the hill surveyed the ___**panorama**___ of the battlefield.

6. The Hall of Fame in Cooperstown, New York, is baseball's ___**pantheon**___.

7. Hitler was a true ___**demagogue**___ who rose to power by ruthlessly playing on the fears and resentments of the German people.

8. When protestors began to drown out the speaker, proceedings on the convention floor turned into ___**pandemonium**___.

---

*Circle the **boldface** word that more satisfactorily completes each of the following sentences.*

1. There was (**pandemonium,** panorama) in the stands when the home team scored a goal in the final minute of the game and won the championship.

2. Before opening a new branch of a chain store in a particular neighborhood, company management makes a careful study of the area's (**demagogues,** **demographics**).

3. Folk songs and dances are part of a country's (**demotic,** pandemic) culture.

4. It is always difficult to predict which contemporary writers will earn a place in the (**panoply,** **pantheon**) of world literature.

5. It can be said that during the Cold War, the fear of nuclear annihilation was (**demotic,** **pandemic**).

6. In developing nations (**demographics,** **demagogues**) may pose a serious threat to elected leaders who are trying to build democratic institutions.

7. The documentary presented the (**panorama,** pandemonium) of the Civil War from the perspectives of both sides.

8. Every year, people flock to New England to view the dazzling (**pantheon,** **panoply**) of autumn foliage.

Read the following sentences, paying special attention to the words and phrases underlined. From the words in the box below, find better choices for these underlined words and phrases. Then use these choices to rewrite the sentences.

WORD BANK				
acquiesce	covet	integrity	pretext	sonorous
askew	endemic	inveterate	profess	tacit
compunction	fathom	lamentable	quell	tangible
conclusive	indelible	placid	sinuous	trenchant

The Gullah People

1. A unique culture, that of the Gullah people, survives on the Sea Islands off the multicurved coast of Georgia and South Carolina.

　　　sinuous
_____

2. The Gullahs are descendants of slaves brought to America from Africa to work on the Sea Island plantations. The way of life that evolved among these people reflects the unforgettable influences of both African and American cultures.

　　　indelible
_____

3. With the signing of the Emancipation Proclamation in 1863, the sorry institution of slavery was abolished.

　　　lamentable
_____

4. After Union troops invaded the Sea Islands and put down forcibly the rebel forces there, the plantation owners fled. Their lands were given to the newly freed slaves.

　　　quelled
_____

5. Efforts are being made to ensure the unimpaired condition and completeness of the Gullah language, which combines many African words with English as spoken by British colonists in the seventeenth and eighteenth centuries.

　　　integrity
_____

6. Storytelling, an important part of Gullah life, is a tool both for handing down ancestral wisdom and for preserving the stylistically impressive language.

　　　sonorous
_____

7. Activists are working to keep the traditions native or inherent to the Gullah people alive despite the encroachments of modern life.

　　　endemic
_____

Analogies

In each of the following, circle the item that best completes the comparison.

See pages T38–T48 for explanations of answers.

1. disreputable is to **esteem** as
a. exemplary is to extol
b. reprehensible is to commend
c. unjust is to redress
d. ludicrous is to deride

2. backbone is to **fortitude** as
a. stomach is to altruism
b. cheek is to temerity
c. lip is to diffidence
d. spine is to adversity

3. explicit is to **tacit** as
a. spontaneous is to premeditated
b. suave is to urbane
c. tepid is to acrid
d. poignant is to ingenuous

4. insuperable is to **overcome** as
a. infallible is to explain
b. omnivorous is to eat
c. indomitable is to tame
d. feasible is to do

5. potent is to **clout** as
a. voluminous is to brevity
b. tepid is to heat
c. squalid is to allure
d. cogent is to force

6. alienate is to **estrange** as
a. quell is to suppress
b. covet is to abhor
c. brandish is to waive
d. profess is to abjure

7. integrity is to **duplicity** as
a. clemency is to mercy
b. animosity is to rancor
c. chivalry is to gallantry
d. candor is to guile

8. placid is to **tranquillity** as
a. fainthearted is to fortitude
b. diffident is to audacity
c. nonchalant is to concern
d. limpid is to clarity

9. covet is to **craving** as
a. abhor is to aversion
b. scrutinize is to apathy
c. esteem is to animosity
d. discern is to antagonism

10. tangible is to **touch** as
a. lamentable is to rejoice
b. amicable is to hinder
c. pliable is to bend
d. feasible is to avoid

Choosing the Right Meaning

Read each sentence carefully. Then circle the item that best completes the statement below the sentence.

See pages T38–T48 for explanations of answers.

s the adults ruminated placidly in the meadow, the kids and lambs frolicked layfully among the hedgerows. (2)

1. The word **ruminated** in line 1 most nearly means
a. meditated   b. locked horns   c. chewed the cud   d. rested

t first I was appalled by the self-serving hype endemic to the film industry, but few years in Tinsel Town made it seem quite normal. (2)

2. The phrase **endemic to** in line 1 is best defined as
a. prevalent in
b. uncharacteristic of
c. confined to
d. resulting from

n a very cold day, it takes a little patience to persuade my car's recalcitrant ngine to turn over. (2)

3. In line 1 the word **recalcitrant** most nearly means

a. lazy   b. unruly   (c. resistant)   d. ancient

During his reign Henry VII made a determined effort to recover royal lands alienated illegally from the crown.   (2)

4. The word **alienated** in line 2 most nearly means

a. stolen   b. seized   c. bought   (d. transferred)

The blithe ignorance of Marie Antoinette's famous remark, "Let them eat cake," reveals both a cold heart and a shallow mind.   (2)

5. The item that best indicates the meaning of **blithe** in line 1 is

a. witty   (b. unconcerned)   c. spiteful   d. genial

Two-Word Completions

Circle the pair of words that best complete the meaning of each of the following sentences.

See pages T38–T48 for explanations of answers.

1. I had always admired the ease and _____ with which he turned out essays and articles so effortlessly, until one day I discovered that he had actually _____ three-quarters of what he claimed to be his own work.

a. duplicity . . . retrogressed
(b. facility . . . plagiarized)
c. temerity . . . alienated
d. diffidence . . . adulterated

2. When the noise of his uncle's drunken _____ interrupts the quiet of the night, Prince Hamlet remarks that such _____ carousing is, to his mind, "a custom more honored in the breach than in the observance."

a. nostalgia . . . culinary
b. indulgence . . . clandestine
c. solace . . . vociferous
(d. revelry . . . nocturnal)

3. At first glance the painting bears a(n) _____ resemblance to something by Rembrandt, but on closer inspection the eye begins to _____ subtle differences in style and technique that show it to be the work of another painter.

a. insidious . . . ascertain
b. unfeigned . . . amend
(c. superficial . . . discern)
d. ominous . . . fathom

4. Though the vision of "striking it rich overnight" held an irresistible _____ for poor Americans in 1849, most of those who were attracted to the goldfields of California ended up as _____ as they had started out.

a. guise . . . parsimonious
b. impetus . . . blithe
(c. allure . . . destitute)
d. pretext . . . bereft

5. He _____ to be learned and refined, but his ideas and attitudes show his mind to be woefully _____ and uncouth.

(a. professes . . . sophomoric)
b. assents . . . urbane
c. abhors . . . suave
d. alludes . . . supercilious

Enriching Your Vocabulary

Read the passage below. Then complete the exercise at the bottom of the page.

Fiery Words

Although civilizations evolved differently in different parts of the world, many of the tools with which people built their societies were the same. One of the most basic and important tools was the natural element fire.

In Greek mythology the god Prometheus defied Zeus, the chief god, by bringing fire to human beings. He thus gave them a means of surviving and of building civilization.

The most notable thing about fire is its contradictory nature. It is capable both of sustaining life and of destroying it. There are many English words for fire that destroys. For example, *conflagration* (Unit 12), a major fire, is derived from the Latin *flagrare*, meaning "to burn." *Holocaust* (Unit 2), a great destruction by fire, comes from the Greek root *caus*, which also means "to burn."

Some fire words are used figuratively to convey heightened states of emotion. For example, *fervor*, from the Latin root *ferv* ("to boil or bubble"), is used to express very intense feeling or passion. *Ignite*, which literally means "to light a fire," also means "to excite or inflame." *Fire* is also used in many common expressions, such as *add fuel to the fire*, *fire up*, and *keep the home fires burning*.

According to myth the first Olympic flame was ignited by the sun.

In Column A below are 10 more fire words. With or without a dictionary, match each word with its meaning in Column B

Column A

_i_	**1.** incinerate
_c_	**2.** smolder
_b_	**3.** arson
_g_	**4.** firebrand
_h_	**5.** extinguish
_j_	**6.** inferno
_a_	**7.** pyrotechnics
_f_	**8.** blaze
_e_	**9.** kindle
_d_	**10.** hearth

Column B

a. fireworks

b. an act of vandalism involving fire

c. to burn sluggishly without flame but often with smoke; to exist in a state of suppressed activity

d. a fireplace

e. to start a fire; to stir up

f. a fire that flares up suddenly; an outburst

g. a piece of burning wood; a troublemaker

h. to put out a fire

i. to burn to ashes

j. extreme heat or fire

Definitions

Note carefully the spelling, pronunciation, part(s) of speech, and definition(s) of each of the following words. Then write the word in the blank space(s) in the illustrative sentence(s) following. Finally, study the lists of synonyms and antonyms given at the end of each entry.

1. antipathy
(an tip' ə thē)

(*n.*) a strong dislike, hostile feeling

Sensible people normally view any form of bigotry with the most profound _____**antipathy**_____.

SYNONYMS: hostility, enmity, aversion, bad blood
ANTONYMS: attraction, appeal, allure, sympathy

2. applicable
(ap' lə kə bəl)

(*adj.*) capable of being applied; relevant, suitable

The protection against being tried for the same crime twice is not _____**applicable**_____ in some cases

SYNONYMS: appropriate, fit, apt, apposite
ANTONYMS: inappropriate, unsuitable, irrelevant

3. asset
(as' et)

(*n.*) something of value; a resource; an advantage

By law, an annual report must include a detailed breakdown of a company's _____**assets**_____ and liabilities.

SYNONYMS: property, possession, holding, endowment
ANTONYMS: drawback, handicap, liability

4. beset
(bē set')

(*v.*) to attack from all sides; to surround, hem in; (*adj., part.*) harassed, troubled; studded (as with jewels)

Every federal administration must grapple with the economic woes that _____**beset**_____ the nation.

The crown worn by England's monarchs is a gorgeous object _____**beset**_____ with fabulous precious stones.

SYNONYMS: (*v.*) assail, harass, badger, pester, torment

5. compassion
(kəm pash' ən)

(*n.*) sympathy for another's suffering; pity

Without the _____**compassion**_____ and generosity of donors and volunteers, many charitable organizations would have to shut their doors.

SYNONYMS: concern, commiseration, empathy
ANTONYMS: indifference, callousness, heartlessness

6. decorum
(di kôr' əm)

(*n.*) proper behavior, good taste; orderliness

Legislative assemblies preserve _____**decorum**_____ by operating under the rules of parliamentary procedure.

SYNONYMS: seemliness, good form, propriety
ANTONYMS: impropriety, bad form, bad taste

7. duress
(dü res′)

(*n.*) compulsion by threat; forcible confinement

Political prisoners are sometimes subjected to a mild form of _____ duress _____ called *house arrest*.

SYNONYMS: intimidation, coercion
ANTONYMS: persuasion, coaxing, sweet talk, cajolery

8. exuberant
(eg zü′ bər ənt)

(*adj.*) high-spirited, enthusiastic, unrestrained; excessive, abundant

Unable to control their _____ exuberant _____ spirits, the fans of the popular singer cheered their idol loudly.

SYNONYMS: lively, ebullient, irrepressible, lavish
ANTONYMS: depressed, despondent, sulky, restrained

9. facsimile
(fak sim′ ə lē)

(*n.*) an exact copy

A _____ facsimile _____ of the U.S. Constitution is displayed in many social studies classrooms.

SYNONYMS: replica, duplicate, reproduction, clone
ANTONYMS: variation, modification, permutation

10. imbibe
(im bīb′)

(*v.*) to drink; to take in, absorb

An inquisitive person can _____ imbibe _____ knowledge from many sources.

SYNONYMS: swallow, gulp, quaff, assimilate, digest
ANTONYMS: eject, emit, expel, discharge

11. implacable
(im plak′ ə bəl)

(*adj.*) not to be satisfied or pacified; unyielding

The peoples of the Arctic have shown that nature need not be an _____ implacable _____ foe.

SYNONYMS: relentless, inexorable, unappeasable
ANTONYMS: lenient, indulgent, permissive, flexible

12. infinitesimal
(in fin ə tes′ ə məl)

(*adj.*) so small as to be almost immeasurable; minute

To a fussy housekeeper, even an _____ infinitesimal _____ amount of dust on a tabletop is unacceptable.

SYNONYMS: tiny, minuscule, microscopic, unnoticeable
ANTONYMS: vast, immense, huge, infinite

13. innocuous
(i näk′ yü əs)

(*adj.*) harmless, inoffensive; insignificant

Conversation at a dinner party may sometimes be confined to pleasant and _____ innocuous _____ generalities.

SYNONYMS: feeble, impotent, unobjectionable, insipid
ANTONYMS: harmful, dangerous, pernicious, toxic, virulent

14. militate
(mil′ ə tāt)

(*v.*) to have effect or force on or against someone or something, fight against

Health concerns _____ militate _____ strongly against the habitual use of tobacco and alcohol.

SYNONYMS: counter, oppose, work against

15. patent
(pat′ ənt)

(*n.*) exclusive rights over an invention; copyright; (*v.*) to arrange or obtain such rights; (*adj.*) plain, open to view; copyrighted

When the _____**patent**_____ on a drug expires, any manufacturer may produce it.

By the time of his death in 1931, Thomas Alva Edison had _____**patented**_____ more inventions than any other American of his time.

During cross-examination a skilled lawyer may catch a key hostile witness in a _____**patent**_____ falsehood.

SYNONYMS: (*n.*) exclusive license; (*adj.*) evident
ANTONYMS: (*adj.*) concealed, hidden, secret, clandestine

16. prowess
(praů′ əs)

(*n.*) distinguished bravery; superior skill or ability

The Greek hero Achilles won fame for his _____**prowess**_____ in the Trojan War.

SYNONYMS: valor, courage, heroism, mastery, proficiency
ANTONYMS: cowardice, incompetence, ineptitude

17. sedate
(sə dāt′)

(*adj.*) quiet, settled, sober; (*v.*) to administer a tranquilizer

At concerts of classical music, audiences generally behave in a _____**sedate**_____ and attentive manner.

A doctor may decide to _____**sedate**_____ a patient who has suffered a severe emotional shock or physical injury.

SYNONYMS: (*adj.*) unruffled, composed, cool and collected
ANTONYMS: (*adj.*) loud, brash, flashy, flamboyant, garish, flighty

18. stentorian
(sten tôr′ ē ən)

(*adj.*) extremely loud

Some public speakers favor a _____**stentorian**_____ delivery and emphatic gestures to drive home their message to their listeners.

SYNONYMS: thundering, booming, deafening, earsplitting
ANTONYMS: hushed, inaudible, whispered, mute

19. stipulate
(stip′ yə lāt)

(*v.*) to arrange specifically; to require as a condition of agreement

A financial institution may _____**stipulate**_____ that all its employees be fingerprinted.

SYNONYMS: specify, contract, provide for

20. ultimatum
(əl tə mā′ təm)

(*n.*) a final proposal or statement of conditions

As a strike deadline draws near, both labor and management can be expected to issue _____**ultimatums**_____.

SYNONYM: final terms

Completing the Sentence

From the words for this unit, choose the one that best completes each of the following sentences. Write the word in the space provided.

1. Her refusal to discuss even the possibility of a compromise convinced me that I was faced with a(n) _____**implacable**_____ opponent.

2. I enjoy his jokes, but he ought to bear in mind that there are certain standards of _____**decorum**_____ to be observed at graduation.

3. American law prohibits police from arresting and holding suspects in any type of _____**duress**_____ without formally charging them.

4. If only he could match his _____**prowess**_____ on the playing field with a high level of excellence in the classroom!

5. The player's chronic shoulder injury _____**militated**_____ against his plan to extend his baseball career for another season.

6. How can you expect them to concern themselves with your problems when they are so _____**beset**_____ with troubles of their own?

7. The "monster" that frightened you so much during the hike last week was just a(n) _____**innocuous**_____ water snake.

8. Centuries-old ethnic _____**antipathies**_____ have more than once led to bloody conflict in the Balkans.

9. We could hear the quarterback's _____**stentorian**_____ signals even above the roar of the crowd.

0. Although the artist's latest work was acclaimed by the critics, it seemed to me to be no more than a(n) _____**facsimile**_____ of a cardboard cereal box.

1. I am well on the road to becoming a millionaire because I have just been awarded the _____**patent**_____ for an automatic homework machine.

2. How quickly their _____**exuberant**_____ holiday mood became quiet and sober when they had to return to work on Monday morning!

3. If the contract is framed by a good lawyer, it will _____**stipulate**_____ exactly when, where, and how payment is to be made.

4. The landlord's _____**ultimatum**_____ was simple and direct: Pay the rent increase or get out.

5. During the long summer afternoons, we used to sit on the shaded veranda, _____**imbibing**_____ iced drinks and talking about life.

6. He has his shortcomings, but compared with his great services to his community and nation, they seem all but _____**infinitesimal**_____.

7. I was amazed to see how a few years had transformed an unruly and mischievous child into a well-bred, _____**sedate**_____ young adult.

18. The reference material you have given me is interesting, but most of it is not _____applicable_____ to my term paper.

19. Her chief _____assets_____ both in business and in social life are her keen intelligence and pleasant manner.

20. Dr. Albert Schweitzer had not only great scientific ability but also a deep sense of _____compassion_____ for suffering humanity.

Synonyms

*Choose the word from this unit that is **the same** or **most nearly the same** in meaning as the **boldface** word or expression in the given phrase. Write the word on the line provided.*

1. **surrounded** by a screaming mob — beset
2. a **reproduction** of a famous painting — facsimile
3. the **evident** stupidity of the remark — patent
4. **fight** against adopting the policy — militate
5. **assimilate** the wisdom of a lifetime — imbibe
6. **specifies** the duties to be performed — stipulates
7. forced to sell all their **possessions** — assets
8. rejected the dictator's **final terms** — ultimatum
9. made only **minute** progress toward a solution — infinitesimal
10. extorted evidence under **compulsion** — duress
11. rules established in the name of **propriety** — decorum
12. argued the case with **relentless** logic — implacable
13. a deep and long-standing **enmity** — antipathy
14. celebrated for her **proficiency** on the tennis court — prowess
15. spoke in a **booming** voice — stentorian

Antonyms

*Choose the word from this unit that is **most nearly opposite** in meaning to the **boldface** word or expression in the given phrase. Write the word on the line provided.*

16. a closet full of **flashy** clothing — sedate
17. judges noted for their **heartlessness** — compassion
18. clear proof that the substance was **harmful** — innocuous
19. greeted the performers with **restrained** applause — exuberant
20. **irrelevant** to the present situation — applicable

Choosing the Right Word

Circle the **boldface** word that more satisfactorily completes each of the following sentences.

1. Mistaking the (**sedate, stentorian**) backfire of the truck for a sudden burst of gunfire, we ducked behind a parked car for safety.

2. They were so (**exuberant, innocuous**) in their praise that I soon began to suspect either their judgment or their sincerity.

3. Someone's most valuable (**prowess, asset**) may be the ability to analyze complex problems quickly and competently.

4. What good does it do to include all those (**stipulations, facsimiles**) in the agreement if there are no provisions for enforcing them?

5. It does little good to feel (**decorum, compassion**) for those less fortunate than ourselves if we are not willing to make sacrifices to help them.

6. Although he was (**beset, imbibed**) by creditors, a tough employer, and medical problems, he never seemed to lose his zest for living.

7. His (**prowess, duress**) as a speaker and debater quickly made him one of the leading figures in the Senate.

8. My study of astronomy gave me a sense of the (**infinitesimal, exuberant**) importance of human beings and their tiny planet in a boundless universe.

9. In this synthetic world of ours, I sometimes wonder if my life is genuine or just a(n) (**ultimatum, facsimile**) of the real thing.

0. Some of the lessons that we learned during the Great Depression are (**implacable, applicable**) to our economic problems today.

1. Her sense of (**compassion, decorum**) is so strict that she often makes other people feel stiff and uncomfortable.

2. "Here's the (**ultimatum, antipathy**)," said Father. "Pass all your courses, or forget about attending the senior prom."

3. The authorities suspected that the hostage's statement was made not voluntarily but under (**duress, patent**).

4. The politician's poor showing in the polls and the failure of her fund-raising efforts (**militated, stipulated**) against her entering the presidential race.

5. The tough leadership we need in this new century will not come from uncertain and (**applicable, innocuous**) personalities.

6. The mistake in identification was so (**patent, infinitesimal**) that the suspect was released with the apologies of the arresting officer.

7. Without actually understanding much of what the speaker was saying, the audience seemed to (**imbibe, beset**) her optimism and vigor.

8. A person's modest and (**stentorian, sedate**) appearance may mask an iron determination and a sharp temper.

9. You are in deep trouble if you combine a strong taste for high living with an equally strong (**antipathy, asset**) for hard work.

0. As he watched his house go up in flames, he felt that he was the victim of an (**innocuous, implacable**) fate.

Vocabulary in Context

*Read the following passage, in which some of the words you have studied in this unit appear in **boldface** type. Then complete each statement given below the passage by circling the letter of the item that is **the same** or **almost the same** in meaning as the highlighted word.*

Far North

(Line

Conditions in the cold and barren lands of the Arctic would seem to **militate** against human settlement. Yet people settled in this region of North America long before the arrival of Europeans. These people, who prefer to be identified as *Inuit* rather than *Eskimo*, are of Asian origin. Most likely the Inuit began migrating from Siberia across the Bering Sea more than a thousand years ago. (5)

The Inuit way of life depended on the sea and its **assets**. Because of their **prowess** as hunters, they could obtain the necessities of life with relative ease. Bowhead whales, seals, walruses, and fish provided meat, blubber, bone, and skin for food, oil, tools, and clothing. As the Inuit moved inland, they began hunting caribou, musk oxen, polar bears, and (10) smaller mammals. The skins of these animals were made into clothes and rugs. In summer the people lived in tents made from animal skins; in winter they built houses made of sod or snow. The Inuit (15) were resourceful and self-reliant. They had little contact with the outside world and no need of it to sustain their way of life.

Traditionally dressed Inuit family inside igloo

All this started to change, however, in the mid-1800s. More and more European (20) whalers and traders began arriving in the north, offering the Inuit manufactured goods in exchange for the animals they hunted. The Inuit were increasingly **beset** by pressures from the outside. Over time they became more dependent on the cash economy and less able to lead (25) their traditional way of life.

In Alaska today most Inuit live in wooden houses. They wear modern, mass-produced clothing and speak English in addition to their native tongue. The kayak and the dogsled have given way to the motorboat and the snowmobile. The nearly **implacable** forces of change have transformed the world of the Inuit. Although (30) some Inuit still hunt and fish, most now participate in the modern economy.

---

1. The meaning of **militate** (line 1) is
   a. argue   c. work ⟵
   b. vote   d. trespass

2. Assets (line 6) most nearly means
   a. resources ⟵   c. challenges
   b. drawbacks   d. moods

3. Prowess (line 7) is best defined as
   a. experience   c. employment
   b. problems   d. mastery ⟵

4. The meaning of **beset** (line 24) is
   a. amused   c. distracted
   b. assailed ⟵   d. shocked

5. Implacable (line 30) most nearly means
   a. toxic   c. harmless
   b. constant   d. inexorable ⟵

Definitions

Note carefully the spelling, pronunciation, part(s) of speech, and definition(s) of each of the following words. Then write the word in the blank space(s) in the illustrative sentence(s) following. Finally, study the lists of synonyms and antonyms given at the end of each entry.

1. alacrity
(ə lak′ rə tē)

(*n.*) a cheerful readiness; brisk and eager action

Neighbors responded with _____**alacrity**_____ to the woman's cries for help.

SYNONYMS: promptness, willingness, dispatch, celerity
ANTONYMS: reluctance, unwillingness, hesitancy

2. alleviate
(ə lē′ vē āt)

(*v.*) to relieve, make more bearable

The doctors and nurses did everything they could to _____**alleviate**_____ the patient's severe pain.

SYNONYMS: lessen, lighten, allay, mitigate, assuage

3. antithesis
(an tith′ ə sis)

(*n.*) the direct opposite, a sharp contrast

Discriminatory practices may be said to constitute the very _____**antithesis**_____ of our nation's democratic ideals.

SYNONYMS: contrary, antipode

4. appall
(ə pôl′)

(*v.*) to fill with dismay or horror

The assassination of President John F. Kennedy in 1963 _____**appalled**_____ the nation and the world.

SYNONYMS: shock, stun, stupefy, horrify
ANTONYMS: please, cheer, gladden, elate, exhilarate

5. bellicose
(bel′ i kōs)

(*adj.*) warlike in manner or temperament; quarrelsome

Teddy Roosevelt's foreign policy was often driven by a rather _____**bellicose**_____ brand of patriotism.

SYNONYMS: aggressive, combative, belligerent
ANTONYMS: amicable, peaceable, conciliatory, pacific

6. disparage
(dis pâr′ ij)

(*v.*) to belittle, speak slightingly of; to undervalue

Don't you think voters are getting awfully tired of listening to politicians _____**disparage**_____ their opponents' voting records?

SYNONYMS: degrade, decry, run down, underrate
ANTONYMS: praise, extol, laud, plug

7. dissonant
(dis′ ə nənt)

(*adj.*) not in harmony; disagreeing, at odds

The clamor of _____**dissonant**_____ voices could be heard clearly through the closed doors of the meeting room.

SYNONYMS: grating, strident, unmelodious, irreconcilable
ANTONYMS: harmonious, agreeing, euphonious

8. droll
(drōl)

(*adj.*) amusingly odd

The hero or heroine of a popular sitcom may be surrounded by a cast of _____ droll _____ eccentrics.

SYNONYMS: comical, humorous, whimsical, zany
ANTONYMS: humorless, solemn, dour

9. edict
(ē' dikt)

(*n.*) an order issued by someone in authority

Only in fairy tales can human unhappiness and misery be banished forever by royal _____ edict _____ .

SYNONYMS: command, decree, proclamation

10. elucidate
(i lü' sə dāt)

(*v.*) to clarify, explain

The precise meaning of a passage in the Bible is sometimes hard to _____ elucidate _____ .

SYNONYMS: interpret, expound, explicate
ANTONYMS: obscure, becloud, muddy, obfuscate

11. laud
(lôd)

(*v.*) to praise

At the assembly the principal _____ lauded _____ both students and teachers for the schoolwide improvement in reading scores.

SYNONYMS: hail, extol, glorify, exalt
ANTONYMS: criticize, censure, belittle, disparage

12. loll
(läl)

(*v.*) to act in a lazy manner; to lounge; to recline, droop

There is nothing I would rather do on a hot, humid summer afternoon than _____ loll _____ in a hammock under a tree.

SYNONYMS: loaf, loiter, sag, dangle

13. loquacious
(lō kwā' shəs)

(*adj.*) talkative, wordy; fond of talking

My dinner companion was so _____ loquacious _____ that our conversation quickly turned into a monologue.

SYNONYMS: gossipy, voluble, garrulous, long-winded
ANTONYMS: silent, reticent, closemouthed, terse, taciturn

14. magnanimous
(mag nan' ə məs)

(*adj.*) generous in forgiving, above small meanness

The general's victory was so decisive that he could afford to be _____ magnanimous _____ toward his former enemies.

SYNONYMS: unselfish, charitable, noble, bighearted
ANTONYMS: petty, selfish, unforgiving, spiteful

15. mandatory
(man' də tôr ē)

(*adj.*) required, obligatory

A union contract may stipulate that members are to receive a _____**mandatory**_____ annual cost-of-living increase.

SYNONYMS: compulsory, requisite, imperative
ANTONYMS: optional, voluntary, discretionary

16. nondescript
(nän də skript')

(*adj.*) ordinary, not outstanding; not easily classified

Fashion critics judged the designer's fall clothing line to be disappointingly _____**nondescript**_____.

SYNONYMS: plain, unremarkable, unimpressive
ANTONYMS: distinctive, remarkable, vivid, prepossessing

17. phlegmatic
(fleg mat' ik)

(*adj.*) slow-moving, sluggish; unemotional

Sloths are such _____**phlegmatic**_____ creatures that they have earned the reputation of being the slowest animals on Earth.

SYNONYMS: lethargic, indolent, torpid, stolid, impassive
ANTONYMS: emotional, sensitive, thin-skinned, excitable

18. rescind
(ri sind')

(*v.*) to repeal, cancel

A sitting Congress sometimes _____**rescinds**_____ statutes passed by its predecessors.

SYNONYMS: withdraw, revoke, retract, annul, abrogate
ANTONYMS: affirm, endorse, uphold, ratify

19. vivacious
(və vā' shəs)

(*adj.*) lively, sprightly, full of energy

A _____**vivacious**_____ individual will certainly never lack for companions.

SYNONYMS: spirited, animated, ebullient
ANTONYMS: dull, spiritless, listless, indolent, languid

20. whet
(whet)

(*v.*) to sharpen, put an edge on; to make keen or eager

In most mystery novels, the first chapter is designed to _____**whet**_____ your curiosity to find out "who done it."

SYNONYMS: hone, excite, stimulate
ANTONYMS: dull, blunt, deaden, stifle, dampen

Completing the Sentence

From the words for this unit, choose the one that best completes each of the following sentences. Write the word in the space provided.

1. When the speaker tried to _____**elucidate**_____ the statement he had just made, I became more confused than ever.

2. His enthusiastic and colorful description of the new series on public TV has _____**whetted**_____ my desire to see it.

3. In a time of fast-talking, slam-bang comedians, is there a place for his kind of quiet, _____**droll**_____ humor?

4. I shall never forget your _____**magnanimous**_____ offer to coach me, even though we were competing for the same role in the play.

5. The principal finally _____**rescinded**_____ the unfair school regulation that prevented new students from trying out for the varsity teams.

6. Is this _____**nondescript**_____ little house the "magnificent mansion" that you've been telling us about all these weeks?

7. Their sarcastic remarks introduced a(n) _____**dissonant**_____ note into what had been a harmonious meeting.

8. I would have preferred to enjoy the paintings quietly, without listening to the explanations of the _____**loquacious**_____ guide.

9. His idle, pleasure-seeking way of life is the exact _____**antithesis**_____ of all that his hardworking parents had expected of him.

10. I'm usually quite energetic, but there are times when I want to do nothing but _____**loll**_____ about and listen to my favorite CDs.

11. Even the state troopers, who had been hardened by long experience, were _____**appalled**_____ when they came on the scene of the automobile accident.

12. Though her friends _____**lauded**_____ her many achievements, her enemies ridiculed them.

13. He may appear to be _____**phlegmatic**_____, but his friends are aware of the strong emotions simmering beneath his quiet exterior.

14. At that dull, stodgy party, her _____**vivacious**_____ personality was like a breath of fresh air.

15. Unlike you, I have never lived in France, but is that any reason for you to _____**disparage**_____ my efforts to speak French?

16. His disposition is so _____**bellicose**_____ that he is apt to turn a simple difference of opinion into a full-scale donnybrook.

17. Instead of waiting for government help, let's do all we can right now to _____**alleviate**_____ the sufferings of the flood victims.

18. In spite of her inexperience as a programmer, she attacked her new job with
_____ alacrity _____ and made good progress.

19. You can make requests and suggestions if you wish, but please don't issue any
_____ edicts _____ .

20. Although in America voting is not _____ mandatory _____ , every qualified citizen
has a duty to go to the polls in every election.

Synonyms

Choose the word from this unit that is **the same** or **most nearly the same** in meaning as the **boldface** word or expression in the given phrase. Write the word on the line provided.

1. the **contrary** of what many people believe _____ antithesis
2. refused to obey the **command** _____ edict
3. agreed to the proposal with **dispatch** _____ alacrity
4. **interpret** fine points of the law _____ elucidate
5. loves to **loaf** around the house _____ loll
6. a series of **strident** chords _____ dissonant
7. **lighten** the tax burden _____ alleviate
8. known to have a **stolid** temperament _____ phlegmatic
9. **revoke** the ban on parking in midtown _____ rescind
10. a truly **unremarkable** personality _____ nondescript
11. artists **underrated** by their contemporaries _____ disparaged
12. joined the **lively** group of dancers _____ vivacious
13. tends to be rather **long-winded** _____ loquacious
14. **extolled** the benefits of daily exercise _____ lauded
15. a book filled with **whimsical** drawings _____ droll

Antonyms

Choose the word from this unit that is **most nearly opposite** in meaning to the **boldface** word or expression in the given phrase. Write the word on the line provided.

16. **pleased** by the economic news _____ appalled
17. **dulls** the blade of an axe _____ whets
18. adopted a **conciliatory** attitude _____ bellicose
19. a party at which formal attire is **optional** _____ mandatory
20. a series of **spiteful** acts _____ magnanimous

Choosing the Right Word

Circle the **boldface** word that more satisfactorily completes each of the following sentences.

1. The cake was delicious, but the serving was so small that it did little more than (elucidate, **whet**) my appetite.

2. I see no reason to (**laud**, disparage) him in such glowing terms for doing no more than his duty.

3. Observers doubted that any coalition composed of such (**magnanimous**, **dissonant**) factions could long refrain from petty infighting.

4. Reporters asked the mayor to (**elucidate**, alleviate) her ambiguous remarks about her plans to seek higher office.

5. Would you rather (rescind, **loll**) in the back seat of a chauffeured limousine or drive your own convertible?

6. Only an unusually (**phlegmatic**, vivacious) person could have remained calm in the face of such provocation.

7. Churchill told the British to be resolute in war, defiant in defeat, and (**magnanimous**, loquacious) in victory.

8. There must be a serious flaw in the character of those who have a constant need to (laud, **disparage**) others.

9. Edna pretended to be indifferent about going to the dance, but I noticed that she accepted Harry's invitation with (antithesis, **alacrity**).

10. In the fight against air pollution, many states have made filtering devices (droll, **mandatory**) for all cars sold within their borders.

11. The only truly effective way to (**alleviate**, appall) the poverty of developing nations is to help increase their capacity to produce wealth.

12. Her manner of speaking is so (phlegmatic, **vivacious**) that even her most commonplace remarks seem to suggest charm and excitement.

13. Although Americans are not a (**bellicose**, mandatory) people, they have proven themselves prepared to defend their nation at any cost.

14. The expression "What goes up must come down" might be termed an (alacrity, **edict**) of nature.

15. It is sometimes said that women are more (**loquacious**, bellicose) than men, but all the men I know do their full share of talking.

16. What (**appalled**, lolled) us even more than the fearful living conditions was the fact that the refugees seemed to have lost all hope.

17. His jokes were actually not too good, but his (nondescript, **droll**) manner of delivering them made a big hit with the audience.

18. Because of the incidents that occurred during hazing week, the school may (whet, **rescind**) the rules that allow fraternity initiations.

19. In the eyes of such leaders as Gandhi and Martin Luther King, Jr., violence is the very (edict, **antithesis**) of a civilized society.

20. The houses in that development are a mixture of (dissonant, **nondescript**) styles, with no particular architectural character or distinguishing features.

Vocabulary in Context

*Read the following passage, in which some of the words you have studied in this unit appear in **boldface** type. Then complete each statement given below the passage by circling the letter of the item that is **the same** or **almost the same** in meaning as the highlighted word.*

A Force for Change

(Line)

In the field of social welfare, few Americans can rival the record of Jane Addams. Born of well-to-do Quaker parents in Cedarville, Illinois, Addams decided to pursue a career in medicine. However, she was forced to drop out of medical school because of ill health. This setback seemed only to **whet** her desire to
(5) **alleviate** human suffering. She was remarkably effective in achieving that goal.

Addams was **appalled** by the poverty and alienation of Chicago's large immigrant population in the 1880s. She responded with characteristic **alacrity**. In 1889 she and a friend, Ellen Gates Starr, established Hull House. This
(10) pioneering institution was a uniquely American version of the European settlement house, a kind of neighborhood center that offered a variety of services. At Hull House immigrants could get safe child care, take useful courses, and overcome their sense of
(15) isolation.

Addams strongly believed that the problem of poverty could not be solved by private generosity or personal kindness alone. She insisted instead that social workers be trained professionals and that
(20) government play an active role in improving social conditions. Among the legislative reforms she championed were the **mandatory** eight-hour limit to the workday for women, the first child-labor law, and the establishment of juvenile courts.
(25) A thinker and writer as well as an activist, Addams encouraged research into the causes of poverty and crime. She **elucidated** her theories and practical

Jane Addams (1860–1935)

experience in a series of books. She was an ardent supporter of a woman's right to vote and was also a leading pacifist. In 1931 she became the first American
(30) woman to receive the Nobel Peace Prize. Jane Addams was truly instrumental in changing the lives of Americans.

---

1. The meaning of **whet** (line 4) is
  a. sicken   (c.) stimulate
  b. modify   d. depress

2. Alleviate (line 5) most nearly means
  (a.) lessen   c. avoid
  b. highlight   d. deepen

3. Appalled (line 6) is best defined as
  a. frightened   c. discouraged
  b. angered   (d.) shocked

4. The meaning of **alacrity** (line 8) is
  a. empathy   c. alarm
  (b.) promptness   d. uncertainty

5. Mandatory (line 22) most nearly means
  (a.) compulsory   c. liberal
  b. crippling   d. voluntary

6. Elucidated (line 27) is best defined as
  (a.) expounded   c. popularized
  b. enlarged   d. disguised

Definitions

Note carefully the spelling, pronunciation, part(s) of speech, and definition(s) of each of the following words. Then write the word in the blank space(s) in the illustrative sentence(s) following. Finally, study the lists of synonyms and antonyms given at the end of each entry.

1. abrasive
(ə brā′ siv)

(*adj.*) causing irritation, harsh; grinding or wearing down; (*n.*) a substance used to smooth or polish

Within every family there are some relationships that tend to be _____**abrasive**_____.

Pumice, a natural _____**abrasive**_____, is a highly porous type of glass that is produced by volcanic eruptions.

SYNONYMS: (*adj.*) chafing, grating, rasping, erosive
ANTONYMS: (*adj.*) smooth, polished, satiny, oily, unctuous

2. acclimate
(ak′ lə māt)

(*v.*) to adapt to a new climate, environment, or situation

You may find it difficult to _____**acclimate**_____ to a new school if you arrive in the middle of the year.

SYNONYMS: accustom, learn the ropes

3. chagrin
(shə grin′)

(*n.*) irritation or humiliation caused by disappointment or frustration; (*v.*) to cause such a feeling

Much to my _____**chagrin**_____, I placed a mere fourth in the 100-meter freestyle.

The lukewarm reception accorded his first and only opera, *Fidelio*, deeply _____**chagrined**_____ the composer Ludwig van Beethoven.

SYNONYMS: (*n.*) vexation, mortification; (*v.*) abash, mortify
ANTONYMS: (*n.*) jubilation, exultation, triumph; (*v.*) exult, delight

4. complacent
(kəm plā′ sənt)

(*adj.*) self-satisfied; overly content

_____**Complacent**_____ individuals are, by definition, overly pleased with their lot in life.

SYNONYMS: smug, pleased with oneself
ANTONYMS: discontented, chagrined

5. concur
(kən kər′)

(*v.*) to express agreement, approve

It is indeed rare for eyewitness accounts of an accident to _____**concur**_____ in every detail.

SYNONYMS: agree, assent, ratify, sanction
ANTONYMS: disagree, differ, part company

6. defamation
(def ə mā′ shən)

(*n.*) slander or libel

Celebrities sometimes find that they have no choice but to sue tabloids for _____**defamation**_____.

SYNONYMS: vilification, calumny, mudslinging
ANTONYMS: salute, tribute, testimonial, praise

7. explicate
(eks' plə kāt)

(*v.*) to make plain or clear, explain; to interpret

The students listened attentively as the math teacher
_____ **explicated** _____ the geometry theorem.

SYNONYMS: clarify, elucidate, untangle, spell out
ANTONYMS: confuse, bewilder, obscure, obfuscate

8. fracas
(frā' kəs)

(*n.*) a noisy quarrel or brawl

Do you think that the _____ **fracases** _____ on
some talk shows are spontaneous or staged?

SYNONYMS: row, altercation, rhubarb, brouhaha
ANTONYMS: agreement, accord, unanimity, harmony

9. grotesque
(grō tesk')

(*adj.*) unnatural, distorted; bizarre

Gargoyles, the _____ **grotesque** _____ beasts carved
on many Gothic churches, are actually drainage spouts.

SYNONYMS: fantastic, outlandish, ugly, deformed
ANTONYMS: appealing, attractive, comely

10. pandemonium
(pan də mō' nē əm)

(*n.*) a wild uproar, din, or commotion

The whirl of activity on the floor of a stock exchange often
looks and sounds like utter _____ **pandemonium** _____.

SYNONYMS: chaos, tumult, bedlam, three-ring circus
ANTONYMS: order, calm, tranquillity, peace, repose

11. raucous
(rô' kəs)

(*adj.*) disagreeably harsh-sounding; disorderly

A _____ **raucous** _____ voice can be a liability for
someone wishing to pursue a career in television journalism.

SYNONYMS: boisterous, clamorous, strident
ANTONYMS: placid, tranquil, peaceful, serene, pastoral

12. receptive
(ri sep' tiv)

(*adj.*) open and responsive to ideas or suggestions

People will generally be _____ **receptive** _____ to
criticism of their work if it is given in a constructive manner.

SYNONYMS: open-minded, tolerant, amenable
ANTONYMS: narrow-minded, intolerant, hidebound

13. renounce
(ri naùns')

(*v.*) to give up or resign something

Throughout history, martyrs have willingly given up their
lives rather than _____ **renounce** _____ their faith.

SYNONYMS: repudiate, disown, abdicate, abjure
ANTONYMS: retain, secure, affirm, assent, aver

14. repress
(ri pres′)

(*v.*) to hold back; to put down or check by force

As history has repeatedly proved, even the most brutal tyrants cannot forever _____ **repress** _____ the human desire for freedom.

SYNONYMS: subdue, curb, stifle, constrain, bottle up
ANTONYMS: liberate, set loose, provoke, excite

15. reticent
(ret′ ə sənt)

(*adj.*) not inclined to speak; reserved; reluctant

She is understandably _____ **reticent** _____ about discussing her most deeply held beliefs with a group of total strangers.

SYNONYMS: taciturn, closemouthed, tight-lipped
ANTONYMS: talkative, garrulous, voluble, long-winded

16. savory
(sāv′ ə rē)

(*adj.*) tasty, appetizing; pungent or salty, not sweet; inoffensive, respectable

Some of the characters a reader meets in a detective story are none too _____ **savory** _____ .

SYNONYMS: delectable, flavorful, aromatic, piquant
ANTONYMS: distasteful, unpalatable, malodorous, bland

17. somnolent
(säm′ nə lənt)

(*adj.*) sleepy, drowsy; inducing sleep

By the end of an enormous Thanksgiving feast, most diners usually feel quite _____ **somnolent** _____ .

SYNONYMS: groggy, soporific
ANTONYMS: alert, lively, wide-awake, stimulating

18. vehement
(vē′ ə mənt)

(*adj.*) intense, forceful, powerful

The defendant's _____ **vehement** _____ protestations of innocence failed to convince the jurors.

SYNONYMS: emphatic, fierce, vigorous, impassioned
ANTONYMS: apathetic, lukewarm, subdued, muted

19. voluble
(väl′ yə bəl)

(*adj.*) characterized by a ready flow of words; glib, fluent

Reporters never give much credence to tips that they receive from _____ **voluble** _____ but unreliable informants, however persistent.

SYNONYMS: loquacious, garrulous, long-winded, prolix
ANTONYMS: uncommunicative, reticent, taciturn, terse

20. zealous
(zel′ əs)

(*adj.*) eager, earnest, devoted

Most members of my family are _____ **zealous** _____ supporters of our local high school's basketball, baseball, and football teams.

SYNONYMS: ardent, fervent, devout, dogged, gung ho
ANTONYMS: reluctant, unwilling, averse, tepid

Completing the Sentence

From the words for this unit, choose the one that best completes each of the following sentences. Write the word in the space provided.

1. You can well imagine my _____**chagrin**_____ at losing such an important election by so few votes.

2. She tried hard to remain awake, but the _____**somnolent**_____ atmosphere of the warm and cozy parlor was too much for her.

3. In an amazingly short time and with only the simplest ingredients, I had a(n) _____**savory**_____ stew simmering on the stove.

4. A free people cannot afford to grow _____**complacent**_____ but must remain ever vigilant in safeguarding their liberties.

5. I was confident that after Dad had eaten a good meal, he would be more _____**receptive**_____ to my request for the use of the car.

6. _____**Raucous**_____ shouts and boos from the stands will have no effect on a good umpire's decisions.

7. The conceited actor was anything but _____**reticent**_____ in discussing his innumerable triumphs on the stage, screen, and TV.

8. We didn't expect such _____**vehement**_____ dislike of country-and-western music from a native of Nashville.

9. He was just an average player when he first joined the team, but everyone admired his _____**zealous**_____ efforts to improve his game.

10. For Halloween the children made _____**grotesque**_____ masks that they were sure would terrorize the neighbors.

11. The carpenter used a(n) _____**abrasive**_____ to remove the old finish from the top of the desk before revarnishing it.

12. The answers the candidate gave at the press conference were rambling and _____**voluble**_____ but contained practically no hard information.

13. The library became a scene of _____**pandemonium**_____ when a practical joker released a number of mice.

14. Both sons agreed to _____**renounce**_____ their claims to their father's estate in favor of their widowed mother.

15. When we reached Mexico City, which is over 7000 feet above sea level, we found it difficult at first to _____**acclimate**_____ ourselves to the thinner air.

16. Although I am afraid of the dentist, I must _____**repress**_____ my fears and go for treatment.

17. An accountant tried to _____**explicate**_____ the new tax legislation to me, but when she had finished, I felt I was even more in the dark than before.

18. Since hockey players often crash into each other at high speed, it's not surprising that occasionally a(n) _____**fracas**_____ develops.

19. The editorial on city government was so unfair and biased that it amounted to _____**defamation**_____ of all the elected officials of this community.

20. I have great respect for your knowledge of our government, but I really cannot _____**concur**_____ with your opinion about the role of the judiciary.

Synonyms

*Choose the word from this unit that is **the same** or **most nearly the same** in meaning as the **boldface** word or expression in the given phrase. Write the word on the line provided.*

1. accustom ourselves to our new surroundings _____acclimate_____

2. mortification over their crushing defeat _____chagrin_____

3. a campaign of **vilification** _____defamation_____

4. tried to break up the **row** _____fracas_____

5. willingly **abjured** worldly things _____renounced_____

6. twisted into **bizarre** shapes _____grotesque_____

7. led to **tumult** on the Senate floor _____pandemonium_____

8. a choice of sweet or **salty** snacks _____savory_____

9. a **fierce** debate on a controversial issue _____vehement_____

10. tends to **stifle** strong emotions _____repress_____

11. a group of **ardent** patriots _____zealous_____

12. reserved in social situations _____reticent_____

13. the siren's **strident** wail _____raucous_____

14. need to **clarify** some of the technical language _____explicate_____

15. not very **tolerant of** a sudden change of plans _____receptive to_____

Antonyms

*Choose the word from this unit that is **most nearly opposite** in meaning to the **boldface** word or expression in the given phrase. Write the word on the line provided.*

16. taciturn traveling companions _____voluble_____

17. a **stimulating** environment _____somnolent_____

18. an extremely **unctuous** manner _____abrasive_____

19. differed with everything I said _____concurred_____

20. aimed at **discontented** voters _____complacent_____

Choosing the Right Word

Circle the **boldface** word that more satisfactorily completes each of the following sentences.

1. With deep (**pandemonium,** **chagrin**), I must confess that I was the one who neglected to hire the orchestra for the class dance.

2. After a lot of persuading, our parents (**repressed,** **concurred**) in our plan to make a bicycle tour of New England.

3. I was startled not so much by your disapproval of my proposal as by the (**fracas,** **vehemence**) with which you denounced it.

4. Some people seem to relish every (**savory,** **somnolent**) morsel of gossip that comes their way.

5. Some politicians are more (**zealous,** **voluble**) in promoting their own careers than in seeking to help the people who elected them.

6. Why is it that some people are so talkative about most things but so (**complacent,** **reticent**) about their own personal background?

7. We all have impulses to violence, but we must learn to (**repress,** **concur**) them if we are to live in a civilized society.

8. The (**receptive,** **complacent**) expression on the antique doll's porcelain face seemed to proclaim "All's right with the world."

9. It's not surprising that after so many years of military service, he has found it difficult to become (**acclimated,** **vehement**) to civilian life.

10. A (**fracas,** **chagrin**) between rival groups on the floor of the convention was swiftly quelled by security guards.

11. Mr. Sanderson is usually a man of very few words, but he was certainly (**abrasive,** **voluble**) when we asked him about his operation.

12. Lacking a positive program of his own, he hoped to gain the support of the voters by (**explicating,** **defaming**) the other candidates.

13. Gloria's kind words put me in such a (**receptive,** **savory**) frame of mind that I agreed to work on the committee before I knew what I was doing.

14. He has a good deal of ability, but his (**zealous,** **abrasive**) personality has prevented him from getting ahead in the business world.

15. In unforgettable words, the prophet Micah called on men to (**acclimate,** **renounce**) the use of armed force.

16. After spending a month in the country, we found the sounds of rush-hour traffic in the big city more (**raucous,** **grotesque**) than ever.

17. (**Pandemonium,** **Defamation**) erupted when the nervous theater manager announced to the waiting crowd that the rock concert was canceled.

18. Will I ever again sleep as deeply as I did on those deliciously (**somnolent,** **raucous**) afternoons on that hot, quiet beach?

19. The figures in the surrealistic painting had the (**grotesque,** **reticent**) appearance of characters in a nightmare.

20. For centuries scholars have argued over how to (**explicate,** **renounce**) certain cryptic passages in Shakespeare's plays and poems.

Read the following passage, in which some of the words you have studied in this unit appear in boldface type. Then complete each statement given below the passage by circling the letter of the item that is the same or almost the same in meaning as the highlighted word.

Down Times

(Line)

On Tuesday, October 29, 1929, **pandemonium** broke out on the floor of the New York Stock Exchange. Stock prices had dropped sharply on the previous Thursday. Panicked shareholders suddenly sold off more than 16 million shares of stock, setting off the longest and most severe economic downturn in the (5) history of the United States.

On October 25 newspapers reported the start of the panic on Wall Street.

Since that fateful day, economists have attempted to **explicate** the causes of the 1929 collapse and the years of depression that followed it. They have pointed out that although many (10) Americans enjoyed a period of unprecedented prosperity in the 1920s, some groups were left out of the general good fortune. President Herbert Hoover did nothing about these inequities. He remained **complacent**, believing that business (15) was best left alone to correct its own problems.

However, conditions did not improve spontaneously. In fact, things got steadily worse in 1930, 1931, and 1932. The collapse of stock prices was just the beginning. Personal bankruptcies, (20) business and bank failures, mortgage foreclosures, and widespread unemployment followed. Hunger and homelessness overtook millions. Across America, the dispossessed huddled together in **grotesque** makeshift huts and gutted automobiles. These shantytowns were called *Hoovervilles*, a name that reflected public (25) anger over the president's failure to find solutions to the nation's woes.

By November 1932, most Americans **concurred** that Hoover had not done enough to halt the economy's decline. They elected a new president, Franklin Delano Roosevelt. He immediately called Congress into special session and pushed through a groundbreaking program of economic relief and recovery known (30) as the *New Deal*. This program did much to restore the country to economic health.

1. The meaning of **pandemonium** (line 1) is
  a. disease   c. chaos
  b. rioting   d. revolution

2. Explicate (line 8) most nearly means
  a. eliminate   c. disguise
  b. debate   d. explain

3. Complacent (line 15) is best defined as
  a. content   c. embarrassed
  b. upset   d. confused

4. The meaning of **grotesque** (line 24) is
  a. gigantic   c. picturesque
  b. ugly   d. dirty

5. Concurred (line 27) most nearly means
  a. doubted   c. suspected
  b. determined d. agreed

Analogies

In each of the following, circle the item that best completes the comparison.

See pages T38–T48 for explanations of answers.

1. complacent is to **disgruntled** as
a. zealous is to indifferent
b. stentorian is to raucous
c. mandatory is to vehement
d. receptive is to retentive

2. stimulate is to **interest** as
a. repress is to laughter
b. whet is to appetite
c. beset is to pleasure
d. imbibe is to mouth

3. facsimile is to **same** as
a. prowess is to opposite
b. antipathy is to same
c. antithesis is to opposite
d. ultimatum is to same

4. voluble is to **much** as
a. loquacious is to little
b. complacent is to much
c. reticent is to little
d. infinitesimal is to much

5. elucidate is to **clearer** as
a. stipulate is to newer
b. alleviate is to milder
c. acclimate is to stranger
d. rescind is to stronger

6. asset is to **liability** as
a. apple is to orange
b. north is to east
c. plus is to minus
d. black is to green

7. jubilant is to **chagrin** as
a. phlegmatic is to alacrity
b. magnanimous is to liberality
c. sedate is to decorum
d. vivacious is to liveliness

8. small is to **infinitesimal** as
a. large is to innocuous
b. fat is to voluble
c. big is to gigantic
d. wide is to vehement

9. silence is to **pandemonium** as
a. dignity is to decorum
b. order is to anarchy
c. quarrel is to fracas
d. force is to duress

10. abdicate is to **throne** as
a. stipulate is to condition
b. deliver is to ultimatum
c. enforce is to edict
d. renounce is to title

11. somnolent is to **doze** as
a. vivacious is to militate
b. implacable is to rescind
c. reticent is to divulge
d. indolent is to loll

12. bellicose is to **threaten** as
a. nondescript is to whet
b. droll is to amuse
c. innocuous is to appall
d. grotesque is to comfort

13. savory is to **taste** as
a. abrasive is to sight
b. raucous is to sound
c. exuberant is to odor
d. patent is to texture

14. patent is to **invention** as
a. product is to brand
b. license is to vehicle
c. copyright is to book
d. title is to name

15. magnanimous is to **favorable** as
a. grotesque is to unfavorable
b. nondescript is to favorable
c. vivacious is to unfavorable
d. raucous is to favorable

16. vivacious is to **phlegmatic** as
a. hearty is to merry
b. carefree is to careless
c. vehement is to grotesque
d. jaunty is to morose

17. receptive is to **take in** as
a. sedate is to wake up
b. mandatory is to wipe out
c. dissonant is to smooth out
d. abrasive is to wear down

18. zeal is to **fervent** as
a. prowess is to valorous
b. chagrin is to exuberant
c. compassion is to reticent
d. magnanimity is to stentorian

Word Associations

In each of the following groups, circle the word that is best defined or suggested by the given phrase.

1. getting adjusted to a new job
   a. sedated   **(b. acclimated)**   c. disparaged   d. whetted

2. a fight on the field soon broken up by the officials
   a. alacrity   b. decorum   c. patent   **(d. fracas)**

3. the proper way to behave
   a. prowess   **(b. decorum)**   c. defamation   d. edict

4. how one would describe a salesman known for his fast, smooth talk
   a. reticent   **(b. voluble)**   c. abrasive   d. phlegmatic

5. overcome with shock and dismay
   (a. appalled)   b. whetted   c. stipulated   d. beset

6. the exact opposite of what was expected
   a. alacrity   **(b. antithesis)**   c. decorum   d. facsimile

7. spend the entire afternoon in the hammock
   a. rescind   **(b. loll)**   c. beset   d. stipulate

8. like the cat that swallowed the canary
   (a. complacent)   b. droll   c. savory   d. grotesque

9. an official proclamation with the force of law
   a. asset   b. chagrin   **(c. edict)**   d. duress

10. sympathy for those less fortunate than ourselves
    (a. compassion)   b. facsimile   c. decorum   d. antithesis

11. This is my final offer. Take it or leave it!
    a. asset   **(b. ultimatum)**   c. antithesis   d. fracas

12. information that is relevant to a research project
    a. savory   **(b. applicable)**   c. mandatory   d. sedate

13. a child who listens carefully and learns readily
    a. sedate   b. implacable   c. nondescript   **(d. receptive)**

14. children at a party running about in wild disorder
    a. chagrin   b. fracas   c. edict   **(d. pandemonium)**

15. "I do not like you, Dr. Fell. The reason why I cannot tell."
    (a. antipathy)   b. ultimatum   c. antithesis   d. edict

16. Please explain what you meant by those remarks!
    a. alleviate   b. rescind   **(c. elucidate)**   d. acclimate

17. what one might try to do with a yawn
    a. rescind   b. sedate   c. whet   **(d. repress)**

18. how one might describe solitary confinement
    a. chagrin   **(b. duress)**   c. ultimatum   d. antipathy

19. I was never so embarrassed in my life.
    (a. chagrined)   b. reticent   c. raucous   d. zealous

20. accept an offer with cheerful promptness
    (a. alacrity)   b. decorum   c. duress   d. defamation

Vocabulary in Context

*Read the following passage, in which some of the words you have studied in Units 13–15 appear in **boldface** type. Then complete each statement given below the passage by circling the item that is **the same** or **almost the same** in meaning as the highlighted word.*

(Line)

Inventor of Worlds

Isaac Asimov (1920–1992) has been **lauded** in many quarters as a master of the science fiction genre, and several of his books reached the
(5) best-seller lists. Unlike some other writers in the field, however, Asimov always **renounced** the view that science fiction should be pure fantasy. Instead, he championed
(10) what is sometimes called *hard* science fiction—that is, science fiction that has a purpose beyond simple entertainment or escapism.

Asimov, who was also a scientist
(15) and an academic, was a **zealous** believer in the usefulness of science to humanity and of the rational approach to solving human problems. He expressed **chagrin** that humanity
(20) often seems unable and unwilling to learn the lessons that science and history have to teach. These beliefs are reflected in his science fiction. He wanted to make readers think about
(25) where society may be heading if present trends continue.

Millions of readers are **receptive** to Asimov's ideas because of the context in which he presented them.
(30) Much of the appeal of his stories lies in the inventiveness of the imaginary worlds he created. His extremely popular Foundation stories were written one at a time for
(35) the magazine *Astounding Science Fiction* in the 1940s; and in the early 1950s, they were collected and published in book form. These stories are among the finest
(40) examples of what has become a familiar science fiction motif: the rise and fall of a galactic empire. Asimov called his galactic empire Trantor. Though it was not a
(45) **facsimile** of any actual empire, its vast size and centralized administration call to mind imperial Rome. This is not surprising, since Asimov read Edward Gibbon's
(50) classic history of the Roman Empire twice before the age of twenty.

Another outstanding element of Asimov's science fiction was the development of the robot as a
(55) concept and a character. Though he did not invent the idea, Asimov imaginatively extended the concept of robotics in his 1950 collection *I, Robot.* His premises came to be
(60) accepted by other science fiction writers and even by researchers into artificial intelligence.

---

1. The meaning of **lauded** (line 2) is
a. quoted　　　　(c. extolled)
b. criticized　　　d. listed

2. Renounced (line 7) most nearly means
(a. repudiated)　　c. acknowledged
b. remembered　　d. embraced

3. Zealous (line 15) is best defined as
a. generous　　　c. halfhearted
(b. ardent)　　　d. fitful

4. The meaning of **chagrin** (line 19) is
a. delight　　　　c. anger
b. fear　　　　　(d. disappointment)

5. Receptive (line 27) most nearly means
a. indifferent　　c. addicted
(b. responsive)　　d. hostile

6. Facsimile (line 45) is best defined as
a. description　　(c. duplicate)
b. variation　　　d. satire

Read each sentence carefully. Then circle the item that best completes the statement below the sentence.

See pages T38–T48 for explanations of answers.

Before working on a tooth, a dentist will usually sedate the target area with some kind of local anesthetic. (2)

1. In line 1 the word **sedate** is used to mean

a. sober   b. isolate   c. quiet   (d. numb)

When viewed from below, the lofty peaks that beset the little village in the valley seem to touch the very gates of heaven. (2)

2. The word **beset** in line 1 is best defined as

(a. surround)   b. worry   c. stud   d. harass

I was interested to learn that my lawyer friend specialized in patent law and made a handsome income from it. (2)

3. The word **patent** in line 1 most nearly means

a. common   (b. copyright)   c. obvious   d. church

"Love, schmov!" I said. "One could hardly expect such a principled woman to marry a man whose past was scarcely savory." (2)

4. In line 2 the word **savory** most nearly means

a. pungent   b. shady   (c. respectable)   d. enjoyable

Nary a ripple disturbed the tranquil surface of our phlegmatic little brook on that lazy summer afternoon. (2)

5. The word **phlegmatic** in line 1 most nearly means

(a. sluggish)   b. impassive   c. muddy   d. unemotional

Antonyms

In each of the following groups, circle the word or expression that is most nearly the **opposite** of the word in **boldface** type.

1. stentorian
a. repeated
b. tiny
c. seated
(d. hushed)

2. stipulate
a. demand
b. take
c. agree
(d. renounce)

3. concur
a. join
b. bring
(c. disagree)
d. please

4. savory
a. ugly
(b. distasteful)
c. settled
d. costly

5. vehement
a. strong
(b. weak)
c. messy
d. convincing

6. nondescript
a. funny
b. lively
(c. distinctive)
d. confusing

7. innocuous
a. kind
(b. harmful)
c. necessary
d. open

8. mandatory
(a. optional)
b. greedy
c. silent
d. needed

9. reticent
a. grotesque
b. receptive
c. voluble
d. applicable

10. imbibe
a. eject
b. hurt
c. help
d. praise

11. droll
a. loud
b. large
c. funny
d. grim

12. raucous
a. small
b. mellow
c. dangerous
d. safe

13. implacable
a. severe
b. flexible
c. laughable
d. poor

14. asset
a. dislike
b. disagreement
c. ability
d. disadvantage

15. defamation
a. praise
b. advantage
c. pity
d. agreement

16. laud
a. appall
b. elucidate
c. disparage
d. beset

Word Families

A. On the line provided, write the word you have learned in Units 13–15 that is related to each of the following nouns.

EXAMPLE: zeal—**zealous**

1. sedateness, sedative, sedation — sedate
2. alleviator, alleviation — alleviate
3. loquaciousness, loquacity — loquacious
4. repression, repressor, repressiveness, repressibility — repress
5. exuberance — exuberant
6. concurrence — concur
7. dissonance — dissonant
8. stipulator, stipulation — stipulate
9. renouncement, renunciation, renouncer — renounce
10. elucidator, elucidation — elucidate
11. disparager, disparagement — disparage
12. bellicosity — bellicose
13. acclimation — acclimate
14. explicator, explication — explicate
15. grotesqueness, grotesquerie — grotesque

B. On the line provided, write the word you have learned in Units 13–15 that is related to each of the following verbs.

EXAMPLE: defame—**defamation**

16. apply — applicable
17. abrade — abrasive
18. receive — receptive
19. mandate — mandatory
20. savor — savory

Two-Word Completions

Circle the pair of words that best complete the meaning of each of the following passages.

See pages T38–T48 for explanations of answers.

1. Edna's _____, offbeat sense of humor proved to be a considerable _____ in the competition for class wit.
   a. nondescript . . . facsimile
   b. grotesque . . . antithesis
   c. savory . . . fracas
   d. droll . . . asset

2. "Since the documents are only _____ of the Declaration of Independence," the salesperson said, "the price I'm asking for them is _____ in comparison with what the real thing would cost."
   a. antitheses . . . grotesque
   b. facsimiles . . . infinitesimal
   c. patents . . . savory
   d. edicts . . . voluble

3. Though the supply of winter uniforms had done much to _____ the hardship suffered by the troops, the continuing shortage of ammunition and the ominous weather forecast _____ against pressing the attack.
   a. beset . . . concurred
   b. alleviate . . . militated
   c. acclimate . . . stipulated
   d. whet . . . elucidated

4. I might not be so _____ about suggesting improvements at the office if my boss were more _____ to constructive criticism. But since he seems to resent it, I keep such ideas to myself.
   a. phlegmatic . . . implacable
   b. zealous . . . magnanimous
   c. reticent . . . receptive
   d. exuberant . . . compassionate

5. Like a Roman emperor of old, the new principal issued a(n) _____ stating that attendance at morning assembly, which had been optional under the old regime, was now _____.
   a. edict . . . mandatory
   b. facsimile . . . applicable
   c. patent . . . complacent
   d. defamation . . . sedate

6. Alexander the Great was a(n) _____ foe of the Persians as long as they posed a threat to Greek security. But once he had conquered them, he proved to be a(n) _____ and evenhanded ruler.
   a. vehement . . . repressive
   b. somnolent . . . innocuous
   c. phlegmatic . . . nondescript
   d. implacable . . . magnanimous

7. Though it didn't rule out mild soap, the warranty expressly _____ that _____ cleansers should not be used on the floor because they would damage the tile surface.
   a. stipulated . . . abrasive
   b. explicated . . . innocuous
   c. rescinded . . . applicable
   d. concurred . . . dissonant

sed, sess, sid—to sit, settle

This root appears in **sedate** (page 152). The literal meaning is "settled," but the word now means "quiet or calm." Some other words based on the same root are listed below.

assess	**obsessed**	**sediment**	**subsidiary**
dissidence	**residual**	**subside**	**supersede**

From the list of words above, choose the one that corresponds to each of the brief definitions below. Write the word in the blank space in the illustrative sentence below the definition.

1. excessively troubled or preoccupied by

A person who is _____obsessed_____ with the details of a project may have trouble seeing the "big picture."

2. matter that settles to the bottom of a liquid; lees, dregs

Catfish and snails will help to keep your aquarium free of _____sediment_____.

3. remaining; left over

After I pay my monthly bills, I deposit some of the _____residual_____ money in my savings account.

4. to displace in favor of another; replace; force out of use

In most homes, compact disks have _____superseded_____ long-playing records and tape cassettes.

5. furnishing aid or support; of secondary importance; a thing or person that assists or supplements

Evening newscasts generally cover major stories but don't have time to examine _____subsidiary_____ issues.

6. disagreement in opinion or belief; dissent

The nominating convention was disrupted by noisy _____dissidence_____.

7. to grow less; become less active; to die down ("*to settle down*")

The candidate could not begin to speak until the uproar _____subsided_____.

8. to estimate the value of; to fix an amount, tax; to determine the importance, value, or size of

A gym or health club may _____assess_____ new members a fee at the time they join.

From the list of words above, choose the one that best completes each of the following sentences. Write the word in the space provided.

1. How accurately can present-day diagnostic tests _____assess_____ the true potential of any teenager?

2. Under the United States Constitution, state governments may exercise those _____residual_____ powers that are not assigned to the federal government and not forbidden to the states.

3. Will solar power ever _____supersede_____ fossil fuels as the major source of energy in the United States?

4. Only when the master of ceremonies finally raised his hand did the giggling in the audience _____subside_____.

5. Party officials sought to quell the growing _____dissidence_____ in the ranks by ousting the leaders of the disgruntled faction.

6. The raw materials needed by that giant corporation are supplied mainly by its own _____subsidiary_____ companies.

7. The elderly are often _____obsessed_____ by the fear of being robbed or injured by young hoodlums.

8. When the floodwaters finally retreated, residents returned to find their little village covered with a layer of muddy _____sediment_____.

---

*Circle the **boldface** word that more satisfactorily completes each of the following sentences.*

1. All departing flights were delayed until the blizzard's strong winds and heavy snowfall (**superseded, subsided**).

2. Prospectors panning for gold sift through rocks and (**dissidence, sediment**) from streambeds to search for nuggets of the precious metal.

3. Government officials visited the site of the earthquake to (**assess, subside**) the extent of the damage.

4. We plan to camp overnight beside one of the river's (**obsessed, subsidiary**) streams.

5. By the late 1920s, talking pictures had largely (**superseded, assessed**) silent films in the affection of the moviegoing public.

6. No totalitarian regime can suppress (**dissidence, sediment**) permanently, no matter how repressive its methods are.

7. One of the (**subsidiary, residual**) effects of a severe cold may be a nagging cough.

8. Some people are so (**obsessed, superseded**) with work that they have little time or energy left for anything else.

Writer's Challenge

Read the following sentences, paying special attention to the words and phrases underlined. From the words in the box below, find better choices for these underlined words and phrases. Then use these choices to rewrite the sentences.

WORD BANK

alleviate	asset	complacent	elucidate	reticent
antipathy	bellicose	decorum	militate	stipulate
antithesis	beset	disparage	repress	voluble
appall	compassion	duress	rescind	zealous

West Point

1. During the American Revolution, colonial forces were <u>pestered</u> by British troops on many fronts, including New York's Hudson River, a strategically vital waterway.

   beset

2. George Washington recognized the defensive potential of a position on a high bluff along the river in the area known as West Point. He set up headquarters there and prepared to repel an attack by the <u>quarrelsome</u> Redcoats.

   bellicose

3. After the war, Washington feared that the new nation might grow <u>self-satisfied</u> about its freedom. He recognized the need for an institution that would teach the art and science of warfare.

   complacent

4. In 1802, President Thomas Jefferson signed a bill <u>requiring as a condition of agreement</u> the establishment of the U.S. Military Academy at West Point.

   stipulating

5. West Point cadets receive rigorous training to prepare them to <u>bottle up</u> armed attacks on the nation and its allies.

   repress

6. The academy has changed with the times, overcoming long-held <u>hostile feelings</u>. Women and other candidates have added to the diversity of the academy's cadets.

   antipathy

7. Graduates of West Point have proved to be among the military's most valuable <u>possessions</u>, serving in America's defense with great distinction.

   assets

Analogies

In each of the following, circle the item that best completes the comparison.

See pages T38–T48 for explanations of answers.

1. poignant is to **touch** as
a. limpid is to stroke
b. droll is to tickle
c. ironic is to brush
d. ominous is to rub

2. claim is to **renounce** as
a. sword is to brandish
b. indemnity is to recompense
c. wrong is to redress
d. right is to waive

3. chaos is to **turbulent** as
a. conflagration is to dissonant
b. pandemonium is to raucous
c. holocaust is to sonorous
d. fracas is to quiescent

4. implacable is to **clemency** as
a. clairvoyant is to sensitivity
b. ingenuous is to guile
c. chivalrous is to magnanimity
d. stolid is to integrity

5. malevolent is to **rancor** as
a. phlegmatic is to torpor
b. stolid is to animosity
c. nonchalant is to concern
d. impervious is to receptivity

6. contentious is to **bellicose** as
a. mandatory is to optional
b. recalcitrant is to receptive
c. squalid is to opulent
d. truculent is to belligerent

7. garrulous is to **loquacious** as
a. sedate is to vivacious
b. parsimonious is to magnanimous
c. scrupulous is to meticulous
d. nocturnal is to culinary

8. pungent is to **smell** as
a. musty is to touch
b. gnarled is to hearing
c. savory is to taste
d. fallow is to sight

9. grave is to **interment** as
a. shelf is to scrutiny
b. buffet is to consecration
c. bed is to repose
d. chair is to sojourn

10. vehement is to **energy** as
a. potent is to edge
b. cogent is to force
c. trenchant is to clout
d. acrid is to insight

11. antipathy is to **abhor** as
a. loathing is to laud
b. fondness is to relish
c. dislike is to esteem
d. partiality is to appall

12. applicable is to **irrelevant** as
a. capricious is to inconstant
b. doting is to indulgent
c. kindred is to incompatible
d. copious is to inanimate

13. complacent is to **smug** as
a. explicit is to tacit
b. urbane is to suave
c. decrepit is to obsolete
d. endemic is to negligible

14. order is to **rescind** as
a. belief is to abjure
b. reference is to allude
c. agreement is to concur
d. problem is to explicate

15. laggard is to **alacrity** as
a. renegade is to duplicity
b. martinet is to discipline
c. bully is to belligerence
d. craven is to valor

16. speech is to **voluble** as
a. food is to palatable
b. income is to multifarious
c. writing is to voluminous
d. thought is to spontaneous

17. abrasive is to **erode** as
a. conclusive is to flood
b. coercive is to plunder
c. tentative is to demolish
d. corrosive is to burn

18. crestfallen is to **chagrin** as
a. elated is to exhilaration
b. complacent is to apprehension
c. blithe is to dismay
d. somber is to compunction

19. perceptible is to **discern** as
a. pliable is to stiffen
b. virulent is to control
c. indelible is to expunge
d. feasible is to do

20. gibes are to **disparage** as
a. platitudes are to deride
b. jeers are to commend
c. condolences are to defame
d. compliments are to extol

21. innocuous is to **virulent** as
a. placid is to turbulent
b. receptive is to amenable
c. disheveled is to unkempt
d. dour is to obnoxious

22. zealous is to **apathy** as
a. ardent is to enthusiasm
b. sophomoric is to maturity
c. brash is to temerity
d. omniscient is to knowledge

Choosing the Right Meaning

Read each sentence carefully. Then circle the item that best completes the statement below the sentence.

See pages T38–T48 for explanations of answers.

Brave is the actress who would take on Scarlett O'Hara after Vivien Leigh's indelible screen performance of the role. (2)

1. The word **indelible** in line 2 most nearly means
a. permanent   b. recent   c. unforgettable   d. sensitive

'Then the people cried out to their captains
For there was dearth in the land of their fathers, (2)
Let us hie to the valley of Glubdub,
Where the honey is sweet and will feed us.' " (4)
(A. E. Glug, *The Clodyssey*, III, 127–30)

2. The word **dearth** in line 2 most nearly means
a. austerity   b. depression   c. war   d. famine

Since a dull blade is likely to cause an accident," the chef advised, "always whet your knives before you use them." (2)

3. The word **whet** in line 1 is used to mean
a. excite   b. stimulate   c. hone   d. prepare

Beset with fewer precious stones, Monomakh's coronation cap is much easier to wear than Catherine's jewel-encrusted crown. (2)

4. In line 1 the word **Beset** is used to mean
a. Hemmed in   b. Bedeviled   c. Harassed   d. Studded

Suddenly the clouds broke, the sun came out, and the whole garden was filled with the suave scent of lilacs. (2)

5. In line 2 the word **suave** most nearly means
a. agreeable   b. sharp   c. urbane   d. polite

As the fatigue of the day slowly overwhelmed me and sleep set in, my head began to loll lower and lower on my chest. (2)

6. In line 2 the word **loll** can be defined as
a. loaf   b. droop   c. lounge   d. loiter

Two-Word Completions

Circle the pair of words that best complete the meaning of each of the following sentences.

See pages T38–T48 for explanations of answers.

1. Copernicus, Galileo, and other ———————— of the sun-centered theory of our galaxy were in the ———————— of the scientific revolution that ultimately led to human beings walking on the moon.

a. misnomers . . . plagiarism
b. clairvoyants . . . retribution
c. wastrels . . . conflagration
d. exponents . . . vanguard

2. The suspect had been observed ———————— furtively in an alleyway an hour before the assault occurred, which suggests that a ———————— crime rather than a chance mishap was involved.

a. skulking . . . premeditated
b. reposing . . . finite
c. plodding . . . truculent
d. brandishing . . . malevolent

3. Recognizing that an enemy assault on the right would put his entire battle formation in ————————, the commander ordered his reserve troops ———————— to reinforce the exposed flank.

a. demise . . . augmented
b. jeopardy . . . deployed
c. holocaust . . . coerced
d. duplicity . . . retrogressed

4. The leering faces of ———————— gargoyles and other bizarre monsters ———————— from the walls, towers, and battlements of medieval churches and castles like so many fantastic hunting trophies hung over a fireplace.

a. blithe . . . ruminate
b. grotesque . . . protrude
c. garrulous . . . gape
d. supercilious . . . skulk

5. After our upset defeat we realized, to our ————————, that our early string of easy victories had turned us ———————— and dulled our competitive edge.

a. prowess . . . implacable
b. duress . . . receptive
c. chagrin . . . complacent
d. alacrity . . . stentorian

6. Although I'd been wide-awake when I'd entered the auditorium, the ———————— effect of the speaker's droning voice and tired platitudes was so ———————— that I began to fall asleep.

a. uncanny . . . infinitesimal
b. lamentable . . . negligible
c. somnolent . . . stultifying
d. averse . . . exhilarating

7. When the weather's fine, I enjoy ———————— on the beach; but when it's ————————, I prefer to bask under a sunlamp.

a. sojourning . . . infallible
b. reposing . . . palatable
c. embarking . . . capricious
d. lolling . . . inclement

8. In Pennsylvania's Amish country a visitor can still see ———————— a way of life that elsewhere in this vast country has long since become ————————

a. copious . . . decrepit
b. multifarious . . . emaciated
c. extant . . . obsolete
d. limpid . . . poignant

9. The account he gave of his actions on that fateful night was so full of
_____ and inconsistencies that I did not think it would be
_____ for him to convince a jury of his innocence.

a. discrepancies . . . feasible   c. precedents . . . cogent
b. panaceas . . . facile   d. gibes . . . scrupulous

10. When the Montagues and their _____, the Capulets, decided to
settle their feud in the streets of Verona, the authorities had to be called in to
_____ the riot that ensued.

a. adversaries . . . quell   c. renegades . . . repress
b. martinets . . . chastise   d. exponents . . . suppress

11. The author was gratified by the lavish praise offered by the many critics who
_____ her new novel, but she was perplexed and disappointed by
the _____ welcome the book received from the public.

a. extolled . . . tepid   c. reiterated . . . insidious
b. scrutinized . . . benevolent   d. deleted . . . dour

12. Though _____ invariably squander their _____
in no time at all, frugal people may often amass comfortable nest eggs over the years.

a. deviates . . . precedents   c. wastrels . . . assets
b. benefactors . . . attainments   d. clairvoyants . . . itineraries

13. The _____ little "difference of opinion" suddenly developed into
an ugly _____ when the two people involved in the dispute started
throwing punches at each other.

a. nondescript . . . antithesis   c. insidious . . . quandary
b. squalid . . . scrutiny   d. amicable . . . fracas

14. The military governor began to grow _____ when the brutal
_____ he ordered against the populace for acts of sabotage failed
to curb their spirit of resistance.

a. recalcitrant . . . condolences   c. corrosive . . . quandaries
b. apprehensive . . . reprisals   d. assiduous . . . indemnities

Read the passage below. Then complete the exercise at the bottom of the page.

High-Tech Vocabulary

Crash! The sound of cars colliding on a highway indicates that something destructive has occurred. A crash on the information superhighway is soundless, but it can be just as destructive. When a computer crashes, a great deal of valuable information may be lost, or the entire system may shut down.

In the world of computers, many familiar words have taken on new meanings. A *bug* is a flaw in a program; a *mouse* is a useful tool. The World Wide *Web* is not a spider's trap but a series of interconnected electronic sites that facilitate the flow of data anywhere in the world. *Delete* (Unit 3) now means more than just "to erase." It also means the removal of data from a computer's memory. The delete function can be used to edit text, to remove unneeded documents, or to destroy confidential information.

English now includes numerous words derived from the language of computers and from the functions of the Internet. The prefix *e-* has been added to common words to describe electronic functions. For example, mail that is sent electronically is called *e-mail*. *E-commerce* and *e-book* have entered everyday

Mobile phone with wireless access to e-mail

speech. As computer technology continues to evolve, it will continue to enrich our language.

In Column A below are 8 more computer words. With or without a dictionary, match each word with its meaning in Column B.

Column A

c	**1.** cursor
d	**2.** menu
f	**3.** cut and paste
g	**4.** hardware
b	**5.** link
h	**6.** compute
e	**7.** icon
a	**8.** desktop

Column B

a. This is the area of your computer screen on which pictures and windows appear.

b. This is a connection to a web site.

c. This moves rapidly across the computer screen.

d. This is the list from which your computer takes your order.

e. This refers to a representational picture on your computer screen.

f. This arts-and-crafts term describes a computer function that simplifies moving material from one place to another

g. This is the physical components of a computer.

h. This means to process any kind of information.

Selecting Word Meanings

*In each of the following groups, circle the word or expression that is **most nearly the same** in meaning as the word in **boldface** type in the given phrase.*

1. his **ominous** appearance
   - a. threatening
   - b. impressive
   - c. attractive
   - d. unexplained

2. a **diffident** visitor
   - a. unexpected
   - b. shy
   - c. rude
   - d. welcome

3. **unfeigned** interest
   - a. businesslike
   - b. private
   - c. sincere
   - d. hypocritical

4. test of **fortitude**
   - a. skill
   - b. courage
   - c. conscience
   - d. intelligence

5. a **commodious** harbor
   - a. distant
   - b. well-run
   - c. costly
   - d. roomy

6. a **malevolent** attitude
   - a. spiteful
   - b. protective
   - c. indifferent
   - d. loving

7. **augment** his income
   - a. insure
   - b. increase
   - c. spend
   - d. waste

8. **apprehensive** feelings
   - a. worried
   - b. elated
   - c. indescribable
   - d. unreasonable

9. an **inopportune** time
   - a. early
   - b. late
   - c. inconvenient
   - d. pleasant

10. **reiterate** an opinion
    - a. express
    - b. attack
    - c. defend
    - d. repeat

11. **squalid** conditions
    - a. healthful
    - b. exacting
    - c. ideal
    - d. wretched

12. guilty of **duplicity**
    - a. murder
    - b. bad taste
    - c. stubbornness
    - d. deceitfulness

13. a **bellicose** personality
    - a. complacent
    - b. boring
    - c. quarrelsome
    - d. kindly

14. **vociferous** protests
    - a. frequent
    - b. subtle
    - c. noisy
    - d. reasonable

15. an **opulent** lifestyle
    - a. luxurious
    - b. dull
    - c. boring
    - d. poverty-stricken

16. **harass** the driver
    - a. help
    - b. accompany
    - c. annoy
    - d. dismiss

17. an **omniscient** deity
    - a. hardworking
    - b. veteran
    - c. all-knowing
    - d. conscientious

18. **voluminous** correspondence
    - a. confidential
    - b. abundant
    - c. infrequent
    - d. official

19. an **invulnerable** position
    - a. safe
    - b. dangerous
    - c. isolated
    - d. important

20. an **infallible** method
    - a. foolproof
    - b. scientific
    - c. fallacious
    - d. unproved

21. become a **culinary** expert
a. science   (b. cooking)   c. music   d. travel

22. averse to strenuous exercise
(a. opposed)   b. accustomed   c. devoted   d. untrained

23. remiss in her work
a. excellent   b. skilled   c. scrupulous   (d. careless)

24. time to **muse**
a. entertain   (b. ponder)   c. relax   d. study

25. place in **jeopardy**
a. jail   b. custody   (c. danger)   d. safety

Antonyms

*In each of the following groups, circle the **two** words or expressions that are **most nearly opposite** in meaning.*

26. (a. incite)   b. organize   c. train   (d. quell)

27. a. wealthy   b. scientific   (c. assiduous)   (d. lazy)

28. (a. deny)   b. embezzle   c. clarify   (d. profess)

29. (a. commend)   b. consecrate   (c. criticize)   d. sacrifice

30. a. asset   (b. unwillingness)   c. allure   (d. alacrity)

31. a. youthful   b. expected   (c. dour)   (d. amicable)

32. a. foreign   (b. unkempt)   (c. well-groomed)   d. charming

33. a. enthusiastic   (b. agreeable)   (c. contentious)   d. attentive

34. (a. infinitesimal)   b. loquacious   (c. colossal)   d. profitable

35. a. obey   (b. antagonize)   (c. placate)   d. remain

36. (a. confirm)   b. attain   c. arouse   (d. rescind)

37. (a. palatable)   b. dangerous   (c. disagreeable)   d. foolish

38. (a. weak)   (b. potent)   c. illegal   d. beneficial

39. (a. scrupulous)   b. glorious   c. natural   (d. cursory)

40. a. intellectual   (b. petty)   (c. magnanimous)   d. disturbed

Supplying Words in Context

In each of the following sentences, write in the blank space the most appropriate word chosen from the given list.

Group A

abhor	vehement	esteem	suave
solace	consecrate	conclusive	trenchant
gibe	sedate	vivacious	suppress
temerity	guile	warily	somber

41. The dismal winter landscape put him in a very _____ **somber** _____ mood.

42. He is so _____ suave _____ that he seems to fit into any social situation without the slightest difficulty.

43. How does he have the _____ temerity _____ to criticize people who have done so much for him?

44. We _____ abhor _____ racism, but we feel pity rather than hate for racists.

45. The dictator was unable to _____ suppress _____ the spirit of freedom.

46. The fingerprints were regarded as _____ conclusive _____ evidence of his guilt.

47. Her _____ trenchant _____ remarks cut right to the heart of the issue under discussion.

48. I find some _____ solace _____ for our failure in the knowledge that we did everything we possibly could.

49. Let's ignore their vicious _____ gibe(s) _____ and do what we think is right.

50. Her _____ vivacious _____ personality did much to enliven the party.

Group B

adversary	ironic	implicate	altruistic
insidious	inveterate	condolence	dearth
multifarious	tacit	impervious	clairvoyant
misnomer	facsimile	feasible	redress

51. He is so sure of his own virtues that he is just about _____ impervious _____ to criticism.

52. Janie's uncanny ability to guess what I'm thinking at any moment sometimes verges on the _____ clairvoyant _____.

53. I'll have to be at my best to have a chance against a(n) _____ adversary _____ such as Ken.

54. Just when strong leadership is all-important, we find ourselves suffering from a(n) _____ dearth _____ of qualified candidates.

55. Isn't it _____ ironic _____ that he resigned from the editorship just before the newspaper received the award he had done so much to earn?

56. The plan was deemed not _____ feasible _____, since we did not have sufficient funds to put it into effect.

57. With all her _____ multifarious _____ activities, it's a wonder that she finds time to sleep.

58. As a(n) _____ inveterate _____ concertgoer, he has seen many great musicians perform.

59. It would certainly be a(n) _____ misnomer _____ to nickname that unscrupulous crook "Honest John."

60. Not a word was said, but there was a(n) _____ tacit _____ understanding that we would go to the dance together.

Words Connected with Law and Government

The words in Column A may be applied to various situations connected with law and government. In the space before each word, write the **letter** of the item in Column B that identifies it.

	Column A	Column B
_f_	**61.** punitive	a. a formal command by a governmental authority
_g_	**62.** bequeath	b. to change or add to a law
_a_	**63.** edict	c. based on the will of the people
_e_	**64.** abjure	d. possessing unlimited power, as a dictator
_k_	**65.** mandatory	e. to repudiate under oath
_h_	**66.** defamation	f. relating to punishment
_d_	**67.** omnipotent	g. to pass on to one's heirs
_j_	**68.** ultimatum	h. unfair injury to a person's good name
_b_	**69.** amend	i. relating to lawmaking
_l_	**70.** precedent	j. a final demand by a government
		k. obligatory; required by law or regulation
		l. a judicial decision serving as a basis for later decisions

Words That Describe People

Some words that describe people are listed below. Write the appropriate word on the line next to each of the following descriptions.

adroit	raucous	chivalrous	implacable
reprehensible	corrosive	august	indulgent
exuberant	meticulous	exemplary	sophomoric
nonchalant	stentorian	brash	officious

71. I admire the cleverness and skill with which Amy handles people in situations in which others might behave extremely awkwardly. _____adroit_____

72. He is an outstanding citizen of this community who can well serve as a model for young people. _____exemplary_____

73. My aunt is so lenient that she lets her children do almost anything they want. _____indulgent_____

74. Bob's foolish chatter and know-it-all attitude make him a total bore. _____sophomoric_____

75. She takes everything in stride and remains calm and unruffled in situations that would upset other people. _____nonchalant_____

76. When he feels that he has been wronged, he will never be satisfied until he gets even.

_____implacable_____

77. Our English teacher encourages us to pay careful attention to every detail of grammar, usage, and punctuation.

_____meticulous_____

78. He has betrayed his trust and should be condemned by all decent people.

_____reprehensible_____

79. I admire the grace and courtesy with which Tom treated that elderly lady.

_____chivalrous_____

80. She's always meddling in other people's affairs.

_____officious_____

Word Associations

In each of the following, circle the word or expression that best completes the meaning of the sentence or answers the question, with particular reference to the meaning of the word in **boldface** type.

81. Which nickname would a **parsimonious** person be most likely to have?
  a. Alibi Ike
  (b. El Cheapo)
  c. Fancy Dan
  d. Calamity Jane

82. A nation that is a **belligerent** is engaged in
  (a. war)
  b. industrialization
  c. land reform
  d. energy conservation

83. A movie that is exceptionally **poignant** is likely to
  a. put you to sleep
  (b. touch your emotions)
  c. get a lot of laughs
  d. fail at the box office

84. An expenditure of money is **negligible** when it is
  a. illegal
  (b. too small to worry about)
  c. excessive
  d. legal but not morally justified

85. You would be most likely to read of **uncanny** events in
  a. a history textbook
  b. a detective story
  c. a novel of social protest
  (d. a ghost story)

86. You would **extol** something that you find
  a. contentious
  (b. commendable)
  c. corrosive
  d. crestfallen

87. If you **concur** in a decision, you
  (a. agree with it)
  b. consider it wrong
  c. are indifferent to it
  d. are not aware of it

88. To **skulk** out of a room suggests
  a. haste
  b. happiness
  (c. sneakiness)
  d. listlessness

89. You would criticize a **wastrel** for
  a. being lazy
  b. talking too loudly
  (c. squandering money)
  d. not telling the truth

90. Which of the following suggests that a team is being **derided**?

a. "We're number one!"

b. "Go get 'em!"

c. "You guys are losers!"

d. "Give us a break, umpire!"

91. A well-known **renegade** in American history is

a. Daniel Boone

b. Abigail Adams

c. Edgar Allan Poe

d. Benedict Arnold

92. The word **demise** suggests that someone or something has

a. won a prize

b. failed an examination

c. passed out of existence

d. gained final approval

93. The word **holocaust** can be applied to

a. a trivial event

b. an amusing misunderstanding

c. a long war that ends in a draw

d. a historical tragedy costing many live

94. Which of the following phrases suggests something that is **disheveled**?

a. something the cat dragged in

b. bright-eyed and bushy-tailed

c. cute as a button

d. ready for action

95. To be **somnolent** implies a desire to

a. eat

b. exercise

c. get out of town

d. sleep

96. A picture that is **askew** should be

a. dusted

b. given a price

c. straightened

d. sold to the highest bidder

97. We may apply the word **stately** to

a. a duchess and a sailing ship

b. a robot and a computer

c. a city and a state

d. a gibe and a grimace

98. Which of the following individuals might be called **innocuous**?

a. a neighborhood gossip

b. a devoted community worker

c. a religious leader

d. a well-meaning but ineffectual person

99. If people refer to Dave as **obnoxious**, he should try to

a. speak more clearly

b. behave more agreeably

c. smile more often

d. learn to play bridge

100. Which of the following might be described as **lamentable**?

a. winning a scholarship

b. visiting a sick friend

c. getting a new car

d. failing to do well on this final test

The following tabulation lists all the basic words taught in the various units of this book, as well as those introduced in the *Vocabulary of Vocabulary, Working with Analogies, Building with Classical Roots,* and *Enriching Your Vocabulary* sections. Words taught in the units are printed in **boldface** type. The number following each entry indicates the page on which the word is first introduced. Exercise and review materials in which the word also appears are not cited.